MW01469795

New Rules to Live By

Parenting One Day at a Time

By

Gay Moore M.Ed. RNC

authorHOUSE

1663 LIBERTY DRIVE, SUITE 200
BLOOMINGTON, INDIANA 47403
(800) 839-8640
www.authorhouse.com

First published by AuthorHouse 06/25/04

ISBN: 1-4184-1316-X (e)
ISBN: 1-4184-1315-1 (sc)

Library of Congress Control Number: 2003098949

Printed in the United States of America
Bloomington, Indiana

This book is printed on acid-free paper.

Cover by Debra Doss
d&b graphics, Chattanooga, TN.

To my husband Sandy, without whose help and support this book would never have been written.

Introduction

Parenting is the most important job most of us will ever do, but it is also the one for which we find ourselves the least prepared. We may feel that because we were once children ourselves, have grown up to be responsible adults, and are capable of having or adopting children that we ought to know how to parent. Nonsense! Most first time and even second and third time parents sometimes feel ill prepared to meet the demands of parenthood. Often, just when we think we have it all figured out, our children pass into another stage of development and the learning process starts over.

The challenge of parenthood is to establish a home in which children grow into healthy, confident adults who are able to leave our home and enter into the larger world ready to meet the challenges of that world. To this end, all families have rules. These rules govern every aspect of family life: household chores, money management, religious practices, how feelings are expressed, as well as which behaviors are appropriate and which are inappropriate. The rules maintain the family system, defining communication and roles within the family. These rules, both spoken and unspoken, are necessary to keep families operating smoothly.

Rules may support a functional family system or they support dysfunction within the family. Since families are neither wholly functional nor wholly dysfunctional, all families have rules that support growth as well as stagnation.

In a more functional family, the rules support the development of the potential of each member of the family, both males and females are respected and valued, as are the feelings and opinions of each family member.

However, in a more dysfunctional family, the rules support the abusive system. Members of the family are not respected and supported in their growth. They are not encouraged to express feelings and talk openly. There may be secrets and taboo subjects. In a functional family the rules are flexible, known to all, and can be changed or negotiated as situations change. While adults and children have different roles and expectations, the rules apply to everyone in the family.

In a dysfunctional family system, the rules are frequently unspoken, not negotiable, and may either be inflexible, constantly changing, or inconsistent. Rules that apply to some members of the family may not apply to others. Roles within the family are either rigid or poorly defined and change arbitrarily.

In counseling those who are seeking to change their current family systems, I have found it helpful to discuss the rules and messages that were present in their family of origin and which continue to affect them today. By bringing such rules into awareness, one can decide to keep those that support growth and emotional health and change those that hinder it. This is the purpose of this daily reading book. It is my hope that you will find in these readings rules that are familiar to you and that by examining them you can begin the process of changing the rules that do not promote the goals you have for your family.

It has been my privilege to be a part of this process of discovery and decision in many families. I would like to thank those who have shared with me their family rules, both old and new. It is to them that this book is further dedicated.

I would like to also thank Haley Chastain for her valuable editorial suggestions and comments.

Note: As you read this book you will find a number of days in which one reading is assigned for more than one day. On those days you might like to re-read the passage on the second day. It is my hope that you will be rewarded with just a bit more to consider. Or you might just take the day off. I have become a great believer in the restorative value of taking a day off from any usual occupation. So relax and enjoy being a parent.

January 1

Old Rule: No matter what you do you will end up parenting just like your parents.

We have all heard this bit of folk wisdom. It says to parents, "You may have ideas about what you want to do differently, but you'll end up parenting just like you were parented. It is inevitable, you cannot change it."

It is true that we learned how to parent from our parents. We may find that when we are tired or stressed our parents' words come from our mouths and we behave with our children much like our own parents did with us. However, we are not locked into any style of parenting. We can change the way in which we rear our children.

Most of us learned beneficial things from our parents that we will want to give to our children. At the same time, there are things that we will not want to pass on, those things that were painful to us or that are simply not workable in the situations that families deal with today.

Changing the way we have learned to parent to the way we would like to parent is hard work. It takes conscious effort to do it differently. Many of us want to rear our children differently from the way we were reared, but we do not have a clear idea of what we would like to do or how to implement those changes. We want to be loving, nurturing parents who rear responsible, self-confident, and caring children who are able to use their talents to the fullest, but we are not sure how to do this on a day-to-day basis.

It is my hope that this book will help you become aware of the rules that are operating in the life of your family. If you decide that you wish to begin to parent differently, I have proposed some ways that you might begin this process. A word of warning, you will not do this perfectly. Sometimes when you most want to be a different kind of parent, to respond differently to your children, you may find that you have reverted back to the old rules. Forgive yourself and keep trying. Just as there are no perfect children, there are no perfect parents. It is unlikely that you have done irreparable harm to your children or your relationship with them. Hang in there! It is our overall loving intentions and willingness to learn new ways of handling problems that make the difference in our parenting. You can do it!

New Rule: I am not locked into parenting as I was parented. With conscious effort, I can be the parent that my children need. I can be the parent I want to be.

January 2

Old Rule: Don't talk about it.

This rule is standard in dysfunctional families. It can apply to any problem or circumstance, including chemical dependency, physical, sexual, or emotional abuse, extra-marital affairs, gambling addiction, and other family secrets. The variations are endless!

The intent is to deny the existence of a problem by not verbally acknowledging it. The beliefs underlying this silence are typically: "If we do not talk about it, it either does not exist, is not that bad, will eventually go away, or nothing can be done."

Tragically, such families harbor dreadful open secrets. Family members know what is happening, but they don't talk about it. As a result, family members die of their addictions, children continue to be abused, and the dysfunction and pain within the family is passed to the next generation.

Breaking the "don't talk" rule is the beginning of recovery and healthy change for the individual as well as the family. It frees us to begin to tell the truth and to verbalize our feelings about what is happening.

Talking about it is not without risk. For when we choose to tell the truth as we see it, we risk the disapproval of family members who are not ready and may never be ready to emerge from their silence and denial. Only you can decide if the risk is worth the gain.

However, it is vital to teach our children the importance of talking about problems within our own families. This is the only way that life's difficulties and conflicts can be resolved. In our efforts to rear healthy, functional children, teaching them to talk about what they see, hear, think, and feel is essential.

New Rule: I refuse to live by the "don't talk" rule and to pass this dysfunctional rule onto my children. I will learn to express what I see, hear, think, and feel in an appropriate manner and I will help my children learn to do the same.

January 3

Old Rule: Don't feel! Be tough!

As children we hear this message in varied forms. "Don't cry when someone hurts your feelings. Be tough!" "Don't cry when you are spanked. Be tough!" "Don't get angry with your parents, be tough, hold it in." "Don't cry when you fall down and get hurt. Be tough!"

As adults we continue to live by this rule, believing that denying our feelings under the guise of "toughness" is appropriate, mature behavior. In the process, we become emotionally frozen and detached from our feelings.

As we grow older, we experience difficulty expressing ourselves to the people we love or suffer periods of depression and intense loneliness. Uncomfortable with the feelings of others as well as our own, we pass this message on to our children. We repeat the same damaging expressions to them, telling them to keep hurt and anger inside, out of the view of others.

Life does not have to be this way. We can change this rule. The first step is to acknowledge that we have been robbed of our own feelings as children and have continued the process by denying their existence as adults. We can begin to free ourselves from the emotional prison in which we find ourselves by first expressing ourselves to those we love. At first, such expression of feelings may be awkward and uncomfortable. Keep practicing! It will get easier and the rewards are tremendous! We can also give our children permission to express their feelings to us, including anger and hurt, without fear of ridicule or reprisal. Remember that a rich emotional life with access to wide variety of feelings is the hallmark of an emotionally hardy, resilient human being.

New Rule: In my home, I allow myself and my children to express feelings. It is essential to the development of a healthy, creative person. .

January 4

Old Rule: Don't trust.

Human beings learn to trust others when parents and other caregivers from infancy through adolescence meet their needs. Children learn the "don't trust" rule when trusting others, including parents, leads to disappointment and hurt.

Children whose parents are neglectful, abusive, and habitually inconsistent come to see the world around them as dangerous and unpredictable. They learn not to trust others, including their parents, in order to survive emotionally. Children reared in homes where they must learn not to trust come to believe that the rest of the world is a dangerous place. Such children often grow up with a deeply held conviction that trusting others, even those who might seem to be trustworthy, is foolish and hazardous. Therefore, they believe, the only way to avoid hurt is not to trust anyone completely. This belief often translates into difficulty forming close relationships as adults.

Inability to trust also stunts the growth of empathy. When we do not experience our own environment as capable and willing to meet our needs, we have difficulty understanding the needs of others.

By their behavior, abusive and neglectful parents tell their children that they are not worthy of loving attention. In other words, children learn to view themselves as unworthy of love when their parents, who are supposed to care for them above all others, are not loving. Such parental neglect results in a lifelong battle with self-doubt and low self-esteem.

Conversely, parents who consistently meet the needs of their children for security and love lay the foundation for healthy self-esteem and the ability to translate this experience into intimate adult relationships. Trustworthy parents also lay the groundwork for the ability to see the world from another's point of view, the ability to empathize. When we view relationships with others as safe and rewarding, we can risk putting ourselves in another's position. When we experience important people in our lives as giving and caring, we learn how to give and care ourselves. In learning to trust, we become fully human and give back to others what we have been given: love and compassion. We learn to trust and then become trustworthy.

New Rule: Trustworthiness is one of the most important traits of a good parent.

January 5

Old Rule: Don't trust those who are different from us.

One of the harsh realities of being a parent is the necessity of teaching our children to be wary of those they do not know and to protect themselves from those who might hurt them.

However, when we, in the words of Richard Rogers, "carefully teach" our children "to hate and fear," we narrow their world and cripple them with our own fears and ignorance.

One of the characteristics of a truly intelligent person is the ability to see that which is different from oneself not with suspicion, fear, and distrust, but with curiosity and interest.

Tolerance and empathy for others is not the same as adopting the behavior or beliefs of others as our own or condoning behavior which is not within our value system. It is accepting that each of us has different experiences, beliefs, and goals. It is living out the Biblical injunction to "love others as we would love ourselves" and accepting others, as we would wish to be accepted.

In appreciating differences, we teach our children to view those who are different from themselves as individuals to be respected, not as members of a group to be distrusted, avoided, or regarded as inferior. How much better to teach our children in this increasingly complicated and diverse world to judge others "not by the color of their skin, but by the content of their character." (Martin Luther King, Jr., 1968)

New Rule: We teach our children to view those who are different from themselves with tolerance and curiosity, not fear and distrust.

January 6

Old Rule: Parenting is serious business.

When my first child was an infant, I read the best parenting advice I ever received in a newspaper advice column. The writer of the column simply stated that childhood was very short and to enjoy the time you have with your children.

It is important to laugh with them and to have fun with them, but it is also essential to enjoy the things they do which you might not want them to know amuse you. You have to laugh when your child puts popcorn kernels in his ears, which have to be removed in the emergency room, or when your little daughter launches into a discussion of her baby brother's penis with your dinner guests.

As they get older, you have to laugh when they become confused and run the bases the wrong way or push the dancer next to them out of the way during a dance recital.

As children become adolescents, you have to laugh when your extremely fair skinned son uses a tanning preparation which turns him light orange except in the folds of his skin which are darker orange, giving him the appearance of a tiger, or when you have a volume discount at the auto body repair shop because of a series of vender benders.

You must laugh or you will cry, bang your head against a wall, or say things, which you will later regret. They do not do these things to make you crazy. They are merely learning about life. It is a messy, inexact process, which can either make you crazy or make you laugh.

New Rule: In order to survive as a parent, it is important for me to keep my sense of humor and to bear in mind that childhood and even adolescence is short, so we might as well enjoy it.

January 7 & 8

Old Rule: Good parents include their children in everything they do. When not earning a living, their focus is solely on the children. Loving, responsible parents are totally child- centered.

I am nearing the end of child rearing. My younger child is going to college next year. He is increasingly independent, learning to care for himself and take responsibility for his life. Every day he needs his father and me less. He is becoming a young adult and I am proud of him. While I am never going to stop being his concerned mother, he is ready to move out into the larger world. This process of letting go and the change it brings to my life, my husband's life, and to our relationship is both painful and exhilarating. This experience, while certainly not unique, represents an enormous change in our lives.

I say all of this to express concern about the families I see who are completely child- centered. Children's activities occupy every weekend, while weekday evenings are absorbed with homework. Recreation is totally child-centered. Even worship services become exercises in keeping rambunctious toddlers quiet.

I am concerned because their lives are out of balance. While certainly well intended, the couple relationship and the personal lives of the parents are lost in this child-centered lifestyle.

During the course of this book, you will often read about balance and the emotional, physical, and spiritual health found in the wisdom of middle way. I believe that the need for such balance is nowhere more evident than in the child-centered life style.

If they are to maintain a healthy family, parents must have a relationship with each other. They need time to talk, time to have fun, and time to make love free from the intrusion of children. They need time to be adults and to do adult things. As individuals, parents need time to themselves, to be with adult friends, and to pursue adult interests. They need to worship without the distraction of restless toddlers.

I realize this seems impossible, when the demands of child rearing and making a living are so great. Fortunately, a little seems to go a long way. An occasional dinner out, even just once a month, can bring new life to a frazzled marriage. An evening out with adult friends, either as a couple or as an individual, is revitalizing. A couple of hours to oneself to read or do a hobby are a wonderful gift that couples can give each other. Leaving small children in the church nursery can provide parents with a blessed hour of peaceful worship. Leaving children in the nursery at the local YMCA while taking an exercise class or swimming helps parents relax and rekindle their energy.

Taking some time for yourself and your relationship with your spouse does not make you a neglectful parent. It might even make you a better one. When my first child was very young, I was a stay at home mother who was totally devoted to mothering and keeping a tidy home. I wanted to be the very best mother and wife ever created. However, I became increasingly frustrated, lonely, and depressed. My husband, bless him, encouraged me to go back to school. I started with one class, two afternoons a week for 90 minutes. I took my child, sometimes over his objections, to a sitter and went to class. What I quickly realized was that the mother who pulled up at the sitter's to pick him up was a much more patient and relaxed mother than the one who left. The opportunity to be with other adults, to learn something new, and to experience meeting short-term goals (something in rather short supply in child-rearing and homemaking) helped me to regain a balance between being a parent and being an individual.

Many times my husband and I have been out of balance, letting child rearing and working consume all of our time and energy. The results were always the same: frustration with our sons and distance between us. We have had to correct our course many times. Now that our sons are grown and have lives of their own and we have to look to our sense of ourselves as individuals and our relationship with each other, it is reassuring to have someone there.

New Rule: Parents are also individuals and part of a couple relationship. It is important to find a balance between being a parent, a spouse, and an individual. Emotional, physical, and spiritual well-being is often found in such a balance.

January 9

Old Rule: You cannot please your parents, but you must keep trying.

Several years ago, I taught a nursing school class filled with exceptionally bright and talented students. During a class concerning self-esteem, I was amazed to learn how many of these talented, hardworking, achievement-oriented young adults felt that their parents, especially their fathers, were not pleased with them. They felt driven to do well in an attempt to please their parents, but they also felt such approval was impossible to earn.

The parents of these successful students would probably have been amazed if they could have heard their children express hurt and confusion concerning their parents' disapproval. They felt their parents were not only critical of their mistakes, but who they were as people. It was painfully obvious that many of them felt they were a disappointment to their parents, despite their efforts and achievements.

As parents we have considerable power. We have the power to foster self-esteem in our children or to decrease it. By our words and actions, our children can sense our approval or our disapproval. Because we have so much power, they will unquestioningly take in our attitudes and opinions about them as reality. These parents may have felt that by not praising their children they were insuring their children did not become conceited or over-confident. The world will hand them criticism after criticism. They do not need regular expressions of displeasure from us in order to remain humble. What they do need is our approval and our non-critical love to armor them against the disapproval of the world. Not that we approve of all of their actions, for this is impossible, but our children do need to hear from us that we approve of them and who they are becoming as people.

Michael Popkin, Ph.D., as part of his "Active Parenting" program, suggests writing a letter of encouragement to our children, telling them what we value and appreciate about them. Whether we tell them or write to them, we need to let them know that we cherish them and we are glad they are our children.

New Rule: I tell my children frequently how much I love, appreciate, and value them.

January 10

Old Rule: We don't show our feelings in this family. Showing feelings is a sign weakness.

Most of us are familiar with the three rules of a dysfunctional family: don't talk, don't think, and don't feel. They have become cliché. They are recognizable because many of us have grown up with these destructive rules.

While we tend to fear anger and label angry feelings as dangerous, we tend to label the expression of sadness and hurt as a sign of weakness, especially in men. Boys in our culture are still conditioned to hide their hurt feelings. If they cry and express hurt or disappointment, they are looked upon as less than manly. Sadly, women, as they move into non-traditional roles, are told they should be more like men and they, too, should learn to hide and deny hurt feelings. "Take it like a man" has come to apply to both men and women.

Repression of sadness and hurt comes at a high cost. When we deny feelings, we short- circuit our emotions, for we cannot repress one feeling without repressing others. In other words, we blunt joy as well as pain when we deny its existence. When we deny our emotions and do not allow their expression, we rob ourselves of a piece of our emotional life. We become less human.

We can help our children to express emotions in a more functional manner, by first adopting the attitude that there are no "good' or "bad" feelings. Feelings are a natural part of being human. Second, we can allow children to communicate their feelings without shaming them. This means that we can allow them to cry, and express sadness, hurt, or disappointment without telling them that they should feel otherwise, or that they are "acting like a cry baby". We can also model the appropriate expression of sadness and hurt while giving ourselves the gift of expressing such feelings. The ability to share feelings is a sign of strength and emotional hardiness, not a sign of weakness.

New Rule: In our family, we permit and encourage the expression of all feelings, including hurt, sadness, and disappointment. We know we are all stronger as a result.

January 11

Old Rule: It is important to be religious, but for heaven's sake, don't base your life on it.

Many of us were given the first part of this rule directly. We were taken regularly to religious services. We were taught to adhere to a set of rules and to behave as though we had a religious foundation. We might have been taught that those who did not practice a religion, especially our religion, were inferior. We were told that it was important to be religious.

However, we were given the second part of this rule in more subtle ways. We saw our parents attend religious services and talk about the "right" way to live, only to return home and abuse us and each other. We heard them criticize and judge others or behave dishonestly in business. Worried and filled with doubt about themselves and the future, they seemed to have no peace of mind. While they were religious, they were spiritually bankrupt.

Religious teachings and practice can provide a framework for spiritual growth and aid in the search for a meaningful existence. However, it is a vibrant and dynamic relationship with that which is greater than ourselves that is truly important. We can base our lives upon such a relationship and help our children to establish values, which guide their lives as well as provide a refuge in times of confusion and despair.

New Rule: My spiritual journey and my relationship with that which is greater than myself is of ultimate importance to me, not the outward practice of religion. I teach my children to practice religion as a framework for their spiritual growth.

January 12

Old Rule: God is watching you. He sees what you do, even when I don't.

When parents use these words, they are not fostering the child's relationship with God. They are using religion and fear to control the child's behavior. This message does, however, affect the child's relationship with and perception of God. The child comes to view God as a punishing extension of the parent: all knowing, condemning, judgmental, and ready to swoop down and punish any transgression.

Completely lost in this form of child control is the concept of a loving God who forgives and accepts us, just as we are. Small wonder that so many adults want nothing to do with God and religion. They may feel they are unredeemable sinners who can never be good enough to go to God, mistakes and all, and experience God's forgiving, loving care.

As adults, we can choose to leave behind the judging God used by our parents to control us and accept God's compassion and guidance. It is to this compassionate and loving God that we can introduce our children. It is to this God that our children can come for guidance when they are uncertain about their choices. It is to this God that our children can come when the world with all of its complexities and choices overwhelms them. This is the relationship with God that will sustain them.

New Rule: I accept the knowledge that God loves us, wants what is best for us, and can forgive our mistakes. This is the God that I want my children to know, love, and turn to.

January 13

Old Rule: Your role in the family is …

In her book <u>Another Chance,</u> Sharon Wesgcheider described the various survival roles played in a family living with alcoholism. These roles, "Hero," "Scapegoat," "Lost Child," and "Mascot," are now a part of the way that we talk about families.

There are many other roles played out in families: the mediator, the peacekeeper, the troublemaker, the sick one, the irresponsible one, and the caretaker. The list is almost endless. The purpose of these roles is to keep the dysfunctional family system operating, even if it harms the individual. Each role has its payoffs or rewards and each has its difficulties. **All** of these roles are painful traps that hurt the family as well as the individual. The more dysfunctional the family, the more numerous and rigidly maintained the roles.

In a healthy, functional family, people do not uphold firmly defined roles in the service of maintaining the family system. They are free to be themselves. In other words, in a functional family, the family exists to nurture the individual. The individual does not exist to keep the dysfunctional system operating. This is an important distinction.

Counselors know that a family is becoming healthier when one person refuses to continue to play their old role and begins to act as an autonomous individual. This puts stress on the family, for when one person refuses to play their role, the entire family feels the tension of change. It is rather like pulling one piece of a mobile, every other piece reacts. Sometimes in the recovery process, family members believe that getting better means adopting a better role.

They usually pick the family "Hero," feeling that at last they will get some of the praise and power that the "Hero" seems to have. Such role switchers soon discover that even this role is painful and restricting.

Healthy families operate not to maintain family roles but to foster the growth of each family member. In other words, no one lives out a role. They are who they are and who they are is valued and respected.

New Rule: In our family we do not insist that people adopt and maintain a role. Our family exists to care for each individual and to allow each one to be all that they can be.

January 14

Old Rule: We are just ordinary people. We are not a creative family.

We are all creative! Each of us has the power to live creatively! While most of us associate creativity with literature, art, and music, it is not limited to what we traditionally call the arts. Creativity can be found in almost every human endeavor, including finding the solution to a computer game, cooking, planting a garden, decorating a room, assembling a unique outfit, or making up a new game.

When children hear "our family is not creative" and its unspoken corollary "therefore, you are not creative," it stifles their imagination and originality. They decide early on that whatever they do is either not good enough or too ordinary to be considered creative. When parents believe that no creative person could possibly come from their family, they may ignore or belittle their children's efforts. They may even suppress children's creativity in art, music, and writing.

Believing this rule, parents also minimize or disregard their own creative efforts and impulses. Adults, like children, need to have their ideas nurtured and respected. We are all creative and can enrich our lives immeasurably when we allow ourselves to express our talents. When parents praise their children's creative efforts, they do not give them an unrealistic appraisal of themselves and their abilities. It is more likely that children will, with such encouragement, continue to create and to explore other avenues of original expression.

New Rule: We embrace the imagination of the adults and children in our family. We encourage creativity in its many forms to flower and flourish.

January 15 & 16

Old Rule: I don't want girls! Girls are too hard to raise!

As a counselor, I heard this rule expressed by those reared in families where females were not valued, while being male or having a male child was valued above everything. I attributed this attitude to a sexist culture, which values boys above girls and dismissed it as ignorance and prejudice.

However, when I began to hear this statement from women who are successful and enjoying the increased choices open to them, I was appalled and distressed. They made statements like: "It is tough to be a woman"; "The demands to be and do it all: employee, wife, and mother are too great. You must to do it all perfectly." "You have to prove on daily basis that you belong in your career"; "You have to be at least twice as good as any man doing your job in order to be promoted and even approach fair compensation and recognition, much less respect"; and "The world is a dangerous place for girls."

In truth, the increasing options open to women have come at a price. We are feeling increased pressure to do "it" all and do "it" all well, often with inadequate support from partners and employers, as well as the culture at large. Furthermore, it is a dangerous world for girls and women. Sexual harassment, even in elementary school, is a pervasive reality. Women are the target of sexual violence as well as pressure to engage in sexual relationships. The freedom to say "yes" often results in extreme pressure not to say "no".

While this maybe a pessimistic view of what it is like to be female in our culture, I frequently hear women express these painful frustrations.

However, we do have little girls and we must prepare them for the world outside of our homes. I believe that those girls who do survive and thrive in the current environment, which is not always female friendly, come from homes where they are appreciated and respected for who they are. Their talents and abilities are valued and they are encouraged to use them to their fullest. They are not reared with an overdose of "What will people think?" or to constantly seek the approval of others. They are taught that

20

ultimately they must please themselves and that it is not only unreasonable, but also life draining to focus solely on pleasing others.

They are also encouraged to be girls, not pseudo-males. They have feminine interests, like pretty clothes and dolls, as well as traditionally more masculine pursuits like sports and computers. They are allowed to express their feelings openly. They are not given the "big, brave, and successful girls don't cry" message. They are also permitted to be angry and are taught to channel anger wisely rather than to suppress it.

These girls are taught a balanced view of their relationship to men. They are not schooled in the old rules that say to find a man who loves you and to please him so he will not leave (for another woman) is the ultimate goal of being a woman. Nor are they taught to view men and boys as the enemy who will use, abuse, and then leave them. Instead they are taught that successful relationships with men, whether friendly, working, or romantic, are best when entered into with a sense of equality and accountability. In other words, they are taught that everyone is worthy of respect, but not subservience. With this sense of mutual respect comes accountability, the knowledge that one is accountable for ones actions and can hold others accountable for their actions.

I am aware of the difficulty of rearing children, male or female, in this manner. Perhaps it is difficult to rear girls, but not impossible, and the rewards are fantastic when they emerge from our homes as confident, independent, self-reliant young women who not only care for others but also care about themselves. Successful parenting produces such adults, male and female.

New Rule: While we acknowledge the difficulty of rearing girls to take care of themselves in a world that is often dangerous for them, it is possible to prepare them to live in that world and not lose themselves. We need not despair when the news is: "It's a girl!"

January 17

Old Rule: Don't question your religion.

Faith and religion are complicated, emotional issues. Many of us believe it is an important parental responsibility to give our children a religious background that will structure and guide their thinking and behavior.

We take them to religious services and may elect to educate them in a religious environment. We want them to know and live by a particular set of beliefs that we believe to be true. For many parents, this is a vitally important part of being a good parent. However, when children begin to ask questions about religious faith, we are often unprepared to answer. Feeling threatened, parents may reply with shaming answers that say to the child that it is wrong to question religious teaching and to be quiet and accept what they are told.

This approach may stifle questions for a time, but it does not put an end to them. It is normal to question one's religious instruction. Indeed, all religions set aside a time in the young adult's life for questioning and exploration. Wise religious leaders expect such questions and are prepared to answer not with the dogmatic reply, "This is what we believe, do not question," but rather with "This is what we believe and this is why we believe it." Such leaders know that questioning and exploration develops mature belief and devotion to one's religious faith.

As our children's first spiritual teachers, we should welcome questions about religious beliefs as evidence that the child is thinking about these serious issues. When our adolescents rebel against what they have been taught and question everything they hear, we might chose to save ourselves a lot of worry and upset if we see this as a natural progression on the path to mature faith. If we feel threatened and respond with "This is what is true, don't ask questions," it is actually evidence of our own inadequate, ill-informed faith. We might take this opportunity to explore our own beliefs. We might find that our children will lead us, their parents, to a more mature faith.

New Rule: I welcome my children's inquiries concerning religious beliefs as an opportunity to lead them to more a fully developed, sustaining faith.

January 18

Old Rule: Children cannot make useful contributions to the family.

Childhood, as a time of school, activities, and carefree play, is a fairly recent invention. Our great grandparents and all of the generations before certainly did not envision childhood this way. Children were important in the family. They were taught to do household and farming chores or to work in the family business.

Children had competencies and responsibilities. They were important, contributing, valuable members of the family.

In truth, we would not wish to return to this way of life. We no longer believe it is appropriate to remove children from school to work on the farm or rear younger brothers and sisters, as so many children were forced to do in the not too distant past. However, we may have lost something positive and instructive when we do not view our children as contributing members of the family.

When we teach our children that running the household depends on all of the members of the family, not just Mom and Dad, we continue this tradition of seeing children as vital to maintaining the home. When we expect that they will assist in the care of younger brothers and sisters who are also given responsibilities, as they are able, we build self-esteem and competencies that will be invaluable to them as they move into the wider world.

Children, like adults, feel important and invested in the family when their contributions are real and valued. They can contribute not just their labor, but also their ideas and their unique perspective. Sometimes out of the mouths of babes will come the solution that will solve the problem. We will not know unless we respect them enough to ask.

New Rule: Children can make useful contributions to the family. When they are encouraged and expected to give assistance to others, their abilities, as well as their self-esteem, develop and grow.

January 19

Old Rule: This is the way you should do it.

When we see our children struggling to master a new skill, it is tempting to tell them how to do it. After all, we certainly know more. We are older, have more experience, and have learned many skills over the years. We know how to do "it."

Yet as our children's earliest and most powerful teachers we need to remember that the lessons in our own lives which were the most meaningful are those in which we figured out matters for ourselves. This does not mean that we should not guide our children. It is our job to guide our children, but guiding does not mean imparting our instructions and expecting children to follow them to the letter. Guiding our children in learning all of the many things that they need to know means that we encourage them to think for themselves. We may well encourage them to explore new solutions and alternatives and allow them to make a few mistakes along the way while they find the solution that is right for them.

To facilitate this process, it is essential to ask the right questions: "What do you think?" "What do you think will happen if you …?", or "Have you tried ….?" Meanwhile we can also insert our own ideas and experiences. Guiding children in this manner does require more energy, time, and patience. In spite of this, the rewards of watching children grow into young adults who can think and reason through whatever difficulty confronts them and who evidence the self-esteem that comes from the belief in one's own competence is worth the time and energy we might spend. After all, isn't our goal to produce sensible, confident young adults who can manage whatever challenge confronts them?

New Rule: "What do you think?" "What do you think might work?" "What do you think might happen if you …?" These questions help us to teach our children to think and act with competence and confidence.

January 20

Old Rule: Figure it out for yourself.

This rule, the opposite of the previous one, is often found in families in which there is constant stress and turmoil. Children from such families are often forced to figure out solutions to problems for themselves. This is most evident in the chemically dependent family in which the parents are so completely absorbed in their own or the other parent's drug and alcohol use that they simply do not have the time, awareness, or energy to teach children what they must know in order to survive.

In these stressed families, children must learn for themselves how to meet everyday challenges. That so many young children do manage to figure out what they need to know in order to survive is a tribute to human resourcefulness, not good parenting.

However, children pay a high price when parents are absorbed in their own turmoil and fail to teach them. Children suffer due to the lack of adult direction. They often make self-destructive mistakes, such as getting involved with criminal activity or drugs and alcohol.

Paradoxically, children who are asked to solve life problems for themselves do not feel competent, for they do make mistakes due to their inexperience and lack of knowledge. Typically, parents who are absorbed in their own difficulties are critical and demanding, thus compounding the problem. Parents who tend to believe that their children should know how to do things without being taught often have enormous expectations which children cannot possibly fulfill because they have not been given the skills. These children, who are not aware of the insanity of being expected to know that which one has not been taught, often believe that they are incompetent, not good enough, and unable to do anything right.

In addition to providing the physical necessities for survival, one of the responsibilities of being a parent is to teach children what we expect them to know. What we take the time to teach them is crucial, not only for their well-being, but also to their self-esteem. It is vitally important that we assume this responsibility.

New Rule: I do not expect my children to figure out what they have not been taught and to know what I have not taken time to teach them. I accept the responsibility of being my children's life teacher.

January 21

Old Rule: There is never enough money to buy the things we want.

I have discovered that there is no end to my wants! Buying new clothes, furniture, jewelry, cars, and antiques inevitably awakens in me a desire for even more and better new stuff. I have come to believe that my wants are almost insatiable! Yet, I do not believe I am alone in this phenomenon. Indeed, the desire for more keeps our economy growing. This is often the driving force behind the ambition to provide more and better for our families and ourselves.

However, we can become consumed by our wants, running up large balances on our credit cards, finding ourselves chronically short of money, and failing to save for the future. We can also pass these habits onto our children, while complaining that they are never happy with what they have and constantly ask for more expensive clothes, toys, and electronic equipment.

In order to change this pattern of desiring more and better while overspending to obtain it, we must first change our thinking. The first step is to accept that happiness ultimately comes from meaningful relationships and using our talents and abilities productively, not from ever increasing accumulations of stuff. Next, we must adopt a sane, rational manner of living within our means. This does not mean miserliness, but enjoying what we have and planning for those things that will genuinely enhance our happiness and quality of life.

Granted, when we adopt this strategy, we will move against the prevailing tide of the culture that holds that satisfaction lies with the next purchase. However, as parents we have the obligation to add our voice and our values to the choices that our children hear.

New Rule: I will teach my children that happiness and satisfaction comes from many sources, not just the acquisition of possessions.

January 22

Old Rule: If I don't have cash, no problem. I've still got money. I'll just put what I want on a credit card.

We Americans are awash in credit card debt. According to "U.S. News and World Report", the average credit card balance is approximately $4500. We believe, even if we do not have the available cash, it is our *right* to have whatever we want so we simply put it on "the card."

As the balances mount, we bemoan our poor financial management and attempt to get credit card use under control. We struggle to get our financial houses in order. This is especially true when we are accustomed to spending freely. We experience great difficulty saying "no" to ourselves and to our children. We may believe that our children are not aware of this, but they are learning the credit card game and they are waiting for their turn to play.

The banks that issue credit cards are waiting for them, too. When they turn 18, young adults are offered credit cards, even if they are not employed. Credit card companies are willing to gamble on them. These companies know that if the young person gets too deeply in debt their parents, not wishing to have their child burdened with a poor credit history, will assume the responsibility.

Parents may complain about the young adult's irresponsibility, charging expensive new clothes, CDs, sport's equipment, or even snack food at convenience stores. However, it is often our own irresponsibility they are imitating, compounded by our failure to teach them about the responsible use of credit.

As parents in a world overflowing with easy credit, we have the responsibility to model its sensible, realistic use to our children. The market place is there to teach them the opposite lesson. If we do not teach our young adults about the responsible use of credit, they may learn these lessons in an effective, yet painful, manner by being overwhelmed with debt.

The first step in teaching such lessons to our children is to model responsible credit management. We need to clean up our own act, before we can teach our children.

New Rule: It is my responsibility to model and to teach wise, rational credit management to my children. The first step is to examine my own attitudes and use of credit.

January 23

Old Rule: Buy it! Hide it! Bring it out later!

When I teach marriage and family classes, we discuss money and what we learned about money and buying as children. I am always amazed at the number of people who where brought up seeing this tactic used in their homes, especially by their mothers.

Women have traditionally earned either no income of their own or substantially less income than their husbands. Therefore, they resorted to all manner of tactics to buy what they wanted. This is one of them. The scenario goes like this: I see it. I want it, but my spouse will disapprove or become angry and make me take it back. So I will buy it, hide for several weeks, and then bring it out. When he asks I'll just say, "Oh, I've had this for a long time." Thus I get what I want and there is no argument.

In addition to a pattern of deception in the marriage, the problem is that children may follow this dishonest example. Instead of learning to be honest with their spouse about money and purchases and work out solutions to disagreements, they learn to be sneaky and dishonest. They also learn that dishonesty is not only clever but also necessary, especially in marriage. Not exactly a belief that bodes well for marital success and harmony.

Knowing that what we do in our relationships speaks much louder to our children than what we say, wouldn't it be better to abandon this dysfunctional, deceitful way of getting what we want and to begin to discuss directly with our spouses more functional and honest ways of dealing with money?

New Rule: In our home we are honest with each other concerning money. When we disagree about how money should be spent, we attempt to solve these conflicts in an honest and forthright manner free from game playing and deception.

January 24

Old Rule: Money equals power.

This rule rules the world. Wealth determines whose ideas are heard and who makes the decisions in government, business, and even religious institutions. Since earliest recorded history, human beings have pursed wealth and its attendant power. Despite consequences to the poor and the powerless, this situation is unlikely to change.

Money also equals power in families. In most families the person who brings in the most income is the person with the most power. Even in the most congenial families we can see that the primary wage earner not only has the strongest and loudest voice in determining how the family resources are spent, but also has the most power with respect to other decisions. Money equals power even in situations that are not financial.

Sometimes the powerful one is more democratic, willing to share decisions. Other times the primary wage earner is more authoritarian, stating firmly and loudly, "I make the money here and I am in charge!" Since men have traditionally been the only or primary wage earners, these differences have led to situations of grossly unequal power within families. As women gain greater access to higher paying jobs and wage inequity changes, shared economic power leads to realignment of the power structures within families. While still in the minority, we are even beginning to see families in which the woman makes more money and, therefore, has more economic power than the man. Occurring for the first time in history, this monumental shift causes additional strain.

There are no easy solutions to the tensions that arise from changes in the family power structure. The first step is to acknowledge the reality of changing power differences and the conflict this brings into our lives. The second step is to work toward open, democratic families in which power is shared, especially between spouses. Third, as they mature, gradually permit children to share in these decisions in order for them to learn to make good decisions about money.

New Rule: Money does equal power in our culture, but in our family we prefer to share power and to make decisions accordingly.

January 25 & 26

Old Rule: It is the school's job to educate my children. Education is not the parents' responsibility.

We send our children to the experts, the educators, whom we believe have the knowledge and experience to teach our children what they need to know to progress to the next level of education and eventually succeed in the workplace. We also expect them to learn to be good citizens of a democracy as well as how to manage successfully in our increasingly complex culture.

While teachers and school administrators have many responsibilities with respect to our children, we, as parents, also have responsibilities in the education process.

First, we have the responsibility to send our children to school ready to learn. This means proper rest, nutrition, and relative freedom from the burdens and worries of family stressors. These stresses may include marital conflict or financial problems that children are powerless to influence, but which often worry and preoccupy them at school.

We also have the responsibility to be interested in what our children are learning and their progress toward achieving education goals. This may mean such practical matters as making a specific time and quiet place for homework. It may include helping with homework or making certain they receive proper tutoring. It means reading to young children and letting our older children read to us. It may involve helping older children with projects and papers. (Notice I said assist with homework and projects, not do them ourselves.)

It is also important to get acquainted with our children's teachers and attend parent-teacher conferences. (It surprised me to hear teachers say that many parents simply do not come to scheduled conferences.) Parents also have the responsibility to model respect for teachers and the process of education.

Education, therefore, is a process that involves three partners, each of whom must fulfill their part if the process is to be successful. While parents have responsibilities, students are responsible for completing assignments and learning the material. (This may seem obvious, but I am amazed at how often students believe that it is their right to be entertained and when they are not entertained they do not need to make an effort to learn.) Learning is the child's job and the child's responsibility. Parents do their children a disservice when they do assignments for them or do not insist on children completing assignments.

Parents also have the responsibility to be aware of what is happening at school. We are all busy. Most parents work outside of the home and our schedules are extremely full. However, it is important that we involve ourselves in our children's school, by attending PTA or PTO meetings, open house, parent-teacher conferences, and reading the newsletter, as well as taking part in school activities. Children, even high school students, like to see their parents involved in school activities. It sends the message to children that their parents are invested in their education, and they are willing to sacrifice some of their precious time to participate.

The years that our children spend in school can be difficult as well as rewarding. If parents, teachers, and children are willing to work together, these years can be productive, esteem enhancing, and even fun.

New Rule: I acknowledge that I am responsible for sending my children to school ready to learn, for supporting their efforts, and for taking an active part in the process of their education.

January 27 & 28

Old Rule: Don't bother me now! Can't you see I'm working?

I am a work addict. When I am not actually working, I think about working. I am constantly preoccupied with what I need to do and if I have accomplished enough today. This is not to say that I am productive. In all of this constant busyness, I tend to be unfocused, trying to do too many things at once.

I work not because I have such important things to do, but because I have difficulty breaking an old parental message that I am lazy and need to earn worth by working and accomplishing. Fun is for rare occasions and only after I have worked hard.

Therefore, when I am not working or when I take a day off, I am uncomfortable and anxious. I feel I should be productive, get things done, earn some money, or at least tidy up the house.

I also work because I have a basic discomfort in social relationships. I am far more comfortable in work relationships; therefore, most of my socializing is done at lunch or in casual conversations on short breaks.

All of this affected my relationship with my children. Having fun with them, just taking it easy, going to the park, or to the swimming pool seemed unproductive. I would become anxious and eager to return home to do some productive housework. Although it was not necessary, I went to work when my children were small, thus adding to the pressure and anxiety I felt to accomplish many tasks during the day.

My work addiction has also affected my relationship with my husband. Predictably, I married a man who has similar beliefs about work and being busy. We tend to reinforce one another, so that our life together included little spontaneous recreation and fun. We have good times as a family but they are planned and happen only after work is done.

I would like to say that I am doing better. At least I am more aware of the problem and work (there is that word again) toward greater balance in my life, but I do continue to struggle with this powerful addiction.

Now that my children are young adults, I look back over my time with them and what I remember most fondly is the time I spent playing with them, the books we read, the trips to the park, how my older son loved to be held and swung when he was a toddler and how much my younger son enjoyed planning for Halloween. My greatest regret is that there are not more of these memories.

I certainly don't regret not spending more time at the hospital or the office, although I do regret not working smarter and focusing on what was truly important in my work and in my home.

If any of this strikes a familiar cord, I urge you to look at your behavior and the feelings and thoughts beneath compulsive over-working. Yes, it is possible to be a work addict and a full-time homemaker, always picking up, cleaning, running the kids to their many activities, and the myriad of other chores that parents do. I urge you to bring balance into your life. Learn to say "no" to some of the demands you make on yourself and that others make on you.

I urge you to bring relaxation, hanging out time, talking, and unscheduled fun into your relationship with your children. Do this not only for yourself, but also for them, for we pass on these behaviors and attitudes. As much as they resent our busyness and lack of attention, they will find that they carry these tendencies into their own lives. We pass this legacy onto them and they to their own children.

Like all family rules, you and I have choices. We have hourly choices about whether this day will be a time of constant work or if there will be balance between work and play, productivity and fun.

An Episcopal priest friend once counseled me to focus on "what is important in my life, not always on what seems urgent." I try to follow this advice and I pass it on to you now for you to examine in light of your own behavior.

New Rule: In our family we do not have to prove that we are worthwhile with constant working. We believe that relationships and the world around us are to be enjoyed. We are human beings, not human doings.

January 29

Old Rule: It is not appropriate to teach children about death.

Parents have a natural instinct to protect their children from those things that will cause them pain. However, death and the accompanying feelings of sadness are as much a part of life as the joy of birth.

Consequently, it is important, when the occasion arises, to discuss death honestly with our children. If we believe that our silence protects them from knowing or thinking about death, we are mistaken. Children do know about death, but our unwillingness to talk about these matters says to them that we are uncomfortable and they ought not to bring it up. Therefore, their questions go unanswered. They are left to figure it all out for themselves and when children are left to figure something out for themselves, not only are they frequently inaccurate but imagine things that are much more frightening than reality.

Death is a difficult subject to discuss. It is our discomfort that keeps us from sharing information with our children. When this subject arises, we might take the opportunity to discuss these matters with them as well as allow them to ask questions. I believe that it is important to allow children, especially school age children, to attend funerals and memorial services as long as we are there to be supportive and to answer their questions.

In addition, it is not necessary to hide our grief from our children. When we express our feelings openly, we give our children permission to express theirs. Grief that is expressed is grief that is easier to bear.

By doing this, I believe we can ease some of the fears children have about death. They do know about death, they do think about it, and they do fear death and loss. As parents it is part of our responsibility to work through our own discomfort so that we can be available for our children to teach them about loss, grief, and going on.

New Rule: It is important for parents to teach their children about the inevitable experience of death, loss, grieving, and continuing with life.

January 30

Old Rule: They have gone to a better place; it is not right to be sad.

Regardless of the truth of this statement, we say this to console others and ourselves when we have lost a loved one to death. We also tell our children this to comfort them and perhaps so that we do not have to witness our children's grief. However, children often hear this as an admonition not to grieve and certainly not to grieve openly. Adults also hear this as a criticism of their religious faith, that one should not grieve the loss of a loved one because the deceased is certainly much happier than when they were with us.

However, grief that is unexpressed does not simply go away. It stays locked inside and the hurt continues unhealed, like an open wound. Grief that is expressed will eventually heal and be easier to bear. This is true for both children and adults.

How much better it is for us and for our children to allow ourselves to acknowledge the pain of loss and the normal feelings of anger and sadness. Loss is easier to bear and heals more completely when we allow ourselves to acknowledge our hurt without the burden of "you shouldn't feel bad, they have gone to a better place" and the unspoken "it is selfish of you to feel bad when their suffering has ended and they are happier now."

New Rule: Even though I believe those who die have gone to a better place, the grief of those left behind, including children, needs to be expressed without guilt or shame.

January 31

Old Rule: We are going to have our children early, so we can get it over with and then we can do what we want.

There are many reasons to have children, even having children early in one's married life or having them close together. However, "getting it over with," like some unpleasant, but unavoidable chore, best done hurriedly so that one can get on to more pleasant things is rather disturbing.

Having been a college instructor for some years and an early parent myself, I have observed that those who complete their education and begin a career before having children or more children are much less stressed and inevitably have fewer conflicts about where to invest their time and energy.

Likewise, those couples that attain some stability in their careers and financial life prior to having children are likely to find parenting more satisfying. Babies, adorable as they are, are expensive and the normal strain of having children is magnified if funds are severely limited.

Being a parent, no matter how desired and satisfying, is restricting. Social life, career, educational options, travel, and even housing arrangements are all greatly influenced by the presence of children. If one has goals that are incompatible with child rearing then perhaps it is best to accomplish at least some of those before having children or additional children.

Becoming a parent is a wonderful, fulfilling, challenging, but permanently life altering experience, which requires maturity in order to do well. Such maturity comes, in part, from accomplishing one's goals and achieving stability in both the marital relationship and in one's personal life before embarking on the long-term commitment of parenting.

New Rule: Having children is only one of the options of young adulthood. I will decide when I am prepared to assume this commitment, knowing that my life will be forever changed.

February 1

Old Rule: Life is serious.

Many of us are terminally serious! Some of us were taught that having fun and experiencing joy was to the suffering of others. Others were taught that children could have fun and play, but adults have serious business to attend to, therefore such diversions should be left behind. Hence, we go through life serious about our jobs, our families, and even our recreation.

Life without humor, joy, playfulness, and even liberal doses of fantasy and silliness is not only dreary but also wasted. Give yourself permission to lighten up, to see the humor in the human condition, to daydream, to do something just because it pleases you, and even risk appearing frivolous to your serious family and friends. Laughter is potent medicine and should be taken several times a day. The price of this medicine is to let go of the "be serious" family rule.

New Rule: I choose to enjoy life and the children I have been given. The years of my life are indeterminate and my children are with me for only a short time. I have balance in my life between seriousness and fun. They are equally important.

February 2

Old Rule: My children don't care. They are failing in school and constantly misbehave. Our home miserable. They just don't care!

When I teach parenting classes, I often hear this lament from exasperated, frustrated parents. Their children are angry, underachieving, and misbehaving. As they grow older and more vocal, their language becomes more abusive toward their parents, particularly toward their mothers. Parents are understandably upset and often interpret lack of response by the children as "not caring."

In reality, children do care. They care about having their way, they care about what they want, and they care about pleasing their parents. When they are labeled "a problem" by their parents who are overly critical, expect too much from them, or are critical of their interests, then children will either give up or become rebellious and abusive.

When children feel that they cannot please or win the approval of their parents no matter what they do, they become what child psychiatrist Theodore Dreikurs called "discouraged children" (Children the Challenge, 1964). Discouraged children feel that they cannot win, no matter what they do. They feel they cannot please their parents, so why not do what they want? In other words, when we do not acknowledge what our children do that pleases us and instead focus on the negative, they will give up trying and seem not to care.

When your child does not seem to care, focus on yourself for a while. Children, as hard as it may be to believe, do want the loving approval of their parents. Ask yourself: Do I praise and acknowledge the efforts my children make? Do I catch them being good and praise their efforts? Am I constantly critical and talk only about what displeases me? Do I support my children's interests, even when I do not share those interests? Do I discipline my children by focusing on the act and not their character? When we begin to change our response to our children, our children will change their response to us.

New Rule: I know my children do want to please me and deeply desire my loving approval. I will find ways to show my children how much I approve of and love them.

February 3

Old Rule: Always keep a good fight going

Some years ago, a friend related to me that every Thanksgiving her parents had what the children came to refer to as "the gravy fight." The script was always pretty much the same. The fight began when the father tasted the gravy and stated that once again the mother had added too much salt. Mother objected and the argument ensued, continuing until everyone was uncomfortable and the expected warmth and good cheer of the family Thanksgiving meal was destroyed. Small wonder that as the children grew older, not only did they not invite friends home for Thanksgiving, they began avoiding these occasions themselves.

Many families have their own version of the "gravy fight," marring what should be enjoyable occasions for both adults and children. Permitting such conflict to continue and playing one's role in a ritual family argument is not only painful, it models poor conflict resolution to our children.

The ritual family fight requires at least two participants and an audience. Consequently, one protagonist or withdrawal of the audience can end the argument. Destructive conflict ends when one participant or a spectator refuses to play their role. When one combatant refuses to fight or an audience member calls attention to the impasse, the argument is effectively concluded.

This manner of defusing a ritual family conflict not only has potential for making family gatherings more pleasant and less tense and stressful, but it may also open the way for family members to relate to each other much differently. Refusing to play one's role in these ritual battles requires courage and maturity. Such action may not always be welcomed by those who are invested in keeping the fight going. Courage is especially necessary when one is confronting parents or other powerful family members, but resolving family conflict in a manner that enhances relationships is a powerful lesson to our children.

New Rule: I refuse to continue to play my part in ritual family arguments either as a participant or as a spectator. I try to model positive conflict resolution skills to my children.

February 4

Old Rule: Keeping the house clean and neat at all times is vitally important.

In her best selling book <u>Simple Abundance</u>, Sarah Branauch talks about "home care" versus housework or house cleaning. This is an important distinction.

Housework is the never-ending drudgery of keeping things looking good. If our goal is to keep the house looking perfect at all times and we spend almost all of our time and energy, both mental and physical, attempting to do this, we are not doing home care. We are not creating a home where our loved ones find a pleasant haven from the world. With all of our worrying and insistence on perfection, we create a sterile, yet clean and attractive environment in which people feel uncomfortable, as if their very presence clutters up the landscape. Have you ever noticed that home decorating magazines never include people in their perfectly arranged rooms? People, imperfect by definition, would ruin the decor.

It is up to the person in charge of the homemaking, (let's face it this is usually the female member of the household) to decide if she wishes to aspire to do the nearly impossible, never ending task of maintaining a home in which "Southern Living" or "Better Homes and Gardens" could do a photo feature and not have to call ahead.

"Home care" creates a haven for those who live there. A place where they can sit comfortably on the furniture. A place where books, games, and hobbies are in evidence. There might be a little dust and people who visit might not choose to eat from the floor, but they would feel at ease and welcome.

"Home care" lets the homemaker relax and focus on those things that nurture the family and herself, instead of the never ending, repetitive, stress producing, impossible task of maintaining a perfect house.

New Rule: Our home is not perfect. There is some clutter and dust and you certainly would not eat from the floor. However, it does reflect the needs and interests of those who live there. It is not perfect. The decorator magazine editors would be horrified, but it is our haven.

February 5

Old Rule: A woman's worth is determined by her attractiveness, especially to men.

We do not like to acknowledge that this rule remains powerful in our culture and certainly do not like to think that we pass this message on to our daughters, but every female is affected by this rule! Why else would we focus so much time, energy, and money on ways to make ourselves more attractive? Why would we be obsessed with weight and attaining the ideal figure? Women do not do all of these things to win the approval of other women. We do these things to win the approval of men.

It is natural that we would want males to view us as attractive and appealing. Animals, including human animals, attract each other visually in order to propagate the species. However, we are often obsessed with appearance and achieving the idealized attractiveness touted in the media. Even in this post-feminist revolution era, our culture values feminine beauty far more than it values the minds or the accomplishments of women. Girls learn very early that while it is good to be smart and talented, it is better to be beautiful. In their desire to help their daughters to be successful and happy, mothers will invest time, energy, and money in helping their daughters to be what our culture says is attractive, even though few girls will attain the ideal. The predicament is compounded by the fact that fathers, brothers, and other males are apt to praise beauty and criticize the lack of it more than any other attribute.

The task of countering the powerful cultural forces that say a woman's worth is based in how she looks is made more difficult when mothers are also ambivalent about these messages. For the sake of our daughters we must try not only to replace the old rules with ones that say that females are more than the attractiveness of their bodies, but also to deal more effectively with those messages by acknowledging their existence and their power. Girls need to be able to express their frustration and sadness about not attaining this idealized beauty. As parents, both mothers and fathers, we need to teach our daughters and sons to value females, not just for their appearance, but for their total being.

New Rule: As a parent I acknowledge the continuing power of the cultural messages concerning female beauty. I will examine my own attitudes and actions and attempt to teach both my daughters and my sons the importance of valuing others for who they are, not merely for their appearance. This is a difficult lesson to teach when the culture so strongly teaches the opposite, but it is the only way I can help my daughter deal successfully with these messages.

February 6

Old Rule: A boy's worth is determined by his athletic ability, while a man's worth is determined by how much money he makes.

This is another powerful cultural rule. Observe the adulation received by men who combine athletic prowess with the ability to command huge amounts of money and there is no denying the power of this rule.

Boys learn very quickly that being a good athlete is the ticket to attention and approval not only from their peers, but from adults as well. They also learn that the lack of athletic ability is a source of shame. As a result, their self-esteem is affected.

As boys grow older they receive the cultural message that their most important task is to develop abilities which will bring them money and that the more money they make the more valued and respected they are. Being athletic is also considered to be an important asset and assists in the ability to make money, even if one is not a professional athlete. These messages are extremely powerful and continue to affect self-image throughout a man's life. Athletic ability and the ability to make money are often determinants of power and the two combined command even more power.

Just as we cannot ignore the cultural message that a woman's worth is directly linked to her appearance, parents must also confront these messages. First, we must examine our own values with respect to athletic ability and the ability to make money, for our own attitudes speak loudly to our children. Second, we need to talk with our children about their feelings and their attitudes and encourage them to question the prevailing cultural messages.

Since most boys are not gifted athletes, we need to value, encourage, and express our appreciation for their other talents, interests, and abilities. As parents we need to adopt a more rational set of values about the worth of men and allow young men to develop and use their abilities and interests even if they do not net large amounts of money. In all of this you will find yourself at odds with prevailing cultural values, but the self esteem, indeed, the very lives of the men and boys we love are at stake.

New Rule: Men and boys are much more than their athletic ability and their ability to make money. Their lives and their abilities are much richer and diverse than this narrow picture and deserve full expression.

February 7

Old Rule: Real men are always ready to have sex.

People of both sexes believe this irrational rule. Women believe it and if a man is uninterested or unable to perform sexually they believe they are undesirable, he has been unfaithful, or question his masculinity, Men believe it and question their masculinity or feelings for their partner when they do not feel interested in sex, are not immediately aroused, or experience episodes of impotence. This rule and the beliefs underlying it are the cause of misunderstanding and emotional pain for both men and women. This is tragic, for this belief is totally false!

Stress, illness, pain, fatigue and depression can affect a man's interest in lovemaking. Unresolved difficulties in the relationship can also lessen a man's desire for intercourse. Indeed, according to a "Time" magazine survey, the majority of men questioned stated that they had had sexual intercourse when they did not want to because they felt pressured. Freeing men to be human and not just performers in the bedroom, lessens anxiety about sex and it enhances love making, especially when men and women feel confident enough to talk about their feelings, desires, and preferences.

As our children's first teachers we need to inform ourselves about sexuality so that we may pass informed, rational attitudes on to them. Our attitudes and unspoken messages about sexuality are just as meaningful, if not more so, than our actual words.

New Rule: Deciding to say "no" does not make a man less masculine. I will inform my children about sexuality and intimacy so that they might use these gifts compassionately and wisely.

February 8

Old Rule: What children don't know won't hurt them.

Some time ago, I was listening to a mother talk about her relationship with her college age son. It had been a difficult relationship and she was relieved that he was now out of the house and in college. During the course of the conversation, she remarked that as a boy he had made the all-star baseball team several times but she had never told him. He still did not know he had been selected. She said she did this because they had another child to entertain during the summer and they had wanted to go on vacation.

I was taken aback. I had never considered this option to my own frustration with what seemed to be an endless all-star baseball season, when I did not know whether to hope that the team would win or lose.

However, the more I thought about her solution to the problem the more uncomfortable I became. Not to tell a child that he had achieved an honor for which he had practiced and played his best seemed to me to inject into the parent-child relationship a basic dishonesty.

From my experience both as a parent and as a counselor, I believe that it is best to be honest with our children. If we simply do not want to do what they are asking us to do, we have the right to say "no." Even though such a stance might be met initially with anger, pleading and rebellion, I believe in the long run such honesty enhances our relationship with our children. Dishonesty, while it may initially allow one to avoid angry scenes, damages relationships. If children feel they cannot trust us in small matters, they may feel that we cannot be trusted with larger ones.

New Rule: I try to be truthful with my children, even when the truth initially results in conflict. Dishonesty leads to mistrust among members of the family. Honesty leads to trusting, open relationships.

February 9

Old Rule: Religion is for fools.

In my counseling practice, I occasionally encountered a young person reared with this rule. They were usually confused and adrift in a world that made no sense to them. They had no anchor and nothing to believe in: not themselves, not other people, and certainly not the all too human parent who pronounced all faith in something greater than one's self as "foolish."

Religion and religious institutions are created and sustained by human beings. As such, they are subject to all of the weaknesses that befall humans. Certainly one can find hypocrisy, pettiness, struggles for power, greed, and ignorance in religious institutions. Wisdom, love, caring, and the spiritual underpinnings of religion are often lost in human weakness and folly. However, a belief in that which is greater, wiser, more loving than human beings is expressed in the lives of people in every culture throughout history.

To arrogantly rob children of all sense of the divine with this rule is to set them adrift in uncertainty and without a framework in which to even begin to make sense of the complicated world they encounter.

Many of us have doubts and disappointments with respect to religion. We experience dark nights of doubt and anger in our religious faith, but none of us has the right nor the wisdom to declare that there is nothing of value there. It is more beneficial to share with our children our beliefs, our doubts, and our experiences - our spiritual journey. Perhaps in our journey they can find something of value to hold on to.

New Rule: Despite my own doubts, I try to share with my children the wisdom and value of religious faith.

February 10

Old Rule: I really didn't want a child (another child), but we had one anyway.

I was talking with a friend whose mother, now in her 80's, had announced to a mutual friend that she really didn't want any more children after her first. My friend, who is the second child, was shocked by her mother's honesty, but also grateful to finally have her questions answered. She always felt she was a disappointment. No matter what she did or how hard she tried, she seemingly could not please her mother. She believed, in her child's logic, that somehow she was defective and not worthy of her mother's love and approval. Finally knowing her mother did not want <u>any</u> additional children, not just her, was a liberating experience.

Sadly, she is not alone. All too often children grow up believing they are defective and a disappointment to their parents, feeling that if they were different, then their parent would love and approve of them. In truth, they were sensing the parent's feelings of being an unwilling parent.

In these days of safe, effective birth control, we have a choice about the number of children we have. Hopefully, we are moving toward a time when every child will be a wanted child. However, I fear that sometimes we have children not because we want them, but because we feel that we should want them. We may believe it is time to have a baby, our friends are having them, our parents want to be grandparents, we want to quit work, it will improve our relationship, or it is not okay to rear an only child.

Parenthood, even when we want to become a parent, is an all-consuming commitment. When we don't want children, parenthood is an onerous burden. We cannot successfully disguise our feelings of being trapped and burdened, no matter how hard we may try.

No child asks to be born. Just as we have the right to determine if we want to be parents, every child has the right to be a wanted child.

New Rule: We take responsibility for assuring that our children are wanted just for themselves and not because becoming a parent is "the thing to do."

February 11

Old Rule: My children must use the talents that they have.

Having a child who is a talented student, athlete, artist, or musician is a wonderful dilemma. We may believe their unique and precious gifts should be used to the fullest, but our children may have little or no interest in expressing themselves in this manner. They may not wish to put forth the energy and dedication necessary to develop their talents.

This can be the source of much frustration and many parent /child arguments. Truthfully, the parental desire to have a child develop a talent that the child does not find important can make home a miserable place.

Inevitably, it is the parent who loses the battle. Not even the most insistent parent can force a child to exert the energy and dedication necessary to develop such talents. We may force them to show up in the class or on the athletic field, but we cannot make them do the work. When we allow this to become a battleground with our children, we also damage our relationship with them. No matter how strongly we feel about their abilities or how much we grieve their lost opportunities, we must let go and let them find their own way to express themselves. (Often it is also our own lost opportunity and dreams that we are grieving.)

We cannot force another human being, even our children, to be something that they do not want to be. All we can do is suggest, support, and make opportunities available. We have at this point exhausted the limits of our power and all we can do is to let go.

Difficult? Very. Realistic and in the best interest of our relationship with our children? Yes!

New Rule: As a parent I know that my power to influence my children to use their gifts and talents is limited. All I can do is recognize, encourage, support, and make opportunities available. They must do the rest.

February 12

Old Rule: A mistake is proof of stupidity and inadequacy.

"You are so stupid! You know better than that! I can't believe you did that! What is wrong with you?!" Many of us can recall all too clearly the sting of those words from childhood, when even the smallest mistake was cause for an angry, shaming attack. As children we were often expected to know what we were not taught, to perform tasks perfectly every time, never ask questions, and above all, never make mistakes.

Many of us continue to live by this absurd rule. We don't take chances. We don't try those things of which we are unsure. We avoid mistakes at all costs, but when we do make mistakes, we berate and shame ourselves with the same words our parents used. We also impatiently berate our own children when they make mistakes.

Good parenting means teaching children what they do not know and explaining and supporting new behavior when the inevitable mistakes occur. We can also re-parent ourselves in much the same way. In a healthy family, a mistake is an opportunity to learn rather than proof of inadequacy. We can choose to stop the old "You sure are stupid" message and instead ask our children and ourselves "What did you learn?" and "How could you do this differently?" When we begin to view mistakes as occasions to learn and grow, we can risk making them.

New Rule: No one need be ashamed of mistakes. We learn our most important lessons from them. They are proof of our willingness to grow.

February 13

Old Rule: If you can't do it well the first time, don't even try. You don't want to look foolish.

Children grow from not knowing what "being foolish" means to being self-conscious and vitally concerned with looking good. If we grow up with this rule from early childhood, it probably continues to affect our behavior. We don't try new sports, hobbies, or even new careers. We don't pursue our dreams because we are terrified of looking foolish.

We know that every new skill requires learning time (at least we should know), but we irrationally feel we should be good at something the first time we attempt it. If you don't know, I'm telling you right now: it is insane to assume that anything worth doing does not require learning time!

This rule is harmful to us and we do not want to pass it on to our children. We want them to explore and learn. We want them to have a wide variety of skills and interests. However, we do pass on this irrational thinking. We expect too much, too soon.

We expect a child to play well who saw the soccer field for the first time last month. We don't not give them learning time, time to make mistakes, and time to look foolish. We don't take risks ourselves. We say, "I couldn't do that" when a new opportunity is presented to us. What we really mean is, "I don't want to look foolish, while I am learning to do that".

Instead, we want to help our children accept that each new skill takes learning time. We want them to know that the fun, adventure, and exhilaration are in learning not in doing things perfectly the first time. Doing something well the first time is boring. It doesn't matter what others who stand on the sidelines say. Actually, we probably need to get off the sidelines in life ourselves and begin to learn to do new things and accept new challenges, even if it means that we make mistakes and look foolish. Only then can we hope to teach our children a spirit of adventure and curiosity about meeting life's challenges.

New Rule: I do not worry about looking foolish to life's observers. I view life as a constant learning experience and am eager to try new things. By adopting this attitude, I can help my children to have the courage to pursue their own interests and dreams.

February 14

Old Rule: Love is scarce.

In practical terms, living by this rule means that if one person in the family is loved then others are less loved or that one child is labeled the "favorite" child while another might be labeled the "problem" child. Love is conditional, fleeting, given for good behavior, and unexpectedly withdrawn.

In truth, real love is not finite, but rather infinite. Love grows as it is given. There are no bounds to true love. It is not given grudgingly to control and manipulate. Love is given freely, not as a reward for good behavior, but for just being who we are.

Love overlooks and forgives mistakes and human failings. Love does not demand exclusivity. Love does not even demand to be loved in return.

Parents find that we love our children in different ways. Although we maybe reluctant to admit it, we feel closer to one child than another, usually the child that mirrors our best attributes. Likewise, we are apt to have difficulty relating to another child, usually the one that mirrors the things we do not like about ourselves. However, as healthy parents we realize that we love each child and that love knows no bounds. Even when they are in trouble or have displeased us, love does not end. It is not scarce and contingent on what our children are currently doing or even end with estrangement. Love is just there, hoping that our children will lead happy and productive lives.

Love is patient; love is kind; love is not envious or boastful or arrogant or rude. It does not insist on its own way; it is not irritable or resentful; it does not rejoice in wrongdoing, but rejoices in the truth. It bears all things, believes all things, hopes all things, endures all things. Love never ends.
1 Corinthians 13:4

New Rule: In our home, love is not a scarce thing. It is plentiful, dispensed freely, and grows as it is given.

February 15

Old Rule: Big boys don't cry.

Men's feelings, or the lack of them, are the topic of considerable discussion. Indeed, the belief that "men do not show their feelings" is a cliché. Like most clichés, it has a basis in truth. Men are taught from earliest childhood that to be masculine is to hide or deny feelings of hurt and pain. Even young boys are taught not to show vulnerability by expressing emotions. However, the cost to men is immense. Cardiovascular disease, depression, and alcoholism are linked to stress resulting from repressed feelings. Men simply do not live as long as women.

Men are likely to feel puzzled and frustrated in relationships when they are asked to share their feelings, including emotional pain. The "don't cry" rule is so firmly entrenched that they maybe at a loss to even identify what they feel. Masculinity is often linked to being emotionally numb.

Nevertheless, men do have a choice. They can choose to begin to express feelings, including tears, with those they love and trust. Although it may seem awkward at first, men are capable of sharing feelings and can reclaim this capacity.

New Rule: For men - I choose to acknowledge and express my feelings, including hurt and sorrow. I allow myself to be vulnerable to those I love.
For women - I give the men I love permission to express feelings without loss of masculinity.
For parents - I give my son the freedom to express his feelings of pain and sadness, even if it means that he cries. I do not shame him for his feelings.

February 16

Old Rule: Nice girls don't get angry.

A therapist colleague believes that while men in our culture suffer from the effects of repressed hurt, women suffer from the effects of repressed anger. I think there is considerable truth in this statement.

Even today, girls in our culture are often taught to be quiet, pleasing to others, and compliant. In other words, girls are taught to be good. Whatever "good" means, it does not mean being assertive and expressing anger. Girls who are "not good" are often chastised for being too rowdy, too loud, too bossy, too pushy, and later in life as "bitchy".

The consequences to girls and women are devastating. When girls are told not to make a fuss and to be "nice and quiet," their self-esteem begins to fall. What they hear in these statements is that their concerns and they, themselves, are not important enough to be heard. As a result, by the time they reach their early teens, low self-esteem is a serious problem for many girls. As women, we suffer conflicts about whether we have the right to be angry when we are taken advantage of or even abused. In essence, we become perennial victims trying to get our needs met through manipulation, constant complaining, playing the long suffering martyr, or waiting for being "good" to pay off.

What we really need are appropriate ways to express this normal human emotion. This begins when parents allow and even encourage daughters to verbalize anger and to take action when they feel they have been wronged, even if others, including other parents, teachers, and their grandparents, may label them as "not nice." As a matter of fact, we might begin to measure our success in parenting our daughters when people cease to describe them as nice, sweet, little girls.

New Rule: Anger is a normal human emotion. I teach my daughter to acknowledge and express herself when she is angry. I give myself and those I care about permission to express the full range of feelings, including anger, without condemnation.

February 17

Old Rule: Stuff your anger until you explode!

Eric Berne, creator of Transactional Analysis, called it "collecting brown stamps." That is, permitting someone to take advantage of you, to violate your rights, until you feel justified in feeling victimized or exploding with rage. This destructive way of handling anger is all too common and the source of many family problems.

The scenario usually goes something like this. I put up with inconsiderate, irresponsible behavior in silence, carefully nurturing and stuffing my anger. I build up resentments, but keep the top on this simmering volcano of anger. I wait for the final straw, the violation to occur when I feel justified in blowing up, spewing out my stored anger, while telling everyone within ear shot, "That I have had enough and just cannot take it any more." Chances are I am out of control and say and do hurtful things I would not ordinarily say or do. After the eruption is over, I feel remorse and guilt, but an unspoken sense of justification because I was pushed over the edge by the bad behavior of others. I vow not to do this again and sincerely apologize to those whose feelings I have bruised. Mistakenly, I avoid any expression of anger and, therefore, begin the process again with exactly the same result. I have used "I" in this description because this is my game. This is the drama from which I have had to recover. I still have relapses, but I am happy to report that I am making progress.

In order to recover, I have had to take responsibility for how I express anger. I have had to abandon the nice girl role and take responsibility for the fact that I do get angry and I have the right to express it. I have learned that unexpressed anger does not go away. It just gets bigger. I have had to admit I do not have the right to collect resentments and then blow up at others. I have learned and continue to learn that when I take responsibility for dealing with a situation in which I experience anger and stay current with anger (not allowing it to build up), I am not abusive to others, and they are more likely to listen to me and respect my desires and opinions.

I hope I learned these principles early enough to model them for my children. I know I am much happier and my relationships are greatly improved when I practice them.

New Rule: In our family, we acknowledge that anger is a normal emotion and unavoidable when we live with others. We also believe that anger that is not expressed only simmers until it finds a way to be expressed. This is true not only for adults but for children as well. Therefore, we know that each of us has the right to express anger in a manner that is timely, responsible, and doesn't injure others.

February 18 & 19

Old Rule: I know they will change if only I can..........

Can what? Wait long enough? Find the right words? Find the right person to talk with them? Be good enough or loving enough?

In counseling individuals and families in crisis, I have noticed that in almost every such family there is someone who is waiting for another person to change in order for the situation to improve.

Waiting for another person to change is one of the most futile and painful situations in which human beings can find themselves. Yet many of us spend years in relationships waiting for another to change. We seldom wait passively. We argue, cry, appeal to reason, try to find the right words, take care of them, get others to talk some sense into them, and manipulate. We do everything except the one thing that is in our power to do - let go and change ourselves.

This waiting can go on for years. Recently, I read about the first wife of an often-married man. She waited for him to "come to his senses and come back to her." Indeed, she spent more than 40 years of her life, not his life, but her life, waiting. When he died, he had been married to another woman for a number of years and had no intention of returning. She was left waiting for him to change until the day that he died. While extreme, she is not unusual.

Co-Dependents Anonymous, a group that knows a lot about the futility of waiting for another person to change so they can be happy, often paraphrases Reinhold Niebuhr's Serenity Prayer. They pray, "God, grant me the serenity to change the person that I can change, the courage to change that person, and the wisdom to know that I am that person."

In reality, the only person we can change is ourselves. When we begin to let go and to change our reaction to another, we change the situation. When we allow another person to suffer the natural consequences of their behavior, we change the situation. When we use our energy to take care of ourselves and our children rather than engage in attempts to argue with, manipulate, reason, or plead with another, we change the situation. When we begin to change our attitude about another person and accept them as they are, we change the situation.

When we stop trying to force another to take responsibility for their behavior and start taking responsibility for our own, then we can begin to reclaim our power from that person. For when we attempt to force another to change, that person has the power in our lives, even though they may appear weak and helpless. If another's behavior is destructive to themselves and others and becomes intolerable, we may be forced to decide to end the relationship. This is difficult and painful, but to spend our lives waiting for someone to "see the light" or "come to their senses" is far more painful and destructive.

Not only is this behavior destructive to adults, but it also teaches our children to enter into their own version of these relationships, especially girls. When we as mothers (this pattern seems to afflict more women than men) stay in destructive relationships waiting for someone else to change, we teach our daughters to find lost souls or self-destructive people, especially men, and enter into relationships in which they wait for another to change.

Only by taking charge of our own lives and using our power where we truly have it, can we teach our children to do the same.

New Rule: I choose not to spend my life waiting for another to change. I accept that it is useless and beyond my power to attempt to change another. I take responsibility for my own life and am willing to teach my children to do the same.

February 20

Old Rule: A normal woman wants children and a good mother never regrets having them.

Mothering is the most difficult and challenging occupation. It is virtually unrelenting! One is never completely off duty, even when asleep. The product parents create is complex, never completed as planned, always imperfect, and the quality is not evident for at least 21 years after the inception of the process. Few of us, if we really knew the depth of the commitment and the demands of the role, would actually have the nerve to undertake the job.

Yet, somehow, we believe that a real woman desires to be a mother and we say as much to our non-mothering friends. We also believe that once we have children we should always want to put their needs and wants ahead of our own, never resent the constant demands on our time and energy, and never question the wisdom of having them in the first place. In short, a really good mother is always loving, patient, self-sacrificing, and thankful to be the recipient of this wonderful gift of children. Yeah! Right!

Get real! Let yourself off the hook! Don't feel guilty about the minutes even days or weeks when you question the sanity of having children. It is perfectly normal to feel frustrated, overwhelmed, impatient, and to wonder if there might be somewhere to go to resign from this job! Such feelings, especially when they go on for an extended period of time, are usually the result of mothering overload that can result in mothering burnout, a state of chronic resentment and martyrdom that is not healthy for mother or children.

If for no other reasons than being a more patient and effective parent and role model of self-care for your children, take time for yourself. Do something, anything, for yourself, even if only for half an hour. You may feel a little guilty at first, taking time for yourself, but you will get the hang of it. The world of mothering will not stop if you get off for while. It might even make a better mother of you! I challenge you to find out for yourself!

New Rule: I accept that at times I tire of being "Mom." I need not feel guilty about my feelings and my need to make time for those things I enjoy that do not involve being a mother.

February 21

Old Rule: Suffer in silence.

I used to believe that my inability to suffer in silence was evidence of a character flaw. Today, I believe that my unwillingness to endure any painful circumstance, which I have within my power to change, is instead a personal strength. Yet many people, especially women, endure distressing situations and relationships at work and at home. They spend years waiting for their turn to have their needs met, their desires considered, or for someone to wake up, grow up, or change. They suffer, but despite their beliefs to the contrary, they rarely suffer in silence.

Such long suffering people complain bitterly to anyone who will listen, often to other sufferers who will not only sympathize but also have their own stories to contribute. Mired in such patterns, they do not talk to the person who is responsible for the difficulty. They don't take responsibility for confronting and changing the situation. They complain and stay stuck.

Such persons unwittingly pass this pattern of passive behavior onto their children. By suffering in silence, we say to our children there is nothing they can do to change the problems in their lives. In failing to assemble the courage to make changes in the way we relate to others, we unwittingly teach this cowardice and sense of helplessness to our children.

"Cowardice" may seem like an excessively strong word to apply to such behavior, but it is cowardly to complain without taking responsibility for what we are able to change. Granted, we are not able to change another person, but we are able to voice our dissatisfaction to the person involved or to accept that others are not going to be as we want them to be and find other ways to get our needs met.

Suffering in silence is not a virtue, but instead an expensive character flaw that we might decide we do not wish to pass on to our children.

New Rule: I do not teach my children to suffer in silence. I teach them to change what they have the power to change and to accept what they, in truth, cannot change.

February 22

Old Rule: Money is the root of all evil, but it is important to have it.

Growing up with this contradictory rule guarantees we will experience confusion and conflict concerning money. Such ambivalence results in our investing time and energy obtaining the skills necessary to succeed in making money and then finding that we feel guilty about having it. We feel that our worth is somehow contingent upon our ability to earn money and yet feel uneasy about spending it, especially on ourselves. As a result, we make irresponsible decisions about money. Unable to account for how we spend it, we turn money management over to our spouse, retaining, of course, the option to complain and criticize if they do not manage it as we would like.

Accepting responsibility for our attitudes about money is just as important as accepting responsibility for the way we spend it. Sorting out contradictions and conflicts in our attitudes is the first step in gaining control over our financial lives. Despite our best lectures about money management to our children, our attitudes and actions will likely determine their money management style. We cannot teach our children to handle their own money in a rational, successful manner until we can do so ourselves.

New Rule: I accept and have pride in my ability to work and earn money. I also accept responsibility for the manner in which I spend money. I teach my children sane and rational money management by doing so myself. I use a portion of our money to help others, a portion to give pleasure to those I love, including myself, and save a portion for later use. As with most of life, balance is the key to success.

February 23

Old Rule: If you want it, buy it. Worry about paying for it tomorrow.

Our consumer culture encourages this rule. Our media, especially television, indoctrinates children early with a "buy now, pay later" message. We are teaching our children from earliest childhood that they are entitled to the "good things of life" and in our consumer culture the "good things in life" mean material possessions.

I learned in early adulthood, as my husband and I increased our earning and buying power, that my wants are literally endless. I drive a dependable car, but would like to have a more luxurious one. I live in a comfortable home, but would like to have one on a lake. Much of what I have today I would not have dreamed of having 30 years ago, but yet I would like to have something a little nicer, a little more luxurious. This may be human nature, but it is certainly the way our consumer economy operates. We have a sense of entitlement about material goods and our children have it too. Most of us live beyond our means. Credit card debt is high and our savings rate in the United States is low compared to the rest of the world.

While we have an enviably high standard of living that attracts people from all over the world, much of our consumer culture is built on a shallow foundation of mounting debt and financial short-sightedness. We feel we must teach our children to manage money wisely, but we face the difficult task of countering the consumer culture messages of "buy now, this will make you happy, you are entitled; pay later." The first step in teaching our children is to put our own financial house in order and begin to live by sane money principles. These principles are simple. The bills will come. I must pay them sometime. Credit cards purchases are made with borrowed money and will have to be paid back with interest. Possessions will not make me ultimately happy. They may make my life more pleasant or please me temporally, but will not bring fulfillment. Possessions do not buy self-worth. Status built on money and possessions is a trap, for there is always someone who has more money and more possessions.

We all know these principles, but it is far more difficult to live by them. Teaching our children these facts is one of the most difficult aspects of being a parent in this culture, but it is essential in order for them to develop into well-balanced competent adults.

New Rule: In our family we try to place money and possessions in perspective - nice to have but ultimately not fulfilling. We also try to teach our children to manage money, especially credit, wisely.

February 24

Old Rule: If you are attractive, you are more lovable

Our culture puts a high premium on physical attractiveness. There are studies that suggest that even small children attribute greater intelligence, virtue, and desirability to attractive people. Attractive people have an easier time finding employment, are waited on more quickly in stores, and even get help faster when they have difficulty. The deck is stacked in favor of those who are physically attractive.

However, any cursory examination of the population says that most of us are not over whelmingly physically attractive. Yet many children, especially girls, are taught that the most important thing about them is whether or not they are pretty. Both girls and boys go through periods of time when they are awkward and not particularly attractive. This can be an especially traumatic time for them. Often they adopt standards of attractiveness that are impossible to achieve and their self-esteem suffers as a result.

While we cannot change the cultural messages that being attractive is not only better but vitally important, we can help our children by devaluing the importance of attractiveness ourselves, and focusing on academic, athletic, and artistic talents.

We might also begin to develop some wisdom ourselves concerning this topic, since most of us have to some extent accepted the messages about the value of looking good. We might begin to value lovely personality attributes, handsome intellectual achievements, graceful athletic performance, ravishing musical and artistic ability, and elegant acts of compassion and kindness.

New Rule: In our family we try to maintain a balance between valuing physical attractiveness and other attributes which comprise beautiful human beings.

February 25

Old Rule: Children are not sensitive about their appearance.

My husband and I were having breakfast in the elegant dining room of an old inn. Next to us was another family also having breakfast. The family included a mother, father, boy about 10, and the mother's parents. It was the grandmother's birthday and she was opening and admiring her presents. She was especially appreciative of the gift from the child and told him so. The family was having a lovely morning.

As the pleasant exchanges continued, the mother suddenly looked at the boy and said, "We have to do something about that hair." The child's happy, confident expression vanished and was replaced by a look of shame. The grandmother attempted to change the subject, but to no avail, as the father chimed in with his own negative comments about what appeared to me to be neatly brushed hair.

It is unlikely that either of these parents would have criticized a friend or even each other in such a shaming, callous manner in the midst of a birthday party, but somehow they believed it was perfectly appropriate to say such things to their child.

As parents, we are our children's most powerful and important mirror of their worth and attractiveness. Therefore, we have the power and choice either to support or destroy their opinions of themselves, including their confidence in their appearance.

One way to support healthy feelings of self-worth is to be aware of what we say to them about themselves. When we feel we must be critical, we can pick a private time to express our opinions about their appearance in a respectful, non-demeaning manner. We should certainly avoid being critical when others are around. The world is very rough on children's self-esteem. As parents we should take opportunities to build self-esteem and avoid diminishing it.

New Rule: Children, like adults, are sensitive about their appearance. When I feel it is necessary to make a critical, instructional comment to my children, I select a private time.

February 26

Old Rule: Women cannot be friends with other women.

This rule, which even some women accept, assumes that the source of the inability of women to have friendships with other women is their competition for the attention and approval of men. According to this sexist stereotype, women are in constant competition in their efforts to attract men. Women are assumed to be dishonest and devious, willing to do almost anything to best another woman or to "steal" another's man. In short, it is a mighty foolish woman who actually trusts another woman. This sexist rubbish does, indeed, lead to distrust and emotional distance among women, especially young women.

Competition is a fact of life for the young, men as well as women. While competition among males is viewed as healthy and even desirable, competition among women is viewed as evidence of basic untrustworthiness. Women are competitive, but many avenues of competition have traditionally been blocked to them, so they do compete in their ability to be attractive and to attract the opposite sex.

However, females of all ages do develop friendships in which they find not only companionship and enjoyment but also understanding and support in difficult times. As friendships continue, shared feelings lead to a deepening sense of trust. The exact opposite of this rule is a more common circumstance, women do establish friendships with other women that support and sustain them through the years.

New Rule: I choose to help my daughters find appropriate channels for their competitive energies. I also teach them that trustworthiness is one of their finest assets. It will help them build strong, rewarding friendships with both men and women.

February 27

Old Rule: I don't want to spoil my baby by picking it up every time it cries.

During a recent conversation with a first time mother about her beautiful new baby, she asked, with obvious concern, if I thought she would "spoil" her baby by picking her up every time she cried. Of all the things new parents might worry about, this should be the last one!

Our instincts tell us that when an infant cries there is a reason and we need to attend to the discomfort, even if the discomfort is the need to be close to us. The only way babies have to communicate their needs to us is by crying. Likewise, we respond to their cries knowing they are totally dependent upon us. Interaction with parents is a child's first experience with other human beings. Babies who experience their needs being met in a timely and consistent manner learn to trust others. They learn that the world is a dependable, safe, and nurturing place. They learn about being loved and are laying the psychological groundwork for learning to love others. Of course, they do not have the verbal skills to express these feelings, but those who study child development have, for some time, placed an emphasis on the importance of meeting infants' needs for touch and closeness as well as for food and bodily comfort in a consistent manner.

As for this "spoiling" business, while it is possible to over-indulge an older child by giving into their tearful demands, it is virtually impossible to "spoil" a crying infant by picking them up.

If you have a new baby, relax and enjoy this time. Pick them up and cuddle them. Enjoy your baby! This time will go by all too quickly. Pay attention to and respect your instincts. They are frequently correct. Learn to use them throughout your life as a parent.

New Rule: I respond when my baby needs my attention. I follow my instincts to pick up, cuddle, and hold my children.

February 28

Old Rule: These new parenting ideas are not for me. They are fads. I'll just stick with what worked for my parents and what seems to work for me.

While there is much value in using the common sense wisdom of child-rearing of our parents and grandparents and certainly wisdom in doing what our intuition says is right for our children, there is also value in being open to new ideas and new ways of doing things. One of these new things is actually an ancient practice that has been updated and studied so that we know it has scientific validity. This is infant massage.

Mothers have been massaging their infants for centuries. It is, indeed, instinctive. When we pick up a baby, we automatically rub its back to soothe or to show affection. In other cultures, women learn from their mothers to massage their infants in order to comfort them.

In the past few years, we have seen an interest in infant massage develop from the work of women like Vimala Schnider McClure. We are seeing a growing body of scientific research that suggests that massaging babies has many benefits. Such benefits include increased ability to sleep soundly, fewer digestive problems, and faster weight gain especially in premature infants. Subjectively, parents report a greater sense of ease and increased bonding with their children.

On a purely practical level, massage gives parents something of benefit to do with their infants as they interact with them, which is not only fun but may also help with some of the sleep and colic problems babies experience. It is also a way for fathers to feel more a part of taking care of the baby, thus increasing their sense of competence.

As babies get older and develop into toddlers and even into young children, these simple, easy-to-learn techniques can provide a framework for special parent/child time. There is literally no down side or drawback to learning and practicing infant massage.

If you are interested, contact The International Association of Infant Massage at 1-800- 248-5432. They will be happy to give you the name of infant massage instructors in your area.

New Rule: We are open to learning new things to help us parent our children.

February 29

Old Rule: Do it right! Daily reading books are supposed to cover all possibilities. You have to give readers their daily reading, even if the day comes only once every four years. So, do it right!

"Do it right, every time" is the old message that lingers in my head. But whose words are they? Who decides what "doing it right" is supposed to be? Sometimes doing it right for me and I suspect for most of us, is to pull back and not *do* anything. Just be, take time to be in the moment. Relax without constantly striving to do it right, do better, do the best that you can, or do it differently. Whatever you are doing, let go, just be, hang out, and know that whatever your circumstances you are probably doing the best that you can on most days and your children will likely grow up to be okay. Give yourself a break, and do it frequently. Just live life. Don't constantly try to change it. Relax!

Think I'll take it easy for a while.

New Rule: Take a break! Hang out! Just be!

March 1

Old Rule: Talk! Talk! Talk! But don't say anything.

Some families talk endlessly. They discuss politics, religion, the weather, sports, and, especially, absent family members. Other families engage in heated political and religious discussions, peppered with liberal doses of disputed family history. Endless chatter marks every gathering.

In all of this chatter, two elements are often lost: listening and the expression of genuine feelings. People talk but never hear what others are saying. When another is talking, they are formulating their response. Actually, they do not really care what others are saying. They only want their chance to talk.

While we would not care to engage in a serious dialogue at every family gathering, to avoid it completely, implying that serious discussions are neither welcome nor tolerated, means that we do not really know what our family members are feeling and thinking.

Such endless, empty chatter may leave us feeling lonely even in the midst of our families.

Breaking this talk, talk, talk pattern requires that we stop talking and start listening. In our silence, we can begin to tune into our own thoughts and feelings and hear what others are really saying. We can then begin to share our thoughts and feelings and invite others to do the same. Like breaking the "don't talk" rule, others might not be willing to join us. We cannot control the behavior of others. We can only control our own. What we can do is pay our family members the most extravagant of compliments - listening.

New Rule: In our family, we take time to listen to what is important to others.

March 2

Old Rule: That was good, but …

This rule sounds like praise followed by helpful constructive criticism, but when used consistently, it fosters discouragement and rebellion and kills self-esteem. If you have difficulty seeing this clearly, recall when your own parents said, "You did a good job cleaning up your room, but the bed could be neater," "The B in math was good, but it could have been an A if you had tried harder," or "Thanks for mowing the lawn, but the yard looks better if it is cut diagonally rather than left to right." The critical parent, who was probably reared with critical parents themselves, seems unable to stop at praise. They must add a critical comment, which is meant to instruct, but instead sends the message to the child, "You just didn't get it quite right."

Eventually, children will internalize this criticism and believe themselves incapable of doing anything good enough to please their parents. Such children either decide to stop trying or rebel and refuse to do what they are asked. Rebelling or giving up makes sense when you understand that what children really hear is not praise followed by encouragement to improve. Instead, they tend not to hear the first part of the message and focus on what follows: the "but." Eventually they decide," No matter how hard I try, I'll never get it right. I'll never please my parents, so why try?" When they decide that no matter what they do they will never please us, we and our children are in serious trouble! Children who feel that they cannot please their parents not only lack self-esteem, but will likely decide to please themselves and in doing so will make serious errors in judgment.

Our children will never perform perfectly. Persistent criticism, no matter how well intended, damages their self esteem and our relationship with them. Remember this the next time you are attempted to say, "That was good, but…"

New rule: I do not routinely couple praise with criticism. Knowing that children respond better to parental praise rather than criticism, I use praise freely and criticism judiciously.

March 3 and 4

Old Rule: We do not want a fat child.

Our culture is obsessed with weight. We spend millions of dollars on diets and weight reduction programs. We idolize thin, waif-like women and insist that they are the ideal. We honor the muscular, trim male athlete. Yet we are an over-fed and undernourished culture that survives on high carbohydrate, fat laden convenience foods. On average we are getting heavier every year. A visit to any public place offers ample evidence of the number of overweight children and adults. Yet, our culture sends numerous contradictory messages about food, eating, being overweight, and ideal body size.

In some, families being overweight is a terrible thing, so terrible that family members of healthy weight and normal size, especially girls, are criticized for being too fat or admonished that they had better watch it because they are getting fat.

While we are fond of saying that we want our children to be healthy, I suspect the true reason that we put pressure on children to be thin is our aversion to overweight people and the belief that overweight people are not physically attractive. We also know that overweight children are teased and suffer from negative stereotyping, including laziness and decreased intelligence and ability. Overweight people in our culture are simply not as well regarded as people who weigh less.

Additionally, we want our children to be accepted by their peers. If they are not overweight, such acceptance is more likely. However, focusing on weight as the total measure of their worth as human beings is a terrible mistake. Berating and shaming an overweight child or adult never helped them to loose weight. It only increases their sense of inadequacy, lowers their self-esteem, and puts barriers of anger and pain between them and others.

We can assist our children in attaining and maintaining normal, healthy weight by first adopting a common sense attitude about what is normal. We should also appreciate that children will go through developmental stages when they will appear to be overweight, typically prior to an increase in height.

Second, we need to look at our own eating habits. When we consume large amounts of soft drinks and junk food and the only vegetable that we eat and offer our children is the tomato on a fast food hamburger, we cannot expect our children to be of normal weight. If we bring high fat snack food into the house, that is what they will eat. If we reward children and ourselves with food ("If you are good I will buy you a soda or a candy bar"), they will learn to equate such food with feeling approved of, comforted, and nurtured.

We can also accept that as a culture we are simply less active. This inactivity creates weight problems for both children and adults. Children who spend many hours in front of the television or computer are not burning many calories. Their metabolism will slow and they will be heavier. The same is true for adults. We all know these facts, but we have difficulty acting on them. If our children are to be of normal weight they must be more active. As parents we need to set an example and become more active ourselves. Just as with food, they learn from us about activity and exercise.

We have all heard these facts many times. We may have attempted to institute them in our families with limited or no success and feel frustrated and angry with our children as a result. We have tried. We are a normal, healthy weight and our children are still overeating, inactive, and overweight. At this point, parents need to let go and give the child the freedom to decide for themselves what they will do about their weight. All of the arguing, criticism, and manipulating in the world will probably not change the child's behavior and will likely make matters worse.

The worst thing that we can do is to permit this issue to become a source of shaming, self-esteem destroying, relationship-damaging confrontation between us and our children. Our children need to know they are valued, loved, and accepted by us no matter how overweight they are. They also need to know that their physical appearance, including their size, does not determine their worth and is not their only important attribute. Our culture says, "Size is your most important attribute and since your weight is not okay, you are not okay." We need to guard against reinforcing this irrational message. In short, we must adopt a reasonable, sane approach to weight if we are to help our children.

New Rule: I maintain my own healthy eating and activity habits in order to teach them to my children. I also maintain a healthy perspective concerning size and weight in order to assist my children in dealing with these issues.

March 5

Old Rule: We are so busy! We live in our car! I'm constantly running the children to their activities.

Many parents can relate to this rule. Their children are involved in numerous activities and parents are constantly on the move making certain that they arrive at the proper place at the proper time. If there are several children in the family, the schedule becomes even more complicated. Mom and Dad sometimes pass each other on the highway, talking on their cell phones, coordinating schedules. The cycle is never-ending! Even Sundays are packed with things to do!

In the middle of all this well intended busyness, children often become tired and ill-tempered. Harried, exhausted parents respond to their children's irritable behavior with resentment and anger, because after all, "We are doing this for them." Lost in all of this busyness is family time, time to be together without running to and from the car going to yet another activity. Time to relax.

If all of this sounds familiar to you, you might consider cutting back on some of these activities so that you will be less harried and will have some time for yourself. (Reading the newspaper in the car while you wait for your kid to finish soccer practice is not time for yourself.) You might also have more time for your spouse, as well as, time to do those things that enhance your relationship with your children.

This change requires that we spend time talking with our children about what activities are meaningful and most enjoyable for them. They might not be the activities that we would choose, but in allowing children to choose their own activities, they can practice setting priorities, making decisions, and maintaining a healthy balance between being active and being over-scheduled.

The number of our children's activities and how much of our time we devote to facilitating these activities does not define good parenting. Competent parenting is defined by the relationship we have with our children. Relationship building and maintenance takes time and attention. Conversations with your kids while you are driving may be good ones (I am a great believer in car conversations), but they do not substitute for time spent having fun together. Moderating activities may just help us to be the parents that we want to be.

New Rule: We help our children to choose their activities wisely so that we have more time to spend as a family.

March 6

Old Rule: It is not important to attend my children's games and other activities. I'm busy with work and I have to have a life, too. Besides, they don't care if I am there or not.

I neither like nor understand football, but my sons played and I showed up at almost every game and hopefully cheered in the right places. I have spent much of my life sitting in the bleachers, not always happily, but it seemed to be important to them.

One year during football season, we traveled to a school that was celebrating senior recognition night, honoring their graduating players, band members, and cheerleaders. The football team played well, the band sounded good, and the cheerleaders were enthusiastic. They marched onto the field when their names were called, but there was only one parent, a lone mother, present for all of these kids. None of the other parents had taken the time to come and be with their kids as they were honored.

Kids learn·how important they are to us by our actions. Our words and the amount of money we spend on them do not speak as loudly as our actions. There is no way to avoid this simple truth.

Although they may not show it or they may even excuse us from going if we ask if it is okay not to, kids want their parents to be there for their activities. Some years ago, as a therapist facilitating "Family Week" in a drug and alcohol treatment center, I witnessed many children, including adult children, voice to their parents their sadness about the parents' failure to attend activities. As a result of this neglect, children felt unimportant and insignificant.

As with most things, a healthy balance between adult interests and commitments and having one's life consumed by children's activities is essential. The middle ground may not always be the easiest way or the most popular way, but is frequently the most productive and healthy way to live and to rear children.

New Rule: We realize it is important for us not only to facilitate our children's participation in their chosen activities, but also to attend and participate in those activities ourselves.

March 7

Old Rule: There cannot possibly be anything wrong with my child.

When we are expecting a child, we dream of a perfect baby. We want to believe that we have that perfect child. If there is a problem, we want to blame someone else or deny it all together. This is a normal initial reaction, but it is not a functional way of solving the problems that all children will inevitably have.

Coming out of denial and facing the reality that our child has a physical, developmental, emotional, or behavioral problem is difficult. It is one of the most difficult things we will do as parents. Such a step requires that we let go of the perfect baby dream and come to accept a less than perfect child, a child with difficulties we need to address.

Parents who believe that if their child has a problem it must be the fault of the teacher and not the child is one of the biggest challenges teachers face. This attitude develops as a result of seeing the child as an extension of one's self and not as an individual who does not always behave appropriately.

Such denial is dangerous because it tends to blind parents to the difficulties that children experience and prevents intervention in a timely fashion. It also says to the child that if someone has a problem with your behavior, you do not need to examine yourself. You simply blame the other person and claim to have been victimized.

While it is true that children are occasionally victimized by teachers and other adults and in such cases parents do need to be an advocate for the child, it is also true that the problems may lie with the behavior of the child. Such situations require that parents spend the time and energy necessary to give children the help they may need in handling these problems and model for them an appropriate problem-solving approach to life's difficulties.

New Rule: When my child is experiencing difficulties, it is my responsibility as a parent to look at the total picture and give my child the assistance needed to help solve the problem.

March 8

Old Rule: Be modest! Don't brag!

At one time I taught a graduate group skills course to prospective counselors. During one of the exercises, students were to share with the other members of the group something at which they were really good. When her turn came, one of the young women stated, "Well, I can tell you what I am not bad at." This young woman was bright and accomplished. She had a bachelor's degree, was accepted into graduate school, and held a responsible job. Obviously, there were many things that she did well, but she was quite uncomfortable sharing her accomplishments. She was living by the "Be modest, don't think too highly of yourself and don't talk about your accomplishments" rule. She was so influenced by this rule that she was unable to clearly identify anything that she did well.

While some boys have this difficulty, I find that girls are more likely to be affected by this rule. We teach girls to be modest and differential, not to make others "feel bad" by being more accomplished and, most especially, not to threaten boys by being more accomplished than them. Even in the 21st century, girls continue to get a healthy dose of these messages from home and society in general.

A realistic self-concept is vitally important to a fulfilling, productive life. If we are too modest, too differential, we do not take risks and do not accept challenges because we have come to believe our self-talk about our limitations.

We need to help our children, especially girls, develop a realistic self-image that allows them to say "Yes, I am good at ..." We begin by affirming our children for their talents and achievements and letting them know that extreme modesty is no more realistic and healthy than extreme pride or grandiosity. Both are out of balance and non-productive ways of operating in the world.

New Rule: I encourage my children, especially my daughters, to acknowledge their accomplishments and achievements as a sign of realistic self-worth.

March 9

Old Rule: I pay the bills and you will do as I say!

While having my hair cut, I noticed a father and his two sons. The boys were likely in late elementary and middle school and they had specific ideas about how they would like their hair to be cut. The father also had specific ideas and the three did not match.

Dad, with great exasperation, stated that he was paying for the haircuts and while he was paying they would be done as he wanted. The boys were sulking and Dad was angry. It was an unpleasant scene for all involved. It was also a perfect set up for future adolescent rebellion.

Although it was true that Dad has financial control, was it really necessary for him to exert absolute control over haircuts? Does a permitting a child to make decisions about their physical appearance mean that Dad relinquishes his power as a parent or did he need to learn to pick his battles and not set up unnecessary situations for his pre-adolescent sons to feel rebellious and resentful? Is Dad's only claim to parental authority his ability to withhold money? Or does his authority come from the respect his children have for his judgment and his willingness to be respectful and fair to them and to allow them to begin to make decisions for themselves?

As parents we need to decide when it is important for us to make decisions based on our willingness to pay for things and when playing the "because I'm paying" card is just too costly.

New Rule: Financial support is a part of parental responsibility. With this responsibility comes power, which I choose to use fairly and judiciously.

March 10

Old Rule: Children should learn about life on their own.

This rule is the opposite of paternal over-control, but the results are equally troublesome. When parents follow this rule, they leave their children to make important decisions without adult guidance.

Such parents do not usually take much interest in schoolwork, feeling that even elementary school children are entirely responsible for their education. These parents often feel that checking homework and teacher conferences are not necessary.

This lack of involvement continues into high school and college as adolescents must make curriculum choices and negotiate the complexities of college entrance and financing.

While we seldom forget the lessons in life that we learn for ourselves, children do need adult guidance to make complex decisions. When left to make crucial decisions on their own, they may make serious errors or miss opportunities.

Once again, healthy families, like healthy people, maintain a balance between two extremes. Good parenting, like sound individual functioning, lies in such a balance. Children need the freedom to make increasingly complex decisions and choices. They also need input from our knowledge and experience.

New Rule: My children need the guidance of my knowledge and expertise in important areas of their lives. They should not be left to make significant decisions totally alone.

March 11

Old Rule: You are not the child we wanted. We want you to be different than who you are.

I wanted scholars. I envisioned children who would love to read and who would be interested in all matter of scientific and intellectual pursuits. I wanted children who were fascinated with human behavior and world events. I wanted them to be what I wanted to be, only better: more intelligent, motivated, and successful. God has a sense of humor! I got two athletes!

It is a challenge for me to accept that they are who they are and that they are not I. I work on being interested in their athletic events. I have spent much of my life sitting in the stands, but it has been a struggle. I am certain that my sons have felt my ambivalence and sometimes my disappointment.

The problems are mine, not theirs. As a parent, it is my task to accept my children as they are. To foster and encourage their talents and interests, to expose them to a wide variety of experiences, but to ultimately let them decide what they are interested in and allow them to pursue their own dreams. It is my responsibility to pursue my dreams and to use my talents so that my children are not burdened with my attempts to be successful through them. All of this sounds simple, but it is far from easy. It requires that I check my frequent attempts to steer them in the path that I want them to take and allow them the freedom to use their own talents and pursue their own path. I need to love my sons enough to allow them to be who they are while supporting and encouraging them. In short, I need to love them enough to let go.

New Rule: I support my children in pursing their interests and using their talents as they see fit. They are not copies of me and need not pursue my unfulfilled dreams and ambitions. They are uniquely themselves and must pursue their dreams with my loving support.

March 12

Old Rule: I must be a perfect parent.

A young friend with two rambunctious pre-school boys wants to be a perfect mother. Believing that loving parents do not get angry with their children, she denies her anger and frustration with them. When the boys misbehave, which is quite frequently, she reprimands them calmly and sweetly. These reprimands seldom have their desired effect. Indeed, they usually ignore her.

Many of us want to do what we believe is the most important task of our lives perfectly. "Perfectly" means we are <u>never</u> angry or irritable with our children, always discipline them in a calm and loving manner, <u>never</u> have days when we feel like doing less than our best, are <u>always</u> concerned solely with their welfare, <u>never</u> wish that we had not become parents, <u>never</u> wish we could attend to our own needs without considering theirs, and <u>never</u> wish to simply take a break. We feel ashamed of feeling frustrated, angry, and tired, because we mistakenly believe that loving parents never have these feelings.

We are human and, therefore, not perfectible. There will be times when we wish we could have just a few days off from this parenting business or wish they would just behave and make our lives a bit easier. There will be days when we are irritable and quick to speak harshly and angrily to others, including our children.

If you are operating on the "I must be perfect" rule, give yourself a break and realize that you will make mistakes and such mistakes will not damage your child. Indeed, children need to learn that others are not consistently concerned about their feelings. They need to know that they are not the center of the universe.

We may even find that we must apologize for something we said in anger. This powerful lesson teaches children that when they make mistakes they also need to take responsibility for them and apologize. Through our mistakes, they may also learn that successful relationships among human beings are a matter of attempting to do the right thing and living in integrity with what we believe, even if we occasionally fail.

New Rule: I accept that I am not and never will be a perfect parent. What my children need is a competent parent, a parent who strives to be consistently, but not perfectly, loving and fair.

March 13

Old Rule: Do the right thing all of the time. Be perfect!

I come from a family in which having an overdue library book or dialing the wrong phone number was a source of shame. Family members' feelings were easily injured so one had to be careful what one said. One also had to be constantly mindful about what others thought, for the approval of others was vitally important. I am not blaming my family, for they passed onto me what they were given and the consequences are just as painful to them as they are to me. They passed onto me what they had: a painful sense of shame and inadequacy and the belief that no matter what they do it is never good enough.

In order to change this painful circumstance, I was forced to face the power of this rule and acknowledge it had its tentacles into every area of my life. Attempting to sever them in order not to pass them onto my children, I struggled to accept and continue to struggle to accept my imperfectable humanity. I try to accept that I do not have to be perfect in order to be lovable and valuable to others and to God. I have learned that those who would insist that I be perfect in order for them to love and approve of me are toxic and dangerous and I need to protect myself from them with strong emotional boundaries. I have learned that when I insist that those around me be perfect in order to gain my approval I am being abusive. I have no right to demand the impossible of anyone, especially my children.

I try to pass these lessons onto my children and can see that while I have not been perfectly successful, they carry less of the crippling shame that I was given. I am not a perfect parent, but I have tried to change this painful family legacy and I have progressed. That is all that is necessary.

New Rule: I have no right to expect perfection from myself, my children, my spouse, or any other human being.

March 14

Old Rule: It is a mistake to have only one child.

Those of us who have had an only child, as I did for ten years, have heard the criticism: "Only children are lonely, spoiled, selfish, spend too much time with adults, and never learn to share."

In reality, only children tend to be responsible, conscientious achievers, and have personality characteristics much like first children. True, some only children are self-centered and have a difficult time relating to others, but so do many first, second or third children. What really matters is the quality of parenting and the life experience of only children, just as with any child.

We had only one child because that is what we wanted at the time. One child was all I could handle while completing my education. He was not socially and emotionally deprived. He had many friends and was afforded a wide variety of experiences. Indeed, he did not really want a brother or a sister. He did, however, go through a period when he was about 4 when he wanted a big brother, one who had an equal number, but different toys who was willing to share. When he understood that this was not possible, he decided that he had it pretty good and was not missing much by not having a sibling. He grew up to be a kind, sensitive, and generous young man. His brother was born when he was 10, well past the time when his basic personality was formed. He was and still is a loving and protective big brother.

Many parents want one child and are happy with that child. The reasons are many and varied and no one's business but their own. If you have only one child and feel that your family is complete, refuse to be bullied and intimidated into having more children for the sake of giving the first one a playmate or a learning tool for life. Children should be wanted only for themselves. For heaven's sake, stop worrying! Your child is likely growing up okay, not perfect, but okay. Only those who rear children should determine how many they want and can competently rear.

New Rule: Parents have the right to decide how many children they want to rear, even if it is only one. No one else has the right to make that decision.

March 15

Old Rule: My new spouse and I can leave the past behind.

One of the biggest changes in family life during the past 30 years has been the increased prevalence of divorce and remarriage. Indeed, they have become so prevalent that today over 40% of all children will live with a stepparent for a portion of their childhood. The "rules" of the next few days are an attempt to deal with some of the problems unique to the divorced and remarried family.

Attempting to "blend" families is difficult! (Indeed, those who have attempted to "blend" would say this is a gross understatement!) Successful blending requires patience, sensitivity to the needs of the children and a realistic acceptance of the many potential complications. Blending families requires adults, real grownups! Unfortunately, when we are still reeling from the hurt feelings of divorce and the optimism of a new relationship, adolescent rather than adult expectations often prevail. We often enter into a new marriage with numerous unrealistic expectations.

One such unrealistic expectation is the belief that we can forget about the past, including a former spouse. In reality, once married and certainly once married with children, a former spouse will always have a place in our lives. We may wish it to be otherwise, but the cold reality is when our spouse has children by another marriage or relationship, there will always be an emotional involvement with that parent.

New Rule: When one has children by a previous marriage, the parent of those children will also be a part of our lives.

March 16

Old Rule: My spouse and I can create a whole new family with children of our own.

As I talk with young people who come from families who have divorced one of the most painful circumstances they face is being the kid from the "old" family. This is especially true when a parent attempts to move on and create a new family, complete with "new" children.

When we divorce there is a temptation to view the previous relationship as a mistake. We may view divorce as rectifying that mistake and a chance to create a new marriage and new family. A way to do it right this time. We try to leave the pain and the regrets of the past behind. One of the cruelest outcomes of this plan is viewing the children of the previous relationship as "mistakes," as part of the past to be left behind. No matter how many regrets we have about a previous marriage and how much we desire to do it differently with the children of this relationship, the children of the previous marriage are not mistakes to be rectified with a new family! They still need us. They have a right to our care, attention, and to be valued for themselves. They are not reminders of our past failures to be left behind and forgotten. It is exceedingly abusive to view them as such.

New spouses often have mixed feelings about the children of their spouse's previous marriage. The fact of the child's existence is a constant remainder that the marriage and the ex-spouse do exist and have been an important part of their spouse's life. Marrying someone who has children by a previous marriage means that we are in relationship with the children of that marriage and have a responsibility to treat the children with respect and regard for their needs, even if we have our own children.

In short, children cannot be divorced and it is cruel to behave otherwise. They are here and will not disappear! They are a fact! They are not mistakes that one can erase with a new family.

New Rule: I accept that my children and my spouse's children by our previous marriages are worthy of our care, love, and attention.

March 17 and 18

Old Rule: We can easily blend together and live as one happy family.

Anyone who has ever tried to blend a family will likely be laughing bitterly at the irony of this statement, but the novices among you may think this is actually true.

Whether this is our first marriage or not, we all get married with the hope and the belief that we will be happy and that what ever problems may arise can be worked through because we love each other and share a commitment to the relationship. While this may be true of the spouses who attempt to blend families, this may not be true of the children who find themselves in a family situation that is not of their own choosing.

Even if the step-parent and the child like one another and are attempting to make the relationship work, learning to live with another person with different habits, values, goals, likes, and dislikes is stressful. These differences require conscious adjustments and respectful acceptance, not just on the part of the children but also on the part of the new stepparent. We cannot hope to make stepchildren into what we want them to be any more than we can expect our biological children to be what we want them to be. Even under the most ideal of circumstances, step-parents and children have mixed feelings about one another. Step-children are less likely to match our expectations because we enter their lives later. The later a step-parent enters the child's life the more likely they are to encounter significant personality clashes and difficulty adjusting to one another.

Children may see the new step-parent as an intruder into their relationship with their own parent, as competition for the parent's love and attention, or as the final curtain on any hope that their parents will reconcile. The child may be resentful of yet another adult in their lives who feels they have the right to "tell them what to do" and may express their feelings with active or sullen rebellion.

The step-parent may see the child as a constant reminder of their spouse's former partner, as competition for the time and attention of their new spouse, ("After all, we are newlyweds.") a drain on their free time, a responsibility that they do not want or were unprepared for, or a financial drain. In the worst case, they may find the child quite unappealing and come to dislike the child. At this point, many remarriages end in divorce because of substantial, seemingly irreconcilable differences over children.

If you find yourself contemplating marriage or remarriage, I hope that the above helps you to go slow, be realistic in your expectations, communicate your feelings clearly, and enter into pre-marital counseling with your intended spouse.

If you are already in this situation, I encourage you to communicate your thoughts, feelings, wants, and expectations to your spouse and to seek professional help in dealing with the many challenges that arise. Although it is ideal to have both spouses and the children in counseling, going alone or with one other member of the family is better than no help at all. As is true for all families, when one member of the family begins to react differently to what is happening in the family, all members of the family will begin to change their behavior.

Remember, what you and your new spouse are attempting to do is difficult and will take patience and time to accomplish. Studies suggest that improvement in the situation is usually evident in two years, if most of the family members are willing to work to learn to live together.

Blending families successfully requires that we communicate effectively and frequently and learn the fine art of compromise and respect for individual differences. In short, blending families is not for the immature, cowardly, or rigid.

New rule: In attempting to create a blended family, I accept that I will need to bring into that situation all of the loving patience and willingness to respect, learn from, and communicate with others of which I am capable.

March 19 and 20

Old Rule: We should not have to give so much money to the other parent of my spouse's children. It takes too much of our family income.

The biggest and most bitter battle ground in divorced and remarried families is child support. New spouses often resent the constant need to pay support to the "old" family and the resulting consequences to the "new" family.

Custodial parents may have difficulty collecting child support on a regular basis. Frequently, friction develops over paying for extras and unexpected expenses. The new spouse may resent that they must work in order to support their family while a large portion of the income of the non-custodial parent must go to the "old" family. The problems that ended the first marriage may continue to be played out in the child support battleground. Caught in the middle of the war, the children often suffer from the immaturity and shortsightedness of the adults in their lives.

There are some cold realities that must be faced and accepted if the war is to come to an end. Before you go on, I warn you these realities are tough! You will not find a justification for continuing the war with the children as pawns.

1. The children of past marriages are real. They have the same needs for food, clothing, shelter, education, and medical care that all children do. Their parent's divorce does not in any way change or diminish these needs.

2. When one divorces, remarries, and starts a "new" family, one does not divorce children of the previous marriage. The responsibility to care for them continues to exist as though the divorce never occurred. The children did not cause the divorce and negative consequences to them should be minimized. The adults in their lives are responsible to see to this.

3. Child support payments are awarded to the child, not to the custodial parent. The custodial parent may be spending the money, but the money is paid and received for the care and maintenance of a home for the child.

4.Children are not responsible to collect overdue child support and should never be placed in the situation of obtaining the child support from the non- custodial parent. This is the responsibility of the parents.

5. Children should never be told "I'll be so glad when you turn 18 and I won't have to give any more money to your mother or father." This statement says loud and clear, "I don't really care about you and I'm only helping to rear you because I have to and I'll be glad when I can wash my hands of you." (Small wonder that most children of divorce have self-esteem problems!)

6. Being the spouse of someone who has children and must pay child support is difficult. It requires maturity and patience to accept that this will be a reality until the child reaches young adulthood and that one does not belong in any dispute concerning child support. The people who must work out the problems that arise are the child's parents.

7. It is costly to rear children, especially in two households, and one's standard of living will be negatively affected.

I warned you that they were difficult! Marrying and rearing children successfully requires that we grow up and face our responsibilities realistically. Marrying, having children, divorcing, remarrying, and blending families requires an even greater amount of maturity. This is an inescapable reality!

New Rule: The care of children by a previous marriage or relationship remains primary in the lives of their parents. These obligations, no matter how complicated and costly, do not end with divorce and remarriage.

March 21 and 22

Old Rule: This is my child and you are not going to discipline my child.

Discipline is among the most difficult challenges that blended families must face. These ongoing issues change with the age of the children, and are seldom easily resolved. Indeed, second marriages often end due to the stress of disagreements over this one issue. This is especially true when the stepparent is placed in the "no win" situation of having to live with children they are not permitted to discipline. Despite the difficulty, parents and stepparents can successfully discipline their children and reduce the conflict and tension in the family. Perhaps these few guidelines will help.

Children respond best to consistent, loving, and reasonable discipline. It is very difficult to maintain consistent, loving discipline when children must adjust to a series of "live-in" arrangements. In this case, it is probably best that the "live-in" not discipline the children except when it concerns matters of personal safety or their own property. If children are exposed to a series of parental relationships, including live-in relationships with parents' boyfriends or girlfriends who are given the right to discipline the child, they will be resentful and rebellious. (If your work supervisor changed constantly and each one had a different set of rules they believed they could arbitrarily enforce, you would be resentful and rebellious, too!) One may chose to allow a "live-in" to play a major role in disciplining the children, but be prepared for the inevitable problems this will cause.

If one marries and brings a new person into this child's life, it should be a person who can be trusted to discipline the children safely and reasonably. If one cannot trust their new spouse to discipline the children in a safe manner, why bring them into the children's lives?!

There will be differences of opinion concerning discipline, just as there are between biological parents. These disagreements are best settled out of the presence of the children. If the children know that adults have differences in this area, they will use the conflict to manipulate the adults and possibly to come between them. Remember, children usually have ambivalent feelings about the relationship and will use whatever power we give them to manipulate and control.

"You are not their real Dad / Mom and you don't have any say here" should not be used to negate a stepparent when the adults have a disagreement about discipline. In other words, once we have asked a stepparent to discipline, we should not undermine them in front of the children. This only causes confusion and frustration for everyone concerned, the children as well as the stepparent. (I knew of a biological mother who used this pronouncement in a disagreement with her husband who had reared her daughter with great love and devotion for over 10 years after her father died! Such damage in a marital relationship is not easily repaired.)

Disciplining in a blended family is difficult, but not impossible. Effective discipline requires a willingness to be fair, open, communicate effectively, and put the best interest of the children before the adults' own desire for power and control.

New Rule: In disciplining the children in our blended family, we recognize the importance of giving them clear, consistent, reasonable guidelines concerning their behavior. The most important ingredient in making this happen is our willingness to communicate openly with each other in order to establish trusting relationships among our children and ourselves.

March 23 and 24

Old Rule: Children are resilient. They bounce back from changes in the family, including divorce and remarriage.

Children <u>are</u> resilient. Human beings are resilient. Human beings have remarkable abilities to adapt and survive even when life deals us difficult blows.

However, divorce and remarriage are difficult for children. Research conducted by a wide variety of social scientists, including Judith Wallerstein's long-term study of divorced families, tells us that while children are less stressed when a marriage ends that involves abuse, chemical dependence, and persistent arguing in the home, they are often negatively effected by divorce. These negative effects include feelings of rejection from at least one parent, anxiety, depression, lowered self-esteem, aggression, increased risk of behavioral problems, lack of achievement in school, increased health problems, and later difficulty in establishing satisfactory relationships with the opposite sex.

While most children survive and some children thrive after a divorce and remarriage, the research further suggests that battles between parents and the willingness of parents to use their children in their continuing war is quite detrimental to them.

Children can survive divorce, but they do need extra help and support from their parents, other adult members of the family, and the community, especially their school. Unfortunately, this extra support is needed just when the parents, due to their own stress, experience a diminished capacity to parent. Research shows that divorcing parents are usually less sensitive to the needs of their children, provide less discipline, and are less attentive because they are caught up in their own painful divorce whirlwind.

This is why it is vitally important for grandparents and other family members to be available for the children. Such persons should not enter into the divorce battle but should be there just to support the children. Just one person who is willing to give this support can provide a real buffer for children against the stress of divorce and remarriage.

It is also important for parents to recognize that despite their desire to do so, they may not be as sensitive to their children. They need to be aware of signs of stress and not to ignore them, thinking, "Kids are tough. They will bounce back." Signs of stress may include trouble in school, increased anger and rebellion, increased isolation and crying, complaints of not feeling well in the absence of any true illness, sleep problems, and regression from age appropriate behavior, for instance bed wetting in a child who has previously been dry. If there are signs of stress, talk to the children, attempt to put yourself in their shoes, get out of your own pain and anger for a while, and get help. See a family therapist or go to counseling yourself. A divorce recovery group can do wonders for both you and your child. You may find that your child's school has a divorce recovery group. Your children will benefit in the short term and such assistance may save both you and your children later difficulties.

The negative effects of divorce can last a lifetime. However, divorce need not cause long-term difficulties. These effects are eased when parents are willing to acknowledge that children need help to adjust to the changes in their lives that affect them so powerfully, but which they are often powerless to influence.

New Rule: In our attempt to survive divorce and build a new life, we need to remember our that children can only survive divorce if we take the extra time and care to assist them.

March 25

Old Rule: Your father didn't pay the child support on time again. Ask him for it when you go this weekend.

Many children are placed in the painful role of child support collector. Since mothers are usually the custodial parent, children are often asked to collect the support while they are spending time with their dad.

Let us deal with some difficult realities concerning child support. Much of it is never collected. It is often the final battleground between two people who could not get along in the first place and still wish to hurt and control one another. It is often the subject of repeated, acrimonious legal battles. Money is a precious commodity, sometimes held in higher esteem than the welfare of one's children. Child support, while awarded for the care of the child, is often viewed by the person paying it as a payment to the former spouse and is a source of enormous resentment. Is this minefield of anger, resentment, as well as attempts to control and seek revenge any place for children?

Child support decisions and payment are adult legal matters and children should not be sent as collectors to parents who have chosen not to honor their responsibilities. Children should not be asked to hold accountable irresponsible parents. This is an adult matter and should be treated as such. This also includes being told to ask the other parent for extras above the child support or being told, "I'm not giving you any more because that is what I pay your child support for." These are adult matters and should be handled by the parents. The financial difficulties and stressors custodial as well as non-custodial parents face are quite real, but they are not remedied by involving the children. The unavoidable difficulties that children face as a result of divorce are more than enough for them to handle and should not be compounded by forcing them to attempt to enforce the financial arrangements for their care.

New Rule: As an adult, I take responsibility for dealing with my former spouse concerning financial arrangements. I do not believe it is appropriate for my children to serve as child support collectors.

March 26

Old Rule: We are the parents and we make the decisions in this house.

One of the goals of parenting is raising competent young adults capable of making sound, independent decisions. Many parents, however, seem to believe that decision making skills will magically appear sometime in late adolescence when they are old enough to leave our homes and go out into the world able to care for themselves.

Learning to make sound decisions is not magical. Such learning begins in early childhood when parents allow children to make decisions that have minimal consequences.

This is not to say that parents should abdicate their decision-making prerogative. Children need and want boundaries and direction. However, if we make every decision for them and pass it down without discussion or a chance to disagree, they will be unable to make competent decisions when they leave our home because they will not have the necessary experience.

Decision making starts when children are first able to talk and identify preferences. For instance, when parents allow them to choose pears or peaches for lunch or the red or blue shirt today. It progresses when we give them the opportunity to choose among alternative recreational activities, the time they will begin their homework, what lessons or sports they would like to participate in, and how they will spend their allowance or money they have earned.

When we give children practice in making decisions and take the time to share with them our reasoning as we make important decisions for them or the family, we are teaching them what they will need to know in order to make appropriate decisions when we are not with them. We cannot expect our children to exhibit competence when they have had no instruction and practice in the complex process of decision making. Like many other life skills, such competence comes with instruction and practice.

New Rule: I teach my children to make good decisions by allowing them to begin to make decisions for themselves early in their lives. I also teach decision making skills by sharing with them my own decision making process.

March 27

Old Rule: If you laugh today, you will cry before nightfall.

When I ask people about their family rules, I am amazed at how frequently they include this one. It is absolutely irrational, but alive and well within many of us. It says to children and adults as well, "Don't be too happy and light-hearted because something bad will happen and then you will be crying and sad." There is also an unspoken message that being too happy may actually bring on adversity and if one is too happy then great sorrow will follow.

As crazy and illogical as this sounds, I think that many of us live this way. We don't want to be too contented or too joyful because the very presence of such joy may bring disaster down on us. Therefore, we restrain our joy with beliefs like "Life may be good now, but that won't last" or "Think about all of the unfortunate people in the world, I don't have the right to be too happy," as if our joy somehow diminishes the portion available to others.

It is though there is a happiness bank account that will be depleted if we withdraw too much. Such strange magical thinking is actually a spiritual belief about the nature of the relationship between human beings and that power which is greater than themselves. Persons who tend to believe this rule often believe in a God who is randomly cruel, arbitrary, and does not want what is best for us.

How would your life change if you adopted a new rule that allowed you to be glad in the moment? How would life be different for your family if you believed that happiness was an infinite commodity and there is no relationship between feeling great happiness and the presence of great sorrow in your life? Something to ponder!

New Rule: Happiness and joy are not limited resources. If we laugh this morning, we might still have reason to laugh by nightfall.

March 28

Old Rule: If you are going to cry, go to your room.

"Laugh and the world laughs with you. Cry and you cry alone." Many parents teach their children this cliché and many of us continue to cry alone. The rule "Go to your room, if you are going to cry," says to the child, "I don't care about your feelings and if you are going to have them take them out of my sight," "Your feelings are not justified. You have no right to be sad," or "You are over-reacting and being silly. Go to your room."

As adults we hide our tears not only behind closed doors, but also behind a mask of "I'm okay. Nothing is wrong." We have hidden our feelings for so long that even we are not aware of their depth. What we are aware of is a persistent feeling of sadness and loneliness coupled with a belief that we have no right to be sad and no one really cares how we feel. Unfortunately, when we live by this rule, we pass this legacy onto our own children.

Breaking this old rule involves expressing our feelings to those we trust and allowing our children to share their feelings with us, even when we believe their problems are trivial and will soon pass. Adopting new ways of acknowledging and handling feelings will help parents and children heal from the emotional numbness brought about by the "cry alone" rule.

New Rule: I choose to express my feelings openly to those I trust and allow my children to express their feelings to me. In my home, we no longer cry alone.

March 29

Old Rule: We are rearing our boys and girls in the same way.

In these days of gender-neutral child rearing, we try to rear our girls to be assertive and our boys to be sensitive. We want our girls to be interested in science and math so we buy them mechanical toys. We want our boys to be less aggressive so we don't buy them war toys. (We usually can't bring ourselves to buy little boys dolls.)

While all of this may be happening in the name of giving children choices and developing a variety of interests, we may be putting unnecessary pressure on our children and ourselves. Boys and girls are different, not just anatomically, but their brains are different and their body chemistry is different. Girls tend to be more collaborative and less competitive and aggressive than boys. These differences are thought to be due to the presence or absence of the male hormone testosterone. Boys are more adept at seeing spatial relationships. Girls are better at multi-tasking, perhaps due to the increased thickness of the connection between the hemispheres of the brain as compared to boys.

Of course, there is a huge range of normal individual differences. Many girls are competitive and interested in math and science. Many boys are not interested in athletic competition and excel in language skills and the social sciences. Boys as well as girls have the capacity to be empathetic and sensitive to the feelings of others. Perhaps we should relax a bit and become more comfortable ourselves with female and male attributes and differences.

Maybe it is time to rear our children as individuals who will express their personalities and interests in any number of ways in their lifetime.

New Rule: We are rearing our children as individuals, supporting and valuing their emerging interests and talents.

March 30 & 31

Old Rule: It is not really important to teach our children manners.

Back in the early 1970's when I first became a parent, there was a good deal of discussion among young mothers concerning the appropriateness of teaching our children manners. Coming from the freewheeling, rebellious 1960's, and reacting against what we perceived to be the repressiveness of our 1950's childhood, we wanted our children to be free to express themselves. We wanted them to be genuine in their communication with others and free of the formal phoniness we perceived had been forced upon us when we were reminded to address our elders as "Mr.," "Miss," or "Mrs.," to say "please" and "thank-you," and to speak only when spoken to.

I always had my doubts about the extreme ends of this attitude. Having encountered a fair number of rude, unpleasant children, whose parents in the name of free expression and equality between the generations did not teach them manners, I became a believer in the value and civilizing effects of teaching and enforcing the use of manners. Such instruction can be accomplished without giving the old message to our children that they should be seen and not heard.

Like most matters, there is a healthy middle ground between the stiflingly formalism of over concern with manners and the lack of social skills. Manners are a demonstration of respect, respect for others and self-respect. Manners say, "I treat you with respect and I expect to be treated in the same manner." Can you imagine what a more civil and pleasant world we would live in if we all treated each other with more consideration? We can begin with our own families. We can say "please" and "thank you" to each other. We can also begin to use better table manners, showing respect for those who eat with us. We can use good telephone manners with our children's friends, expecting that our children will do the same.

On a more pragmatic note, having manners often means we make a better first impression on others. Teachers, other adults, and even playmates find children more appealing, when they treat others with respect.

Knowing what to do and how to act in social situations also allows us to feel more comfortable. In other words, knowing how to act in a restaurant where they bring your food on a plate as opposed to passing it over a counter in a paper sack allows us to enjoy and feel comfortable in our surroundings.

You will, of course, need to make your own decision, but I believe that it is important to teach children to respect others, to acknowledge gifts and kindnesses, and to behave appropriately in a variety of social situations.

New Rule: It is important for parents to teach their children to show respect and consideration for others and to be comfortable in social situations. One of the ways I can teach these values is to use "please" and "thank-you" and to practice good manners at home as well as in public.

April 1

Old Rule: If it isn't important to parents, it isn't important.

Parental concerns are serious. Parents have responsibility for the health, education, and welfare of their children as well as the financial well being of the family. Finding enough time in the day to meet all of our obligations, to keep all of the balls in the air, is difficult. Many of us feel stressed and sometimes overwhelmed by our many concerns and responsibilities.

Children's concerns are also serious. They may include: "Am I smart enough to do my school work?", "What if the other kids don't like me?", "Will I ever be popular?", "Will I play well enough to make the team?", "Do I look okay?", "Will I ever grow?", and "Will boys/girls ever like me?" The list of childhood and adolescent worries goes on and on.

Parents can become so preoccupied with our own responsibilities that we disregard or make light of children's concerns. Thus we might fail to appreciate that children need to be reassured and guided as they encounter new situations and demands. Parents cannot always fix the problem nor look into the future, but briefly putting aside our own concerns and listening may be all that is needed. Sometimes we will need to reassure. Other times we will need to guide with a few words of encouragement. (Actually the fewer words the better, for what is needed is not a lecture but words of understanding and guidance.) "Listening" times are typically not lengthy, but in these brief moments when we pay our children the loving compliment of listening to them and responding to their concerns, we say to them, "What you are thinking and feeling is important to me. Your concerns are my concerns."

New Rule: I take time from my concerns to hear those of my children. In this way, I share with them my knowledge, experience, and love, acknowledging to them that what is important to them is also important to me.

April 2

Old Rule: Children don't need to participate in decisions concerning how we spend our money.

Learning to handle money appropriately is one of the most important things we can teach our children. Even young children can comprehend that money is a limited resource and we cannot purchase everything we want. While it is not appropriate for parents to burden their children with all of the details and worry them about family finances, (unfortunately, that is our job) it is appropriate for them to learn about money as soon as they are capable of understanding its purpose.

We can begin to teach them by letting them participate in planning family expenditures like vacations, family outings, and new purchases. Children can certainly learn the need to plan for the things we want. If possible, children should be given an allowance, perhaps as early as age 4 or 5, to spend as they please. With this allowance comes accountability. The allowance is gone when it is spent or lost through carelessness (this does happen as most parents know) and not replaced until the child's next payday. Children need to know that money is a finite resource and spending had best be done wisely.

Just as children learn other powerful lessons from observing their parents, children learn to handle money from watching and listening to us. It is important that we look at our own attitudes about money and actively involve our children in this important area of family life. Family meetings, as described in the October section of this book, are an excellent time to involve them in planning purchases and other expenditures and to teach the importance of responsible money management.

New rule: It is important to actively involve children in family financial matters. By including them, we are teaching our children to handle money wisely.

April 3

Old Rule: "I am so disgusted with you! You are not my child!"

A magazine television show taped parents disciplining their children. One father, attempting to get his child to eat, yelled at the little boy, "I'm so mad at you! You are not my son!" The child's offense? He did not eat his vegetables! Heaven knows what the father would say about a lost coat! Later, the father said he did not realize what he had said.

What we say to our children, especially in anger, does matter. Children take in what we say and they believe it. Even when children do not appear to be listening, the words that come out of our mouths when we are angry have enormous power, often more power than our loving words when we are more controlled. It is likely that a thousand "I love you's" does not undo the damage of one "You are not my child."

Adults are responsible for what we say and do when we are angry. We are responsible for controlling our anger so we do not hurt others either physically or emotionally. When we know we are getting out of control, we have the responsibility to remove ourselves from the situation until we have calmed down enough to handle it nonabusively. Vegetables that are not eaten and coats that are lost are not worth damaging our relationship with our children, as well as their self-esteem.

New Rule: I am an adult and I am responsible for controlling my anger so that I do not verbally assault my children.

April 4

Old Rule: Parents should never apologize to their children.

This is an old rule, dating back to the time when parents had absolute, unquestioned authority, and children had no rights. This led to scenes like the one a friend related to me: his father lined up the four children in the family following the disappearance of an item from the home and spanked each one of them in rotation until the guilty party confessed. One of the daughters did confess, just to stop the abuse. It was discovered later that the thief was a neighbor's child. The father never apologized until the children were adults.

We are going to make mistakes. Perfect parents, like perfect children, do not exist. When we make a mistake, we need to apologize even if the mistake involves our children, just as we would apologize to another adult. Apologizing to our children when we err, shows the love and respect we have for them. It teaches them the power of saying, "I was wrong. I am sorry."

New Rule: When I make a mistake, I am confident and mature enough to take responsibility and apologize, even to my children.

April 5

Old Rule: Regret the past.

Most of us have some regrets about the past: things we should have done or not done; paths we should have taken or not taken; things we should have said or not said. To live is to make decisions. The longer we live, the more decisions we make, and the more opportunities we have for regret.

Regret is a painful, non-productive habit that drains the energy we have for living today. Yet for too many of us, regret is our constant companion. We also introduce our children to this companion, passing on this habit to them just as surely as if we had purposely instructed them. In order to teach our children to live differently, we must first free ourselves.

The first step toward such freedom is to mentally remind ourselves, and keep reminding ourselves, that we have no power in the past. Our only power lies in today. If we free ourselves from dwelling on the past, then we have more mental energy to put toward today's decisions. When making decisions, all we can do is gather information, consider it thoughtfully and perhaps prayerfully, make the decision, take action, let go, and move on. It sounds so simple, but for many of us this means breaking the energy draining habits of second guessing ourselves and recalling regrets. By breaking these habits ourselves we can teach our children to live in the present, not storing regrets like a squirrel collecting useless, rotten nuts.

One way to avoid piling up regrets is to go through the open doors of opportunity. Many of us pass by these open doors, refusing to go through them, due to fear of the unknown, fear of failure, or lack of confidence. We permit opportunities to go by, thus collecting years of regret. Go through the open doors, take risks, and teach your children to have the confidence and courage to live free of the dreadful power of regret.

New Rule: I have developed the mental habit of making the best decision with the information I have, then letting go. I also make a habit of going through the open doors of opportunity. In doing these things I do not collect regrets. By my example, I am teaching my children to live happier and more productive lives.

April 6

Old Rule: Worry about the future.

A close cousin of regret, worrying about the future is another energy depleting mental habit we teach our children.

When we worry, we are actually spending our energy attempting to do the impossible - live in and somehow control the future. Furthermore, that future is always gloomy, for we never worry about the good things that might happen. Full of pessimism, worriers instead conjure up disastrous outcomes and make ourselves miserable in the process. We rob ourselves and those around us of the pleasures of today with our fears about the possible disasters of tomorrow.

If we are willing to admit it, many chronic worriers have some magical thinking left over from childhood when we thought that we could control events with our thoughts. Our magical thinking generally goes something like: "If I worry about it, maybe it won't happen." or "If I worry and expect the worst, I will be prepared." I know of no greater stress in life than attempting to deal with a crisis that has not yet and may not occur. Yet many of us live with this nonsense and pass these habits onto our children.

Like recovering from the habit of regretting the past, recovering from chronic worry requires that when we find ourselves dwelling on the possible disasters of the future, we begin the habit of turning our worries over to God, our Higher Power, or to whatever we chose to call that which is greater and wiser than ourselves. In this process of turning our concerns over and letting go, we will find the increased mental energy to live more fully and effectively today.

By letting go we can begin to teach our children to live in today while planning for the future with optimism, courage, and confidence, not with the constant fear that underlies worry.

New Rule: In our family, we live in today. We also plan for the future, work toward our goals, and look forward to the outcome. We do not permit fear and worry to drain us of the strength needed to live our lives to the fullest.

April 7

Old Rule: We have to take it.

In every family suffering from abuse, whether the abuse is physical, emotional, or sexual, there is an adult who believes they have the right to do whatever they wish regardless of the effect on others and another adult who believes that they must take the abuse. In order to be a victim, one has to believe that one has no choice and must endure the abuse. The tragedy is compounded because the adult victim is training the children to continue this pattern.

Several years ago, I was employed as a counselor conducting family therapy weekends at a chemical dependency treatment center. Part of the therapy included an opportunity for families to participate in a psychodrama depicting what was happening in the family. One of the families who volunteered to do this included a father who was an alcoholic and drug addict, a mother who had left and come back many times to this relationship in which she had been physically and emotionally abused, and several children. The father frequently abandoned the family, was unfaithful, and used the family finances for his drug abuse. He had had the disease of chemical dependency for many years and had been in treatment several times. Despite his current presence in treatment, he obviously did not intend to change his behavior. His wife and children, which included an adolescent daughter, were there for yet another family session. During the session, as I realized it was unlikely that the father was willing to change, I focused my attention on the mother and told her directly that she was teaching her daughter to be a victim. She was training her to find a man who was not only chemically dependent, but also abusive and to believe this was normal and what one should expect from marriage. She was teaching her daughter by her behavior that she had to take it.

There is a saying among adults who are recovering from the effects of abusive relationships: "The first time something happens to you or when you are a child you are a victim, the second time you are a volunteer."

When we "volunteer" for abuse and allow ourselves and our children to be abused and behave as though we have no options, we teach them to "volunteer." We perpetuate the cycle. Only an adult can end this cycle for themselves and their children. It may be difficult, but finding the courage to take action makes real change in the family possible.

New Rule: Although it may be difficult, I refuse to live and keep my children locked in a cycle of abuse. We do not have to take it!

April 8 and 9

Old Rule: Victim, abuser, rescuer - we all have our place on the triangle.

Family therapist, Salvador Minuchin, described it. Many families live it. It is called the "drama" or "victim" triangle. In one corner of the triangle is an abuser who does something to violate the rights of the victim, who occupies another corner. This violation can be physical, verbal, emotional, or sexual. The form of the abuse does not really matter. What does matter is that the victim does not take responsibility for dealing directly with the abuser. Instead, the victim turns to a third party in the remaining corner, frequently a child, to rescue them. This rescuing can take many forms, listening to the problems and pain of the victim and the stories about how they have always been badly treated by others, sending the child to attend to or talk to the abuser, or telling the child not to anger or upset the abuser lest the situation become worse. The possible rescue scenarios are endless, but the drama and the message from the victim is always the same: "Look at how I have been abused. You need to take care of me and make it better."

The rescuer tries. Many of us have grown up listening to our parent's painful difficulties and trying to make it better. Assuming the adult role, we formulated ideas and made suggestions and plans to rescue our parent from an abusive situation, only to experience confusion and frustration when the parent refused to do that which they said they wanted and needed to do. All the while the victim consistently puts out the message: "You must keep trying." The rescuer continues to try and feels more and more inadequate, unable to fix the situation.

Eventually the rescuer will be blamed by the victim for not being good enough, for being just like the abuser, for being selfish and having needs of their own, for wanting to leave home (who wouldn't?), or creating problems themselves. The abuser may blame the rescuer for siding with the other parent. Much to the rescuer's confusion and dismay, they become the victim or maybe even the abuser when they add to the stress in the family by having needs or experiencing difficulties themselves.

The family continues to go round and round on this painful triangle. The plot of the drama may change over time, but the underlying script is always the same and can extend over generations of the family.

The drama ends when one person refuses to play their role and begins to take responsibility for their behavior and to give others responsibility for their behavior as well. Ending the drama is that simple and that difficult.

We need to teach our children with our behavior that each of us is responsible for what we do, that we have choices about how we deal with an abusive situation, and that we cannot help or fix anyone who refuses to take responsibility for their own healing. When we break the cycle of the triangle, we claim the freedom to live outside of this painful drama. When we chose to continue to play out this drama, we pull our children into our pain and teach them to create abuser, victim, rescuer triangles in their own lives.

New Rule: I choose to end the drama triangles in my life by taking responsibility for my behavior, refusing to be a victim, or expecting someone to come to my rescue. Only by taking responsibility for myself can I teach my children how to avoid their own participation in these painful dramas.

April 10 and 11

Old Rule: We don't talk about our problems outside of the family.

In the United States, we consider privacy to be a constitutional right. However, like most concepts, privacy when carried to the extreme becomes detrimental. When families are in trouble, when they most need assistance, this rule keeps them from seeking help and support. Indeed, it is an axiom among counselors that "the sicker the family, the more closed the system." That is, the more the family needs help the greater the need to conceal from others the extent of the difficulty.

Many of us can clearly recall as children being told, "not to tell anyone else what was going on," "it was no one else's business," and "what would people think if they knew." With this rule firmly in place, we carried around with us dreadful secrets that we could not share with others. To share such information with others would have been a betrayal of the family. The isolation increased as we continued to hide the secrets and to feel that our family must surely be the only one where such shameful things happened. Since it was not okay to talk about family problems, we did not receive help in understanding and coping with these difficulties.

As adults we continue not to talk about what was going on. Living by the old rule of "keep it in the family," we continue to feel shame and experience a sense that to speak about our experiences would be a betrayal of the family. The difficulties do not go away just because no one else knows. (At least we think no one else knows.) Even as adults, we continue to react out of our past pain in our emotional lives and in our current relationships. We may experience depression, chronic anxiety, alcoholism, and drug addiction. We are often frustrated by our inability to maintain successful relationships and to be the kind of parents we want to be. Tragically and unintentionally, we pass on to our children the pain and difficulties we were not allowed to talk about as children.

The only way to break this cycle is to talk about it. Find a counselor, another trained and trusted person, or a support group to share the pain that we were told never to divulge. Share the secrets. Then and only then can we begin to heal from the past. Only then can we break the power the past has over our feelings and our behavior. Only when we can begin to shrink the monsters of our past down to manageable size by talking about them can the secrets and traumas of the past cease to have an effect on us and our children.

I know that such intimate disclosure even to a counselor or clergy person is difficult and painful. We feel as though we are betraying our families, but it is quite true that families are only as sick as the secrets that they feel they must keep.

Having broken this rule for ourselves, we are then able to give our children the freedom to be honest about what is happening in our own families and to talk about things that trouble them. In healthy, functional families no subject is taboo or too dangerous to talk about. In such families, children can also seek what guidance they need in dealing with family problems. It is in living by the new rule, "If it bothers you, talk about it." that problems are solved, traumas are healed, and children grow up free of the ghosts of the past.

There is no shame in admitting that our family experiences difficulties, for all families do. No matter how severe the problems, no situation is truly unique. There is also no disgrace in admitting that one does not have all of the answers and needs outside assistance in resolving difficulties. The real tragedy occurs when one allows shame and embarrassment to take over and dictate silence, for then problems are not solved. They are just buried to fester and continue to hurt the next generation.

New Rule: If there is a problem within this family, we can talk about it among ourselves. If we cannot solve it, we seek help from outside of the family.

April 12

Old Rule: People who sit down and rest are lazy.

When many of us think of our parents, especially our mother, we recall that she "never stopped." She was always busy. Even when she sat down, she was busy. At first glance, this looks quite virtuous, but in constant busyness is a wall of unavailability and a message that says, "Don't bother me. Can't you see I'm busy? I have more important things to do than pay attention to you."

By becoming a "human doing" rather than a human being, we not only rob the people we love of our attention, but we also rob ourselves of closeness and intimacy with others. Indeed, busyness is a way to look virtuous and responsible while keeping ourselves emotionally distant. Constant busyness also fuels the martyr stance. It says to others, "Look at all I'm doing for you. I never take time for myself. How can you ask more of me?"

Letting go of constant busyness means risking hearing the "your lazy" self talk in your head. It also means risking increased intimacy with others. Getting past the initial discomfort of slowing the pace of our lives not only frees us to enjoy ourselves and to take better care of ourselves, it also frees us to be emotionally available for those who are important to us.

New Rule: Taking time to relax not only rejuvenates me, it also rejuvenates relationships with those I love.

April 13

Old Rule: Those who focus on taking care of themselves are selfish.

We play many simultaneous roles: spouse, parent, and employee. When we add child to our own parents, sibling, friend, and volunteer, small wonder that we feel overwhelmed. It seems that we are on a treadmill of doing, doing, doing, with multiple important obligations vying for our time and our energy. Many of us feel exhausted, frantic, and burnt out. The last thing that we do, if we have a bit of time left over, is take care of ourselves. If this situation is allowed to go on for too long, not only does our physical health suffer, but our emotional health is affected as well, contributing to resentment, depression, and anxiety.

We know this painful pattern, but when we try to do something about it and start to take some time out for ourselves, we begin to feel guilty. Our internal critic and maybe our external critics start to tell us that we are "being selfish", "should make better use of our time," and "have too much important stuff to do to be spending time on ourselves." As a result we put self-care on hold again, telling ourselves that when this job or this child-focused activity is done, then we can take some time for ourselves.

Living in a family means that there is always another seemingly urgent demand upon our time and energy. It is all too easy to postpone taking care of ourselves indefinitely, until some health or emotional crisis forces us to do otherwise.

Along with all of the other roles that we play, being a parent is only part of us. We are human beings before we are anything else and human beings need to spend time having fun, exercising, and focusing on our spiritual and intellectual development. We also need time to simply do nothing and rest.

This sounds impossible to many of us, but it is essential that we factor ourselves into all of our duties and responsibilities. Time for self-care is not selfish. It is good, sound mental and physical health maintenance. If you are having difficulty beginning, try reminding yourself that you will be a much better parent if you take some time on a regular basis to renew yourself. If you cannot do it solely for yourself, then begin doing it for those who depend upon you. Happily, you will find that the world does not cease spinning if you "get off" for a while. This is not selfish indulgence. This is sanity.

New Rule: I regularly make time to take care of myself. By taking care of myself, I can better fulfill the many roles and expectations in my full and busy life.

April 14

Old Rule: Promises mean nothing.

From time to time, all parents must break a promise to their children. Nonetheless, when promise breaking becomes a pattern, it has disastrous effects on our relationship with our children and, ultimately, on their other relationships.

Children learn to trust the world around them by experiencing their parents as trustworthy. When parents are not trustworthy, when they make promises lightly and just as lightly break them, children realize some significant things about the world and their role within it. First, they learn that adults, especially their parents, are not to be trusted. This is a frightening realization for children. If the people who are supposed to be taking care of them cannot be trusted, then children, who are dependent on those parents, are alone and adrift in the world.

Second, children realize that they are not worthy of keeping a promise. They become aware that they are not important to their parents. The tendency is to believe that if they are not important to the parent, who is supposed to love and want to take care of them, then they must not be very important, lovable, or worthy of care by anyone. This accounts for many of the problems with self-esteem we see with children of divorced families whose non-custodial parents make promises concerning visitations they do not keep.

Third, they learn not to trust others. If one's parents, who say that they care about you, are not dependable then others who say that they care are not likely to be dependable. If one trusts too much and believes what others say, then one is headed for painful disappointment. Therefore, it is best not to trust any one too much, especially those who say they love you.

Just as it is important to follow through with discipline (see October 14), it is equally important to take our promises to our children seriously. They do not forget when we break a promise, they remember and they learn.

New Rule: When I make a promise to my children, it is important that I do my best to live up to that promise.

April 15 & 16

Old Rule: If at all possible, blame someone else.

In Bill Keane's insightful cartoon series about family life, "The Family Circus," a little ghost causes trouble for innocent children. At least that is what the children claim. It is human nature to want to blame our mistakes or misbehavior on someone else. Even the writers of the Bible recognized this desire to avoid responsibility. Adam blamed Eve for giving him the apple and Eve blamed the snake. Both denied responsibility for their own behavior.

Blaming others, denying, or even lying when something goes wrong is a normal childhood developmental stage. It also has a frustrating resurgence in adolescence. Ask an adolescent why their grades are poor, the trash was not taken out, the car dented, or the homework not done, and you will hear a remarkable array of creative excuses, none of which imply that the adolescent is at fault.

While laying blame on others and circumstances in general is normal during childhood, assuming responsibility for our behavior is a developmental task that proceeds throughout our adult lives. If we honestly examine our thinking we would all love to blame someone else for our mistakes. Growing up and taking responsibility when we have messed up is difficult. Our world is filled with examples of people avoiding responsibility for their behavior: government, business, the entertainment industry, and sports provide some outstanding examples. Human beings just find it much easier to blame others for what happens rather than accept responsibility.

In some families, blaming is a way of life. When a mistake is made, all fingers point elsewhere. Typically, there is one person who gets the brunt of being the guilty one or problem child. In such families, no one ever says, "I did it. I am sorry. I'll try to learn and not do it again." No one takes responsibility.

This is a powerful lesson for children. When they grow up exposed to this pattern of blaming their mistakes and irresponsible actions on others, they will continue to do this as adults when the consequences of their mistake are much greater than when they were children. When we fail to take responsibility for our actions, not only do we hurt others, we do not learn from our mistakes. In order to learn from our mistakes, we must first admit we are in error and responsible for the resulting problems.

What we do and say in our daily interactions is a far more powerful lesson to our children than all of the paternal lectures concerning right and wrong. If we are to teach our children to be responsible, we must first accept responsibility for our own lives. When we make a mistake, we admit it, make amends where possible, and try to learn from it. When we say hurtful things to others, including our children, we apologize, and try not to repeat the offense. When we fail to keep our promises and obligations, we don't make excuses. Instead, we take responsibility and attempt to improve. These are powerful lessons that can help our children in their own efforts to become responsible and successful adults.

New Rule: I teach my children to take responsibility for their actions by taking responsibility for my own.

April 17 &18

Old Rule: If others are not happy, then I must be at fault. I need to take care of them and do something to make them happy.

We used to call it "codependency," the feeling that everything is basically my responsibility. If someone is wounded or unhappy then I must take care of him or her and make it better. The word "codependency" has been trivialized and, therefore, lost its original meaning. However, the concept and the painful lifestyle that comes from living by these rules are certainly valid and widespread, especially among women.

During the normal self-centeredness of childhood, we believe that the world and the people in it, especially our parents, revolves around us and our wants and needs. Very young children even believe that others can read their thoughts and that they can control the behavior and feelings of others with those thoughts. Most of us believed that if our mother or father was unhappy it must be because of us. As we mature, these beliefs are gradually resolved. Yet many of us continue to feel that we are responsible for the feelings of others. Some of us were even told that we were the cause of family problems and, being a child, we accepted this verdict. We tried and continue to try to make others feel better.

Accepting this belief, we go through life not only blaming others for how we feel and behave, but also accepting responsibility for the feelings and behaviors of others. For instance, we accept as valid statements like, "You made me angry and forced me to hit you." We became "people pleasers" who worked hard at making others happy. We don't allow others to feel hurt or rejected. We make excuses for them and never say "no" to even the most outlandish and unreasonable expectations. We lost our own identity in our people pleasing efforts. We often feel harried, unappreciated, and angry, because we are attempting to do the impossible: change the feelings of others and make them happy by taking care of them. We are often amazed that despite all of our hard work and sacrifice others are never satisfied and maybe even angry with us.

This painful muddle has dire effects on our families, including our children. We teach them, especially girls, to behave in much the same way with the same consequences. In other words, we teach girls to be victims of the behavior and demands of others in order to be considered loving and giving. We teach them that their worth is contingent upon pleasing and making others happy, especially men and later their children.

We may also teach our children not to take responsibility for their own feelings and actions. If we are taking all of the responsibility and not allowing them to feel unhappy or frustrated, then they will not learn to take responsibility for their own happiness and will blame us and others when their world is not pleasing and bountiful. If you feel exhausted and confused reading this, imagine living by these irrational beliefs.

Recovery from this painful and destructive set of circumstances begins when we accept the reality that we cannot make others happy. We are not even responsible for trying. If others around us are unhappy, then they are responsible for making the changes that will make their lives better. Growing up is a continual process of moving away from the dependence of the infant when we, indeed, must rely on our parents for all of our needs, to accepting responsibility for our own lives and happiness. Not to allow our children to move through this growth process by attempting to meet their every want and soothe every uncomfortable feeling is damaging to them.

Recovery continues when we learn to say "no" and stick to it, when we allow others to be displeased with us and not feel that we must somehow change to meet their expectations, and when we focus on our own care rather than exclusively on the care of others. Recovery from this destructive pattern does not mean moving back to the self-centered days of infancy. It is not about becoming selfish, which is the worst thing you can call a practicing codependent. It is about finally growing up and living up to the obligations that we make to others, while refusing to waste our time and energies taking responsibility for the well-being and happiness of those who can and need to do this for themselves.

Living in this reality, we can then model these productive and life enhancing behaviors and attitudes for our children. However, like most of the lessons we teach our children, we must first learn to live them ourselves.

New Rule: I try to teach my children that they are ultimately responsible not only for their own behavior, but also for their own feelings and satisfaction with their lives. I know this can only be accomplished when I attempt to live by these truths myself.

April 19

Old Rule: Don't upset your mother/father.

This rule comes up frequently when I ask counseling clients to look at the dysfunctional rules that prevailed in their homes when they were children.

It operates most strongly in families when a parent has serious problems, especially a mental or physical illness. Their illness becomes the central focus of family life and the needs of everyone else, including the children, are secondary to the parent's problems.

Frequently, the problem is parental alcoholism, drug addiction, or inability to control anger. In these families, one parent becomes the filter or peacemaker, repeatedly warning the children that they are not to upset the other parent because some feared, negative consequence will occur.

As a result, the parent that is "sick" or "not to be upset" is not held accountable for their behavior and the filtering parent, in the name of keeping peace, becomes quite powerful. The children learn to consistently put their needs after those who appear to be weak, sick, or unable to control themselves. This pattern can last a lifetime and is often recreated in their adult relationships. Children also learn to lie and manipulate. They learn not to give information that may have negative consequences. Instead, they learn to live by a "What others don't know won't hurt me" rule.

Practicing this damaging rule allows dysfunctional, irresponsible behavior to continue in a family until either the peacekeeping parent finds the courage to upset the other parent and begins to change the system or the "upset" parent begins to take responsibility for their own recovery and becomes a full participant in the family.

New Rule 1: I refuse to protect my partner from the realities and responsibilities of family life. I treat my spouse as an equal parent.

New Rule 2: I am willing to be "upset" by the behavior of and information given me by my children. I am an adult and can handle the realities of family life.

April 20

Old Rule: Don't be a problem child.

What constitutes a problem child? Is a problem child the one who doesn't always behave and does not sit quietly, but is instead moving about and exploring the world? Is it the child who asks "why?" when adults make pronouncements? Is it the child who speaks their mind and is independent, not sweet and compliant?

Granted such an independent, articulate, opinionated child takes more energy and time to rear. However, the very traits that may constitute a problem child are the traits that we want our grown children to have - a questioning mind, an independent spirit, autonomy, and the ability to express themselves.

Rather than viewing this child as a problem, why not see this child as one with great potential to achieve and flourish, a child who needs our guidance to channel their energies and abilities appropriately. As parents of this special child, our job is to foster that child's potential with loving approval and support.

New Rule: My inquisitive, opinionated, and active child is not a problem. This child is my challenge as I attempt to facilitate their growth and provide them with the guidance necessary to channel their abilities appropriately.

April 21

Old Rule: My child must not fail.

In the past few years, we have seen a closer examination of our schools and the quality of the education given our children. We place an emphasis on standardized testing and there is a great deal of discussion concerning educational standards and curriculum. As a response to the demand for higher tests scores and the expectations of parents, the amount of homework has increased dramatically.

For some parents this is not good news. They were having difficulty getting their children to do the homework they already had! Homework time for many parents and children is a battleground. The child stalls, pleads ignorance, or has forgotten the assignment and the textbook. The parent, who is likely angry and frustrated, attempts to help. All too often the parent winds up doing more work than the child, because the parent is unwilling to let the child suffer the natural, logical consequences of not doing schoolwork - failure. This pattern can go on for years. The child does not take responsibility for homework and their school projects, so the parent picks up the slack and helps. This scenario does not help the child learn the material or take responsibility for their education. It does teach irresponsibility, dependence, and often manipulation.

Perhaps the best solution is to permit the child to suffer the consequences of not doing homework. When the inevitable failure occurs parents can then create logical consequences at home - lack of desired privileges. It is far better for them to suffer these consequences in elementary school rather than in middle school, high school, or college. They will eventually have to learn that their education is their responsibility. Their achievements or the lack of them must ultimately be their own, not their parents'.

New Rule: I make a place in my home that is conducive to studying. I help my children with homework when they are having difficulty, but the ultimate responsibility lies with them.

April 22

Old Rule: Childhood is a carefree time. Children don't have any worries.

We tend to idealize childhood and remember it as a time when we did not worry about job, money, or family. We see childhood as a time free of responsibilities, a time of fun and joy. While it is normal for human beings to remember the pleasant and forget the unpleasant, childhood is not always carefree. It was not for us and is not for our children.

As parents we want them to enjoy themselves, to play and have fun and to be free of adult concerns. However, children do have worries and concerns. They worry about their parents, especially when we are ill or unhappy. They worry about other family members, like their grandparents. They worry about their schoolwork, their athletic abilities, and their performance in other activities such as dance or music. They worry about being smart enough, attractive enough, or popular enough to measure up to their peers. Children are increasingly worried about their safety in school and in their neighborhoods.

All of these concerns make childhood a less than carefree time. However, we can lighten their load by being alert to when they seem abnormally concerned. We can keep the doors of communication open and allow them to express these worries. We can also lessen their concerns about us by taking care of our own problems, demonstrating our ability to be responsible for the family, and protecting them from adult concerns over which they have no control. We can also talk with them about events, such as school violence, and help them to understand what they see and hear in the media. By doing these things, perhaps we can make childhood, even a 21st century childhood, less fearful and more carefree.

New Rule: I know that my children worry about any number of situations. I try to decrease their concerns by keeping the doors of communication open and taking responsibility for my family and myself.

April 23 and 24

Old Rule: This parenting stuff is so complicated! Most of the time I don't know what to do! I dread when they become teenagers. Then I really won't know what to do!

This parenting business can be overwhelming. Especially when you are reading a book that offers a different thought on parenting for each day of the year! In truth, parenting is the most difficult job I have ever tried to do! I have often felt quite inadequate, even clueless, about what to do next.

Some time ago a student from my Marriage and Family class gave me an article from "Better Homes and Gardens" which might help us all to simplify this parenting business. In their October, 1998 issue, they published an article entitled "Six Secrets to Raising a Successful Teen."

They surveyed 47 high school junior and seniors who were doing well. They asked these successful kids what their parents had done to help them succeed. After reviewing the results they found that the key to rearing successful kids could be broken down into six parenting strategies.

1) Come to my game. Taking the time to come to a child's game or other activities seems to say to kids that they are very important to us.

2) Give the gift of responsibility. When parents establish a trusting and mutually respectful relationship early in the child's life, the child is more likely to feel an obligation to live up to parents' positive expectations.

3) Give them something to believe in. Just as with most successful adults, successful teens are likely to have a strong relationship with God and are encouraged to practice a religious faith.

4) Loosen a tight grip. The teenagers in the survey indicated that they did not consider their parents strict disciplinarians. Instead, they indicated that their parents listened to their wants and were willing to negotiate.

5) Teach kids how to set goals early. Helping kids to set clear, achievable goals at an early age helps foster increased self-confidence and a positive self-image.

6) Listen and then listen some more. These teenagers felt that they could talk with their parents about anything, even difficult issues. The most important part of communicating with kids, or anyone for that matter, is to really listen. This kind of respectful communication does not mean we formulate our response while the child is talking or we spend most of the time giving our latest lecture. It means that we are truly willing to listen to our children. It is in such listening that a positive relationship with anyone, including our children, can flourish.

These strategies may seem simplistic, but they have a dramatic effect on our children. By practicing them we can build positive relationships early in their lives, so that when the stresses of adolescence come our job is made easier because we are parenting out of a strong, positive, and mutually respectful relationship.

New Rule: This parenting business isn't so tough! I can do it, not perfectly, but good enough!

April 25

Old Rule: I just tell my kids, "Don't have sex until you are married." That is all they need to know.

Don't do "it" until you are married. You don't need to know anymore. This is actually an old rule that, thank goodness, most parents do not follow today. Most parents would agree that adolescents certainly do need to know about sexuality and reproduction.

Yet even today, parents struggle with how much and what to tell their children as they grow into late childhood and early adolescence. Unlike many of their parents and grandparents, most parents do not have much difficulty with the facts of pregnancy and birth. What gives them the most difficulty is explaining sexual desire, intercourse, contraception, sexually transmitted diseases, and values.

Some parents opt for the strict, just the facts, anatomy and physiology information leaving out a discussion of sexual desire and sexual values. Often parents focus strictly on the values of abstinence, leaving out information on sexual desire, contraception, and sexually transmitted disease. Our children need the whole package of information, including acknowledgment of their normal sexual desires.

They need to know our values with respect to sexuality. They need and in truth want our help in developing their own values concerning this powerful issue. They need to know that it is not okay to use someone else's body solely to gratify one's desires. They need to know that allowing one's self to be used sexually is not an effective way to keep a relationship. They need to know that not every one is "doing it", that it really is okay to wait, and that saying "yes" does not mean that one must keep saying "yes."

In short, they need our information and our guidance in this very important, powerful, and potentially dangerous part of being human.

New Rule: I would not withhold from my children information, including information about my values, concerning any other important area of life. Therefore, I share with them, early and often, information and my values concerning sexuality.

April 26

Old Rule: We don't talk about sex. My children are too young.

Americans deal with sexuality in some very strange and inconsistent ways. On one hand, most television programs, movies, and music videos give the message that having sex is the usual thing if one is young, attractive, and over the age of 16. Indeed the popular media says that sex is the goal of all relationships between males and females, married or unmarried, committed to a relationship or just casually acquainted. Sexual innuendos fill our entertainment. "Sex is expected and has no consequences," is the often-repeated message. Media sexuality tends to be silly, adolescent, and preoccupied with doing "it". Even young children learn these powerful lessons on an almost daily basis. They almost cannot help but be exposed to a generous dose of sleazy, juvenile, leering, consequenceless sexuality.

On the other hand, parents know the truth about sexuality, but are often reluctant to talk with their young children about the importance of sexuality in the context of love, commitment, and marriage. When we are silent all they will hear is the voice of the media saying, "Just do it, it's fun! There are no consequences."

When we treat sexuality as an adult expression of love and commitment that has both positive and negative consequences, we are assuming our right and responsibility to teach them sexual values and give them accurate information.

New Rule: I give my children accurate information about sexuality. I am alert for those teachable moments when I can add my voice concerning responsible sexuality, love, commitment, and marriage to the other voices they hear.

April 27

Old Rule: "I'm not angry! What makes you think I'm angry?!"

Our jaws are set. Our teeth are clenched. Our entire body is tense and our voice is strained and tight. Yet we deny to our inquiring children that we are angry. We think that we are disguising our anger, protecting them from our feelings, and being "nice," but children are perceptive, especially when it comes to their parents. They know when something is wrong.

The content of our spoken message may be that we are not angry. However, our bodies and tone of voice say we are, indeed, angry. Our children are on target with their perceptions of our emotional state. However, we deny our children's accurate perceptions and tell them they did not see what they saw. When we send these contradictory and confusing messages, we encourage them to believe that they are mistaken and not to trust their observations about others. This is especially true in families in which there is a great deal of stress, and parents feel they must keep many of the difficulties from the children.

Lately, we have become aware of the value of emotional intelligence in successful interpersonal relationships, not just within families but also in the larger world. The ability to accurately interpret the feelings of others is an important part of emotional intelligence. When we deny our children's accurate perceptions, we stifle their natural abilities to perceive others correctly. We teach them not to rely on their own impressions and feelings, but instead to discount them. We are not allowing this important ability to grow and develop.

When we are willing to confirm our children's perceptions, even when the situation does not concern them, we are facilitating the growth of their emotional intelligence.

New Rule: "Yes, I'm angry about … You are very perceptive."

April 28

Old Rule: Get what you can.

When we have a "get what you can before anyone else gets it" set of values we are expressing our belief that there is not enough of the good things in life for everyone. We are saying there is not enough money, possessions, praise, appreciation, success, and even love to go around.

When we believe that we must scramble for everything, we become greedy and we teach our children to be greedy. The more we operate out of these beliefs, the more greedy and frightened we become. The belief that there is not enough is rooted in fear: fear of not having what we believe we need, fear of not getting what we want, fear of being without. When we have these fears, we teach this philosophy to our children and they emerge from our care convinced that they must grab all they can lest they find themselves without. A truly dreadful way to live! Such greed leads to feeling that nothing is ever quite enough, whether it is possessions, money, praise, success, or love. What self-created misery!

New Rule: There is no scarcity of the good things in life. We have enough of what we need or want, even if others also enjoy abundance.

April 29

Old Rule: Winning is everything. Win at all costs.

Competitiveness, particularly athletic competition, is a fundamental component of our culture. Therefore, we must equip our children to handle it appropriately. We would not want our children to be without a competitive spirit. This would take away the fun and the enjoyment of team and individual sports. However, we have all seen the nasty results when competition is carried too far and winning at all costs takes over.

Like most functional behavior, appropriate competition is in the middle ground between non-competitive behavior, which renders games or individual sports pointless, and winning at all costs. It is our responsibility to teach our children the balance between these two extremes. If they choose to participate in athletics we can help them discover the joy of doing one's best, contributing to the team effort, learning and refining new skills, and celebrating when these efforts result in winning. On balance, we also need to teach them that athletic competitions are, after all, only games and winning should not come at the expense of fair play and good sportsmanship.

Sportsmanship, that is maintaining a balance between fair play and competition, is an important lesson that parents both model and formally teach their children. Failure to maintain good sportsmanship teaches children that winning is everything and one must win by whatever means necessary, including cheating. It also teaches children to pout, blame others, and pitch temper tantrums if one does not win, an unpleasant spectacle we see all too often in sports.

Good sportsmanship also entails being a gracious winner, putting the game in its proper place and shaking hands at the close of the competition. Examples of good sportsmanship by parents and coaches model appropriate behavior in competition. Parents have many opportunities to teach important life lessons in the context of competition: doing one's best, the joy of learning and perfecting new skills, playing as a member of a team, putting fair play before winning, and being a gracious winner and an honorable loser.

New Rule: I accept the opportunity to teach my children the lessons of fair play, good sportsmanship, and competition.

April 30

Old Rule: We just do not have enough hours in the day to do all that needs to be done.

In her book <u>To Everything A Season -A Spirituality of Time,</u> Bonnie Thurston encourages us to rethink our relationship to time. Focusing on our use of time, she proposes that we consider a return to Sabbath time. A time set apart for contemplation and rest, Sabbath time is a part of most religious traditions. Yet many of us have come to view Sabbath as time of enforced inactivity that we have, for the most part, abandoned.

Ms. Thurston, however, urges us to think of Sabbath time as a time apart from our usual activities to rest, renew our spirits, and rejuvenate important relationships. In other words, she encourages us to abandon our practice of filling each day with busyness and work and setting aside time for personal renewal and rest.

I realize that the idea of setting apart an entire day is impossible for most of us. We live in families with two working parents or single parents who have much more to do than they can ever accomplish. I have certainly been part of the group that trudges wearily to the grocery store on Sunday evening, resenting the lack of personal time and feeling guilty that I have not attended to the important relationships in my life.

Despite the reality of our over-scheduled lives, perhaps it is time to do what a priest friend of mine suggested: focus on what is truly important rather than on what <u>seems</u> urgent. Is it important to go shopping today to get new shoes or does it seem urgent? Is it important to clean the house, get the lawn mowed, and wash clothes or does it seem urgent? Does it feel urgent to spend some time reading to our children or taking them to the playground or is it important? Does it feel urgent to spend some time alone today taking a walk, reading, or reviving some long neglected hobby or is it important?

Time is a gift, but it is a limited gift. We are free to choose how we use at least a portion of it. Perhaps we can reserve a few hours on the weekend for a family activity or one parent can have an hour or so to do as they please while the other parent takes over. The choices are endless, but we must make a conscious choice if we are to use this gift wisely.

New Rule: We take time in our family to focus on what is important rather than what seems urgent. By focusing on the importance of personal time as well as family time, we refresh our souls and enrich our relationships.

May 1

Old Rule: It is vitally important that others think well of you. Always look good!

My friend's mother was dying. Having ignored the warning signs of her serious illness, she waited until it was too late.

At her mother's home, the yard was flawlessly maintained and manicured. The summer annuals were planted in neat beds and the shrubs were trimmed, a sign to the world that all was well. Inside the house, however, the walls and carpets were dirty. Parts of the ceiling were beginning to fall. The closets and drawers were stuffed with the unsorted debris of many years. "This was my mother's life. Outside everything was perfect. Inside it was a mess," sighed my friend.

Wanting others to think well of us is a normal human desire, but to live only to impress others guarantees that, while the outside may look good, the inside will be unkempt, filled with debris, and shabby.

New Rule: While I would like for others to think well of me and my family, it is far more important to be pleased with myself. I can choose to spend my time and energy attempting to look good to others or to focus on building loving relationships with those close to me, expanding my knowledge, exploring my spirituality, and having fun. This is a powerful example for my children on how to be truly happy and successful in life.

May 2

Old Rule: That is okay, but …

A friend was dressing her 5-year-old daughter for a birthday party. Dressed in a colorful summer dress, Mother gave her the choice of two colors of sandals. The child went to her room and chose a pair of pink sandals that matched her dress. Mom was doing well. She had allowed her daughter to make a small choice between two alternatives. However, Mother, who is quite invested in the appearance of perfection, had wanted the daughter to choose the white sandals and said to her, "Those shoes don't look very good. Go put on your white ones." Surprisingly, the child went upstairs and put on the white sandals without protest. Perhaps she had come to expect such arbitrary behavior from her mother and was not in a mood to fight about it that day. Nevertheless, you can bet she will not always be so compliant.

Obviously, this was about more than pink vs. white sandals. The real issue is teaching our children to make decisions by giving them choices when they are young while the decisions are small and inconsequential and then respecting those decisions. Actually, Mom unwittingly made an even more serious error than if she had controlled the decision from the very beginning. She allowed her daughter to make a choice. The daughter made the choice and then Mom disrespectfully discounted that choice. In this situation, the child absolutely could not win. She could not initially say to Mother "you choose" and she had only a 50% chance of reading Mom's mind and making the right choice. In either case, the decision was not about what the child decided was right for her, but what Mother thought looked acceptable to others. Now, Mom did no permanent damage with her behavior in this instance. Yet, given enough of these episodes of allowing the child to make a choice and then invalidating her choice, two things are likely to happen. The child may come to question her ability to make choices and feel that no matter what she does she can't do it right. Her self-esteem will suffer and she will refuse to make any decisions for herself. Or the child may angrily rebel against Mother, leaving Mother to complain, "What is the matter with this child? I do everything for her and still she is not happy."

Effective parents begin in early childhood to allow their children to make choices among appropriate alternatives. They encourage their children to practice decision-making by gradually increasing the consequences of those choices, preparing them for the inevitable time when they will make important choices without parental advice.

New Rule: I give my children opportunities to make appropriate choices and respect the choices once they have been made. In this way, I teach my children to trust their own judgment and make wise decisions.

May 3

Old Rule: You'll never amount to anything!

A colleague related this poignant story concerning a former student. The student was a bright woman in her early thirties. Having come to college for the first time, she was feeling the exhilaration of knowing that she could, indeed, handle the demands of college work. She was only one semester from graduating when she announced that she was leaving school to return to her factory job because her family needed money. My colleague encouraged her not to leave school and attempted to help her find another way to support her family while completing her degree. During the course of this discussion the student stated, "My mother always told me I would never amount to anything anyway." This woman was living out an old childhood message and in a way she was leaving school rather than move into uncharted territory and risk proving her mother wrong. She was also terrified of failing and actually proving her mother right. Therefore, it was safer to quit rather than take the risk that she might fail to achieve her dream of becoming a nurse. A dream that always remains a dream never encounters the risk of failure.

As a teacher, I have encountered other students who are struggling against parental messages that they "would not amount to anything." These students not only suffer from low self-esteem, but fear success as well as failure. No amount of success convinces them that they are capable. Instead they seem to feel that they are one test or one course away from finding something that will cause them to fail and thus confirm their parents' beliefs. Even if their parents are long dead, they seem driven to prove them wrong. At the same time, they engage in self-sabotage. Just as they are about to succeed, they may simply stop coming to class or become involved in an intense personal situation that saps their time and energy. Such is the power of parental messages to children. They last a lifetime, whether negative or positive, encouraging or discouraging.

New Rule: I am aware of the power I have to influence my children's self-esteem. Knowing I have this power, I attempt to use it wisely to build self-confidence and a sense of positive self-worth in my children.

May 4

Old Rule: Girls have more responsibility and boys have more freedom.

Every parent knows there are differences in boys and girls in how they grow and what they need from parents. Historically, we have given more responsibility to girls, often without much freedom, while boys are often given more freedom as well as tolerance for irresponsible behavior. (Boys will be boys.) This double standard persists today even as we attempt to rear children in a gender-neutral fashion.

On the surface these standards would seem to favor boys, but we also know that being a boy in our culture is dangerous. Boys are more at risk of being injured or killed. They are more likely to kill themselves (even though more girls attempt suicide, more boys actually kill themselves), and they are more likely to commit crimes and to be incarcerated for an extended period of time. Yet we continue to give boys a great deal of freedom, often without expectation or preparation for responsible behavior.

On the other hand, parents know that being a girl can be dangerous. Girls are for more likely to be a victim of assault, especially sexual assault. They continue to bear the brunt of the consequences of pre-mature sexuality. Girls are more likely to see their self-worth reflected in their acceptance by males, which brings on self-destructive behavior such as eating disorders, pre-mature sexual activity, and even criminal behavior with a boyfriend. No wonder parents want to protect girls and teach them to be responsible and careful.

This may not be the best way to rear our children of either sex. According to neurobiologist Deborah Blum in a "Life" magazine article dealing with brain development and the resulting behavioral differences in boys and girls, girls' intellectual and emotional development is negatively impacted when they are restricted and prevented from engaging in a wide variety of activities and pursuits. Boys, on the other hand, may be emotionally more fragile than we realize. They do need emotional support and guidance, even if they protest. Often it is boys who need protecting from the general culture and girls who need to be allowed, with support from parents, to explore the larger world. Once again wise parenting is found in the middle ground between two extremes: too much protection and too much freedom.

New Rule: We try to prepare our daughter to move out and explore the larger world, while we support and protect our son from moving too quickly into that same world.

May 5

Old Rule: Be quiet! Go and play! Can't you see I'm on the computer?

It seems we have a new addiction - the computer, specifically computer games and the Internet. Spending large amounts of time at the computer, even if we are "chatting" with others, is just as much an addiction as over-working or compulsive gambling. Computer use addiction has the same effect as all addictions. It takes us away from the real world of our relationships with others and transports us into an artificial world that is easier to control and make into what we want it to be. Family relationships are messy, unpredictable, and emotionally demanding. On the other hand, computer relationships, surfing the Internet, and computer games are tidy, predictable, easily controlled, and require no emotional energy.

When used in moderation the computer is an entertaining and useful tool that enriches our lives. When used compulsively, computers impoverish our lives. Like all addictions, they can become a substitute for human interaction.

Our children need our attention. They need to interact with us. You may choose to include them in a portion of your computer time, but they do need and deserve to have our attention when we are not preoccupied with other things, including the computer. When we spend time with them without other distractions, we are telling them that they are important to us. Practicing an addiction, even a computer addiction, tells them that they are not as important to us as the focus of the addiction. Do we want to teach our children that they are less important than our computers? The choice is ours.

New Rule: In our family we try to balance the use of the marvelous technology of the computer with human interaction. No computer game or website, no matter how fascinating, is more important than our relationships with each other.

May 6

Old Rule: Worry! It means that you are paying proper attention to your life.

Chronic worry, what a sneaky, subtle obsession! Yet many of us are caught in the trap of compulsive worry. We worry about what we did or did not do yesterday or even in years past. We worry about tomorrow and what will happen to those we love. We tell ourselves that we are responsible, conscientious people who are prepared for any contingency and that we see life and all its catastrophic possibilities clearly and rationally. Baloney! We are addicted to worry!

We spend so much of our time and energy worrying about "what if…" that we completely miss today. Not only do we miss the pleasures of today, but constant worry also allows us to avoid today's challenges. This sneaky addiction enables us to focus on difficulties about which we can do nothing, while ignoring those things we can change. It allows us to tell ourselves that we are serious, responsible adults while we are being actually quite irresponsible. Unconsciously, we pass these destructive mental habits onto our children, teaching them to be frightened, chronic worriers.

Focusing on the present not only frees us from the pain of chronic worry, but it also enables us to deal more effectively with today's challenges. There is great freedom in letting go of the past and turning tomorrow and all of its possibilities over to our Higher Power. When we free ourselves from chronic worry, we can teach our children to live in the present with all of its joys and possibilities.

New Rule: I choose to let go of compulsive worry and live in the present. I have decided to let go of the regrets of yesterday and turn over to my Higher Power concern about tomorrow. I elect to live in the freedom of today and help my children to claim this freedom for themselves.

May 7

Old Rule: Now settle down! Take your medicine!

Medicating children who are diagnosed with hyperactivity, attention deficit disorder, and more recently depression and obsessive-compulsive disorder is a controversial and complex issue that must be decided by parents in consultation with health care professionals.

However, I believe when we give children the message that the medicine is controlling their behavior, we are setting a dangerous pattern. When parents believe children are incapable of controlling their actions and, therefore, not responsible for their behavior, children will come to believe this also and will not learn to take responsibility for controlling themselves. When parents believe that medicines are a magical solution taking the place of discipline and teaching self-control, children do not learn to control their own behavior. They learn, instead, to make excuses for their lack of responsibility.

Having a child with behavioral problems caused by a brain abnormality is difficult for both child and parent. Finding medications that work to help alleviate these complex problems is a godsend. The correct medication can substantially improve the child's life and school performance. However, problems may arise when children learn that if they feel uncomfortable or emotionally distressed something outside of themselves, a psychoactive chemical, will make them feel better. This is addict thinking. Many children are introduced to addiction thinking by well-intended parents who tell them to take their medicine when they are experiencing even minor distress.

I am certainly not suggesting that parents abandon the use of medicines, but what I am suggesting is that we must also teach our children that ultimately they are in charge of managing their feelings as well as their behavior. While these medicines can help, children must ultimately learn to take responsibility for themselves. Grandparents, teachers, and others who are involved with the child can also help them to learn self-control by reinforcing discipline and teaching impulse control.

Having a child with these disorders is a challenge. It can be exhausting and frustrating. I would suggest to parents who are faced with these difficulties to seek support and assistance from all available resources. Supportive help can lighten the load for both you and your child.

New Rule: Even though my child takes medication for a brain disorder, I need to help my child learn to mange and take responsibility for their behavior.

May 8

Old Rule: Lecture! Our children need the benefit of our experience

My father was a lecturer, but I could not repeat any of the thoughts expressed in those lectures. However, I can tell you about the times when he listened and responded to my concerns. I can also recall the times he responded with a lecture that indicated he was not really listening. I am a lecturer, too. As a college instructor, I'm a <u>professional</u> lecturer! However, what may work with the students in my classes definitely does not work when I am attempting to communicate with my children. (Actually lecturing probably does not work all that well in the classroom either.)

Kids seem to be able to sense a lecture coming. When we start the conversation with "When I was your age …" or "When you get out in the world you will realize …" they tune us out. They get that glassy-eyed look and if their little lives depended on it, they could not repeat what we just said. Even if they wanted to listen, the very nature of the communication would not let them.

Communication with children, or anyone for that matter, is first and foremost about listening. Listening is vital to effective communication. Listening not to formulate our reply, but listening to understand what the other person thinks and feels. A good communicator is respectful and slow to pass judgment. Instead, they respond with their own thoughts and feelings in a way that does not block the flow of communication. They tend to be brief and talk with, not to, others. They do not deliver lectures. Effective communication is difficult. It requires energy, even more energy than delivering a lecture, but is far more beneficial in establishing a positive relationship with our children in which every one can truly be heard.

New Rule: Please, Lord, help me to keep my big mouth shut and listen!

May 9

Old Rule: We don't have to talk with our children about drugs and alcohol. They are too young to be exposed to them.

Although we are frequently exposed to information concerning alcohol and drug use by children and adolescents, many of us maintain a state of denial about our own children and the availability of alcohol and other drugs.

In reality, drugs and alcohol are widely available to children in grade school. Many alcoholics and drug addicts will admit that they first began to use these substances when they were young children, some younger than age 12. Where did they get their drugs? Who supplies a 10 or 12-year-old?

They get them in school from other children, from older brothers and sisters, or when they go to a friend's house. They take drugs and alcohol from their parents' supply. Many children begin to use alcohol or marijuana, two of the most prevalent drugs of abuse in our culture, by stealing from or being given these drugs by their parents or other adult acquaintances. In truth, by the time children reach 13 or 14, they have to make a decision not to use drugs rather than to seek out a source in order to use them.

Many children are given prescription drugs, especially tranquilizers by their parents who take them when they are "upset" or "nervous." These parents lack the ability or willingness to cope with anxiety in ways other than tranquilizer use. They teach their children the same dysfunctional way of coping by giving them the quick fix of tranquilizers when their children are "upset."

It is vitally important that we talk with our children early about drugs and alcohol, but having just one "drug talk" will not get the job done. In order to do this we must be knowledgeable ourselves. Frightening them with half-truths and lies will not do either. The truth is frightening enough. We cannot misinform them and expect that they will believe the rest of what we say. We must be straight with them.

It is also important, perhaps even more important, that we look at the message we are giving them by our own use of drugs and alcohol. What we do and the decisions we make are far more powerful teachers than what we say. In order for our children to make wise decisions about drug and alcohol use, we must first make them ourselves.

New Rule: I accept the responsibility of teaching my children about drug and alcohol use, not only with what I say to them, but what I show them by my example.

May 10

Old Rule: We are in control of our children. Our children will never do some of the things that other children do. We simply will not permit it.

Yeah! Right! Pity the poor parents who believe they are in control, who believe that by pronouncement, threat, and parental power they can effectively control their children. It simply does not happen and the older our children become the less control we have. In reality, by the time our children enter adolescence our control diminishes rapidly, even if we are quite vigilant and attempt to enforce strict rules.

Parenthood is about the gradual process of letting go. When they are infants we have a great deal of control, but we can't stop them from crying. We have to fix the problem before they stop crying and so it goes throughout their lives. We don't have control, but we do have power.

Our power is based in our children's desire for our approval. All children seem to have the basic desire to please their parents. They try hard not to disappoint us. Indeed, I have heard many kids say that they did not do something because they knew their parents would be terribly disappointed. A loving, trusting, potentially disappointed parent seems to be a powerful incentive for staying out of trouble. They want our approval and will do most anything to get it – until they feel that it is hopeless. Then they usually decide that they might as well do as they please, for it is useless to try to please us.

They look to us to help them to understand and to negotiate their world, even as adolescents when they seem to resent our every suggestion and rebel against even the most common sense rules. They do not need our lectures and dictatorial pronouncements; they need our help in thinking through their decisions and choices. They need our support when they make mistakes and learn painful life lessons, but they need the freedom to make these mistakes. We have only the illusion of control, but we have immense power.

New Rule: I know that control over my children is limited and grows smaller with each day, but I have the power to help my children develop into competent, responsible adults.

May 11

Old Rule: I'm going to finance my retirement by winning the lottery.

Gambling fever has swept the United States. Millions upon millions of dollars are spent every year in this country on gambling. States are financing their governments and their education systems with lottery money. According to a recent newspaper article, twenty-two percent of us seem to believe that we can actually finance our retirement by winning the lottery. Yet the odds are against us. We are more likely to be struck by lightning than to win a substantial amount of money by gambling. Yet we continue to play, hoping for that big win, hoping to cash in and get a huge prize for a small investment. When it does happen to a player, we are fascinated, wanting to hear what the big winner will do with the money and speculating what we would do with it if we had won. Even those who do not play talk about what they would do if all that money suddenly became theirs. It is fun to talk about it and to speculate even if we know the odds.

However, our children are listening and watching and what they are getting from all of this might not be what we intend. Are they learning that having money is the most important aspiration? Are they learning that the best way to make money is to win at gambling not by education and hard work? Are they learning that it is possible, indeed likely, to make a great deal of money for doing nothing other than buying a ticket and picking a few numbers? Are they learning that buying weekly tickets is more important than paying the bills, buying food, or saving money for emergencies?

People have been gambling for centuries, and it is unlikely that the legalized gambling genie once out of the bottle in the United States can ever be put back. Therefore, we must teach our children the truth about the gambling odds. We need to talk with them about gambling as recreation not as a substitute for education, working to earn money, and sound financial management. In short, they are hearing a lot of messages in our culture right now that touts gambling as a way to be successful. We need to be honest with them about the odds of that actually happening. We also need to model responsible behavior with respect to gambling - that we view gambling as a recreational activity that we do after bills have been paid and we have set aside money into savings. Since gambling is a fact in our current way of life, we need to be as honest about it as we are about drugs and alcohol, for out of control gambling is just as dangerous as any mood altering substance.

New Rule: It is my responsibility to educate my children about gambling, even if I do not engage in it myself.

May 12

Old Rule: Children don't need privacy from their parents.

Like adults, children need privacy even within their families. In some families, however, parents do not respect this normal desire. Parents not only walk in when children are using the bathroom well past the age when they need assistance with the toilet or bathing, but also fail to allow children privacy in their own bedrooms.

One of the characteristics of a dysfunctional family is a lack of appropriate boundaries. This lack of boundaries results in the repeated invasion of children's privacy, including intellectual privacy. Parents often read diaries, letters, and notes from school friends. They question their children repeatedly about their thoughts, actions, friends, and events at their grandparents or other parent's home. Children, like adults, need a sense of "this is mine and I get to chose whom I let into this private space." They also need a place to keep possessions that is not available to others without their permission. As children become adolescents, they need even more physical and intellectual privacy.

As a former drug abuse counselor, I have talked with parents who have searched their children's rooms for drugs or drug paraphernalia. This may be necessary if parents have evidence that their children are using drugs and alcohol or engaged in other harmful or self-destructive behavior. Absent such evidence, parents would do well to bear in mind their children's need for privacy.

If parents are overly invasive, children will become more guarded. Their need for privacy is so intense that if they feel it is invaded, they will become even more reluctant to share with us. They may keep things from us we should know. If children feel they have a choice about what they will disclose, they are more apt to confide in their parents.

We need to respect the privacy of our children and their right to have a portion of their lives which is uniquely their own, a right whose boundaries we do not traverse. In an article in "U.S. News and World Report", (11/20/95, Probing Family Harmony), therapist Maggie Scarfe states, "We are born with a double need - one is to love and link and connect. The second is to have our personal turf, to be who you are. In a good family you have both."

New Rule: Children, like adult members of the family, need and have a right to privacy.

May 13 & 14

Old Rule: Children are just short adults.

This sounds like a completely irrational rule that no one would accept as true, but in reality parents for generations believed it. They did not believe that childhood is a discrete time of life, totally different from adulthood. They did not believe we should study and honor this time and treat children differently. While children were, of course, seen as physically different than adults and dependent for a period of time, children were considered small, inferior adults who would soon have the necessary physical development to take their place in the work of maintaining the family. There was little appreciation of the unique emotional and intellectual needs of children. Indeed, the concept of childhood as a discrete time of life having specific developmental tasks at each stage is a relatively new concept, developed only over the past 100 years.

Today we consider childhood a unique and precious time. In many countries, for instance, child labor is illegal and school attendance mandated. Yet, there are remnants of past beliefs in our treatment of children. When we expect our children to perform like adults on the athletic field, we are not taking into account the time needed to develop the necessary skills to hit a ball with a bat or to run down a soccer field while kicking a ball. When parents become upset over a missed ball, they are not taking into consideration immature coordination and rapidly, but unevenly, growing bodies. (We would also have a tendency to trip, drop things, and miss balls thrown to us if we had gotten 4 inches taller and our feet had grown 2 inches in the past six months.)

Believing this rule, we expect our children to understand adult matters, to think through problems, and to reason like adults. Children want to meet parental expectations and win our approval. Yet when we ask them to do the impossible and criticize them when they do not meet our unreasonable expectations, children may become discouraged or rebellious and angry. Certainly their self-esteem suffers.

Children think differently and experience their feelings differently from adults. They think more concretely and have a different sense of time. They live in the here and now. Postponing gratification and being patient is a notion that develops gradually throughout childhood. In early childhood, everything that is happening now is what is happening. Something that is not happening now will never occur. Parents may find this particularly annoying. Especially if they believe children are deliberately demanding and unreasonable. In truth, they are only thinking like children. While we need to teach children to be patient and to postpone gratification, this is a long-term lesson learned as children's intellectual abilities mature.

The tendency to live in the immediate present causes children to forget what they are supposed to be doing, to be easily distracted, and fail to plan for the future. All of these concepts develop gradually during childhood and on into adolescence and young adulthood.

Children's feelings are also different. Children live life intensely. Hurt feelings are totally hurt, disappointment is total disappointment, and anger is total anger. Joy and elation are also total. This total joy in the moment is, of course, what makes being with children so wonderful.

While we accept that children are physically dependent upon their parents, we are less likely to consider their emotional dependence. This emotional dependence means that they rely upon us to explain the world to them, to protect them from that which they are emotionally unprepared, and to nurture their understanding of themselves and others.

Children's fears are different. They do not have an adult's experience with potentially frightening events. They have vivid, unsuppressed imaginations. They fear the monstrous shadows in the closet and under the bed, as well as new and unfamiliar situations. We know they are safe, but due to their imagination and lack of experience they feel frightened and need our reassurance.

Small children are self-absorbed, pleasure seeking, intense beings who live totally in the present. This is normal, but parents often find this difficult and exhausting. As parents we must teach them to consider others, postpone gratification, and think before they act.

They must also learn from the past and plan for the future. A pretty tall order! Of course, such maturity cannot be accomplished in a short period of time. Growing up is tough, sometimes unpleasant work, and most of us will continue the process throughout our lifetime.

We are our children's earliest, most powerful, and effective teachers. Teachers not only impart information, but are also patient and tailor instruction to the maturity of the student. We cannot fail to teach our children. Our choice is whether or not to be a wise, loving, and patient teacher who respects the needs, developmental stages, and previous experiences of the student.

New Rule: Childhood is a unique, special time deserving of parental respect.

May 15

Old Rule: After all I have done for you; you owe me.

In amazement, I watched a court television show in which a mother was suing her adult son and his wife for the money she had spent "helping" them. It was obvious she felt that because she had given them money they should live according to her standards and meet her demands for attention. Moreover, she seemed to feel that her son owed her devotion and loyalty before his allegiance to his wife. While few of us would go to this length to emphasize to our children that they "owe" us for all that we have done, some parents do expect to be compensated for what they have done to rear their children.

Our children do not owe us anything as a result of what we have chosen to do for them! What we do for our children, we do because we are their parents and parents do things for their children. This may seem to sanction children taking from parents without being accountable or giving anything in return. Far from it! Our children do not owe us anything as a result of decisions we have made to take care of them, but as parents we have the right to expect the respect and consideration due any human being. If we do not wish to do something for our children we have the right to say "no." If we are unwilling to say "no," then we have no right to demand repayment. Furthermore, we have no right to demand payment in the form of never questioning us, never leaving us, or not holding us accountable for our mistakes no matter how grievous.

Parents give because this is what parents have always done. Wise parents know that giving to children does not mean they own their children. Love and respect from children comes from giving of ourselves, not demanding repayment for our chosen sacrifices.

New Rule: What I give to my children I give freely without expectation of being repaid with unquestioning loyalty. My repayment comes by watching them become fulfilled, competent adults who give to their own children and to their fellow human beings.

May 16

Old Rule: Look at all that I do for my children.

This rule is often operative in "What will the neighbors think?" families. That is, among parents who focus primarily on what others think of them. Such parents may sacrifice to buy things for their children. They do this not so much because they wish to take care of their children, even though there is an element of this. Instead, they wish to show others what good, self-sacrificing, devoted parents they are. Thus they win approval for themselves from others.

Although such parents do not believe their children know the difference, children are perceptive and do come to realize that such behavior does not come out of regard for them, but rather out of seeking status and approval from others. The message to the children that usually accompanies this belief is, "Look at all I have done for you. You owe me." As a result, children become either manipulative or react defiantly to parental over- control.

Parents who are secure and self-confident do not need to impress others and seek approval by making a spectacle of what they do for their children. Parents who have low self-esteem and a fragile sense of their worth use their children and what they are able to provide for them as a badge of worth for others to admire. Mature, confident parents do not need such approval.

New Rule: I do what I do for my children not to win approval from others, but because I believe what I do is important for them.

May 17

Old rule: All women are… All men are …

We all play this game: "Isn't that just like a woman." or "All men care about is …" For many of us this is an amusing pastime, but some of us actually believe that there are certain innate personality characteristics that come with being male or female and that all members of that sex are afflicted with them. They are never positive, but always reflect some liability or shortcoming.

When I teach marriage and family classes, I sometimes ask students to participate in an exercise in which they can tell members of the opposite sex what they would most like them to know about their gender. Men often express anger at being labeled with negative stereotypes. They want women to know that not all men are abusive, inconsiderate, and interested solely in a sexual relationship.

Women, on the other hand, want men to know that they are not helpless victims of their menstrual cycle and they can be legitimately angry even if it is not "that time of month." They also want men to know that thinking and feeling simultaneously is not evidence of an absence of rational thought.

Of course, we know that all men or all women do not do anything. However, parents need to be aware when children are listening to us as we play this game. Sometimes children do not know when we are joking or merely passing the time and when we are serious.

New Rule: Negative stereotypes about men or women are not positive ideas to pass along to our children, so I am careful about when I engage in the "all woman are…"or "all men are…"game.

May 18

Old Rule: A woman's greatest achievement is to marry a man who achieves.

This is a very old rule, dating back to a time when women were dependent on men for status and survival. We might think that this relic is dead, but it survives in many cultural messages and role models.

Despite the many advancements made by women in the areas of education and employment, women still make only about two-thirds as much as men for comparable work and encounter many obstacles in their path to success and achievement.

Our media continues to project messages about the good fortune of young women who can attach themselves to wealthy, successful men in business, entertainment, or sports. (Attach is the appropriate word as there is no implication of a meeting of equals.) These messages are often supported by the media images of young, successful women leading difficult, lonely, waiting for the right achieving man to come along so they can make a home for him, have children, and be taken care of. It continues to be an occasion for celebration and a mark of female achievement when a young woman marries a high status, achieving man.

If all of this seems a bit over dramatized and cynical to you, please reserve judgment until you watch some of the television shows that are aimed at those under 25 or examine how you would feel if your daughter came home announcing her plans to marry a man with a high status profession.

It is far better for parents to teach daughters to rely on their own abilities and to focus on their own career goals. It is better to foster their self-esteem and to appreciate their independence and talents rather than allow girls to absorb unchallenged the cultural message that a truly smart girl (not woman, for it is hard to grow up in such relationships) finds herself a successful, wealthy man.

New Rule: I do not permit these cultural messages concerning female success and marriage to go unchallenged. I support my daughter in using her abilities to be successful in her own right.

May 19

Old Rule: Women make the marriage work.

I am always surprised at how often this rule comes up when I teach marriage and family classes. Apparently, women continue to be told by their own parents and by the culture, in general, that they are the ones primarily responsible for holding together a marriage.

Frequently, this "make it work" message gets translated into messages that they must put the relationship ahead of themselves, defer to their spouses, attend to the sexual needs and desires of their partner, and tolerate all manner of inappropriate behavior. Although these messages are changing and women are less likely to settle for a marriage in which they feel that their needs are not being considered, there are still significant cultural messages telling young women that they need to accommodate themselves to the needs of their partner in order to maintain relationships.

Today many of these messages come from self-help, relationship advice books that tell women they are the relationship experts. Many popular books emphasize that women are more sensitive to the subtleties of emotional relationships and that men, those poor lovable oafs, are simply clueless and inept. Therefore, it is the woman's responsibility to make the relationship successful. Young men hear this and when their partner objects to their behavior may reply, "What can you expect? I am after all just a man."

In a mutually satisfying marriage, both partners take responsibility for its success. Both partners take responsibility for being mindful of the needs of their partner, considerate of their feelings, and tolerant of their human failings.

By modeling true partnership in a relationship, we teach our girls to seek out such partnership in the men that they choose, not a one-sided, "I have to make this work myself" relationship. We also teach our boys that successful, satisfying marriage relationships can only happen when they, too, assume responsibility.

New Rule: Successful marriages develop from partnerships in which both spouses take responsibility for making it work.

May 20

Old Rule: A mother's success is measured by how her children behave, how they look, and what others think of them.

Some years ago I had a neighbor with two young boys. They were busy, inquisitive, and not prone to play quietly or watch television for long periods of time. They played with all kinds of toys, combining and recombining them into various games. While seldom rude, they did not automatically obey adults, frequently asking "why?" Actually, they had somewhat of a reputation in the neighborhood.

Their clothes were clean, but seldom perfectly matched as they were allowed to choose what they wore, especially their play clothes. They were expected to get dirty when they played out of doors.

Babysitters came and went quickly as their mother asked the sitter not to watch television, but rather to play with or read to the boys until bedtime.

Their home was not neat and flawlessly decorated. Instead it was filled, actually rather cluttered, with books, magazines, puzzles, maps, art supplies, and a wide variety of toys with many pieces that the boys could use in an infinite number of imaginative play situations. Their mother invested little time in housework. Friends were usually welcome, but she never apologized for the state of the house. Instead, she invested her time in reading and talking to the children as well as taking them to all kinds of interesting places in the community.

As they went to school, she kept up with their progress and insisted that the environment be challenging and interesting, asking that those copied worksheets be kept to a minimum. I suspect that the teachers both respected and resented her involvement.

These children, who were taught to question, to love learning, to think for themselves, and to spend little time worrying about what others thought, became successful young men with promising careers and independent spirits. Their mother, whose goal was to rear such children, is indeed very successful!

New Rule: A parent's worth is measured not by her children's perfect, quiet behavior and stylish dress, but instead by how they use their abilities and talents.

May 21

Old Rule: If you don't like it, you can leave and we will get a divorce.

For the next few days, the readings focus on teaching children to handle conflict effectively.

Every family experiences conflict, even those families who are usually quiet and pleasant. It is our responsibility to model for our children how to manage conflict in a productive, assertive manner so that unresolved or improperly resolved conflict does not destroy their relationships.

One of the most nonproductive ways of dealing with marital conflict is to threaten divorce whenever there is an argument.

As a counselor, I saw many couples, who in the heat of battle, became infuriated and one or both of them threatened to end the marriage. The couple didn't really mean it and when used often, the threat became meaningless. It, nonetheless, damaged the relationship because it ends any efforts at productive problem solving. Children, who have no idea that it is an idle threat, often overhear these arguments and fear that their parents might just mean it this time.

I encourage couples not to say the words "I want a divorce" unless that is exactly what they intend. For many couples this is the first step toward effective conflict resolution.

New Rule: My spouse and I do not threaten divorce when we have an argument. This idle threat stops our ability to resolve our difficulties and unnecessarily frightens our children.

May 22

Old Rule: Children participate in adult conflicts and arguments.

Over the years, I have heard many stories from clients and students about their attempts to defuse arguments between their parents. The scenarios include taking weapons from parents, attempting to separate battling parents, trying to protect one partner from another, or creating a diversion so they would stop fighting. The list is endless, but the results were always the same. The children felt frightened, powerless, or inappropriately powerful in the lives of their parents.

Out of control arguing is frightening to children. When their parents do not handle conflict responsibly, children will try to resolve the situation in order to restore a sense of safety.

Children do not belong in adult conflicts. It is damaging to them and robs them of their childhood. It is absolutely inappropriate for one partner to depend upon a child to protect them or resolve adult conflicts. This includes having a child "talk to" the other spouse about disputes.

A responsible parent handles conflicts with other adults without using children as mediators and protectors, even if the children seem to assume this powerful role themselves. It is inappropriate for children to have such power over their parents. Involvement in adult arguments also detracts from other more suitable activities.

If your children have this role, dethrone them now, give them back their childhood, and assume responsibility for your conflicts with other adults.

New Rule: In our family, adults resolve adult conflicts. Children have no place in the midst of them.

May 23

Old Rule: I try to control my anger, but sometimes I explode.

One way of handling anger is to hold in angry feelings and then explode when the pressure builds up. During the explosion we say and do things that we later regret, things that if we had been in control we would never say or do. After the explosion is over, we feel genuinely remorseful and swear we will never allow ourselves to become so out of control again. So, we stuff anger down without a word of complaint or disagreement. Eventually, we feel entitled to an explosion after having "taken it" for so long. This method of stuffing anger and periodically exploding rarely resolves conflict. It simply continues the cycle.

Through our behavior, we teach our children to repeat the same pattern of self-defeating conflict management. They learn that it is not okay to express anger until one simply cannot stand it any longer and then one has a right to explode. They also learn that conflicts cannot really be solved, that they simply go on and on without an effective and productive end.

Is this what we want our children to learn? Or do we want them to learn to express anger, dissatisfaction, and disagreement in a calm, rational manner and work to resolve conflicts? In order to teach this more functional style we must begin to practice it ourselves. We must break the old pattern of stuffing anger while silently smoldering and have the courage to admit that we are angry. We need to model ways to disagree while we are still in control and able to rationally solve problems. This means that we have to let go of the martyrdom of never getting angry and the adrenalin surge of self-righteous out of control anger. It is worth breaking this dysfunctional pattern to improve the quality of our relationships and help our children learn better ways to handle their own feelings and solve problems effectively.

New Rule: Through my behavior, I try to teach my children to stay current with anger and disagreement by verbalizing my feelings while I am rational and in control. I want them to know that conflict can be resolved rather than postponed until the next explosion.

May 24 and 25

Old Rule: We don't communicate directly with each other.

All families have habitual ways of communicating with one another. Some methods work well, others do not. These differences in style are why some families seem to operate smoothly and produce emotionally healthy children who can go out into the world and form satisfactory relationships, while others do not. Learning to communicate effectively is vital to our ability to establish successful relationships both inside and outside of the family.

In their book, Family Talk: Interpersonal Communication in the Family, Beebe and Masterson identified four different communication patterns used in families. The first is the "chain" network. As the name suggests, information is passed from one family member to the next until the message reaches its intended destination. Children do not talk with their parents; instead they talk with the next brother or sister who passes the message down. The last one is usually the one who has the most influence and can talk to Mom or Dad. Problems result as the message is passed from one person to another. Information becomes garbled as each person adds his or her own interpretation. Misunderstandings abound, communication breaks down, and little is accomplished as information passes along the chain.

The second communication pattern is the "Y" network. In this pattern one member of the family serves as the gatekeeper, controlling the information that gets passed from one family member to another. Typically, Mother serves as the gatekeeper, controlling the flow of information from the children to the father. This pattern is often found in "don't upset your father" families in which Father is viewed as unapproachable and not to be communicated with directly, but only through Mother as an intermediary. In truth, the gatekeeper has much of the power in the family, as she not only controls what gets passed on to Father, but also what gets passed back to the children. An unintended consequence of this pattern is a lack of relationship between the father and his children, as they do not communicate directly and honestly with one another, a necessary condition for a close, loving relationship.

The third communication network is the "wheel" pattern. In this pattern, all communication and decision-making ability rests with one person. Found in authoritarian families, decision-making power resides with one central person who is expected to be all wise and must hold the family together. Looking to the central figure for solutions, children do not learn to make decisions for themselves. If this pattern predominates in a two-parent household, the other parent also looks to the center of the wheel for decisions and has little personal power. This pattern distorts the partnership necessary for a successful marriage and good parenting.

The fourth communication network is the "all-channel" network. In this pattern family members exchange information freely, communication flows in all directions, power is shared, and communication is clear. There are fewer misunderstandings and less tension in the household. Children learn to deal directly with the person with whom they have difficulties and are more likely to have positive relationships with both parents.

While it may seem strange at first, especially if you have lived for several generations using another pattern, the "all- channel" network results in less stress and tension within the family. It also teaches children more effective communication skills that they can take with them into all of their relationships.

New Rule: In our family we use the "all-channel" pattern of communication. Each person talks freely and openly with everyone else. We find that the family just works better that way.

May 26

Old Rule: I don't like conflict. If it arises, I walk away, ignore it, change the subject, or have a drink.

Conflict is a normal, inevitable part of human relationships. It is unavoidable when we live in the same household with other human beings. Therefore, we need to manage conflict effectively and productively, so that differences are resolved and do not damage relationships. It is also important to teach these skills to our children.

Many people find conflict frightening and uncomfortable, usually because in their childhood homes conflict lead to verbal and physical violence. Conflict was dangerous and they learned to avoid it to keep themselves safe.

While I am not suggesting that we seek out conflict, we need to learn to handle it so that our relationships are not damaged by unresolved disagreements. For conflicts that are not resolved do not just go away, they fester and eventually poison the relationship.

When we ignore, walk away from, absent ourselves emotionally by using alcohol or other mood altering chemicals, we leave the other person frustrated and doing the work of the relationship alone. Such conflict avoidance behavior is often learned in childhood from parents who likewise view controversy as dangerous, bad, and to be avoided at all costs. This behavior says to the other, "I don't care enough about you and our relationship to risk attempting to resolve this disagreement." Many relationships are destroyed as a result.

What do you want to teach your children about resolving differences? The first step is to face our own fears and stop running away. The next step is to learn to resolve disagreements in a productive, healthy manner. Only then can we teach these important skills to our children.

New Rule: While I do not enjoy or seek out conflicts, I do not run away from them. I attempt to resolve differences in a way that meets the needs of all the people involved. This is the behavior I want my children to learn.

May 27

Old Rule: If Mom says "no," go to Dad. He might say "yes."

During my marriage and family classes, we often discuss family communication and discipline patterns. Invariably, several students describe families in which parents undermine each other and teach their children that if one parent does not give permission then the other parent just might. Indeed, one usually finds such patterns in families where there are significant problems among parents and children. Growing up with these patterns children learn that if they ask the right parent at the right time a "no" might turn into a "yes." In the process they learn to manipulate others and this affects their relationships outside of the home.

The young adults who say that their parents talk with each other, support one another, and present a united front even if they did not always agree are more likely to identify their families as functional. From an instructor's point of view, they spent more time and energy working, rather than manipulating the system and attempting to get by.

When disagreements arise between parents about what is appropriate for the children, wise parents do not allow children to manipulate them. They talk to each other, out of the children's presence, and present a united front to the children, not allowing themselves to be separated and out-maneuvered. They do not allow power and control issues between themselves to supercede their responsibilities as parents. They do not allow issues about who is the "bad guy" or the "good guy" who is the one willing to say "no" and stick to it, or who is the one who seeks the children's favor and wants to be the "buddy" override their judgment.

This approach takes more time and energy, but in the long run it teaches children to accept parental discipline more easily and it models a pattern of communication that they are more apt to follow when creating their own families. While it is difficult, it is even possible to maintain this communication pattern even if parents are no longer married, if they are able to put the pain and anger of their relationships aside and focus on the best interest of the children.

New Rule: When we disagree about giving our children permission, we talk about it, reach a conclusion, and speak with one voice to the children.

May 28

Old Rule: Mom/Dad can't stand up for you, because she/he can't stand up for themselves.

In these troubled, often abusive families, one parent is rigidly in control, makes all of the decisions, and hands them down not only to the children, but also to their spouse. This parent has absolute power and like all absolute power in the hands of human beings, it corrupts absolutely. This parent is the family despot. The children are powerless and the other parent feels powerless to change the situation. Even if it is not explicitly stated, children are aware of the power difference and view this parent as weak and incompetent. They also view the other parent as a dictator to be feared, avoided, and worked around if they are going to be able to do what they want.

Living with this situation, children learn to rebel against authority or to acquiesce without question. They do not learn to think for themselves, nor do they learn effective communication and problem solving skills. They usually do not respect the parent who will not assert him or herself. Their reaction to this parent is often a mixture of pity, anger, and contempt. They may carry these negative opinions into their relationships with others of the same sex.

Parents who create functional families know that parental power is shared power. They not only respect their spouse and look to them for help in making decisions, but they also foster respect in their children by sharing decision-making power with the entire family. Such parents know that they cannot control what their children do, especially as they get older and spend more time away from home and out of direct parental supervision. They know that children must be taught to think for themselves. Children learn these important skills from parents who are able to assert themselves while respecting the opinions and rights of others.

New Rule: Dad and Mom share power in the family. Even when they disagree they respect one another.

May 29

Old Rule: Don't get mad! Get even!

The media and others in positions of power often espouse this method as the smart way to handle conflict. Movies and television shows glamorize those who are wronged and then formulate elaborate schemes to get even. We have all felt wronged and powerless and enjoy the vicarious pleasure of watching someone get revenge. It is gratifying to see the good guys really put one over on the bad guys. However, when we model this pattern in our families, concealing our displeasure and then getting even with family members when they least expect it, we are modeling a dangerous, dysfunctional, passive-aggressive pattern.

Living by this rule, we do not fight fairly. Rather than stating our displeasure, we hide our angry feelings until they harden into resentments. We then feel justified in doing something that we know will hurt and anger the other spouse. We make an expensive purchase, get drunk, come home late, or refuse to do household chores. If we really want to play this game for high stakes, we have an affair. All of these ways of getting even are destructive to the couple relationship and may eventually destroy the family. None of this game goes unnoticed by our children. We are teaching them powerful lessons in how to handle anger and conflict that will harm their relationships as they become young adults.

Do we really want to teach such dishonest, destructive behavior or do we want to teach our children that conflict can be successfully resolved while maintaining relationships? We have the power to do either. The choice is up to us.

New Rule: When we have a conflict, my spouse and I get it out in the open. We are honest about our feelings and our point of view. In this way, we either resolve the conflict or agree to disagree. We want our children to learn to do the same.

May 30

Old Rule: We are not a touchy-feely family.

As a therapist, I encountered many people who cannot recall having been touched by their parents except in anger. Such people are usually struggling with low self-esteem and experience considerable emotional pain. As adults attempting to recover from their painful rearing, they often relate that they go to their parents and almost force them to hug them. Usually the parent's initial reaction is a stiff straight-arm pat or brief hug. Their parents, often touch deprived themselves, have passed this discomfort with affection down through the generations.

It is difficult to underestimate the importance of being touched by another human being throughout our lives. According to the anthropologist Ashley Montague, "Touching is the first communication a baby receives and the first language of its development is through the skin." Scientific studies suggest that babies who are not held and given physical affection fail to thrive and may actually die. Certainly, their emotional, intellectual, and physical development is negatively affected without warm, affectionate, frequent touch. This is one of the benefits of breast-feeding and why Dr. Benjamin Spock, long ago, recommended that we not prop bottle-feed babies, but hold them instead.

The need to be touched, kissed, hugged, and held does not end with early childhood. It continues throughout our lives. Indeed, one of the losses of old age is the lack of affectionate touch. Affection from both parents is vitally important to children. Boys, as well as girls, need affection. It will not feminize a boy to receive a kiss, hug, or an arm around the shoulder from his parents. Physical affection from parents increases self-esteem, a precious commodity in childhood and adolescence when self-esteem receives so many attacks from the world outside of the family.

So just like the bumper sticker urges - hug your kid today. Even if they seem a little embarrassed, you and they will learn to love it.

New Rule: We are an affectionate family. We all get and give generous portions of hugs, kisses, pats on the back, and arms around the shoulder. We all need it!

May 31

Old Rule: Don't praise your kids too much. They'll be conceited.

Most parents want their children to have high self-esteem and self-confidence. We also want them to have a realistic view of themselves, both their assets and their liabilities. Just as we do not want them to lack confidence, we do not want them to feel superior to others.

I believe that it is nearly impossible for parents to praise children too much, as long as this praise is reality based. While it is necessary to correct our children when they make a mistake or behave inappropriately, the world, including school, other adults, and their peers is only too willing to point out to them their liabilities and shortcomings.

The challenge is to balance the more negative feedback with our positive feedback in order for our children to continue to believe in themselves and their abilities. In reality, the most important determinant of children's achievements is their perception of how we, their parents, perceive them. If they feel that we do not believe in them and do not perceive them as competent and talented, they will not view themselves as capable. Conversely, if they believe that we find them valuable, capable, and competent, they will view themselves in the same manner.

The rest of the world may not always view our children positively, but if we view them positively and praise them we can provide them with some insulation against the negative comments of the world at large.

New Rule: Praising my children does not make them conceited, but it does help build healthy self-esteem even in the face of criticism from others.

June 1

Old Rule: A good mother always puts her children first.

Being a mother is hard work! The culture, the church, parenting books, the media, child development professionals, other mothers, and our families all have ideas about what constitutes good mothering. All of this information makes it even more difficult.

Being a mother is a constant balancing act. Balancing the needs of children against work, housekeeping chores, being a wife, and sometimes caring for our own parents is a never-ending process. In this constant busyness we lose sight of our own needs, interests, and pleasures. No wonder so many of us are frustrated and exhausted with the demands of motherhood. This chronic frustration and exhaustion may harden into episodes of anger and depression.

However, when we do take those occasional moments for ourselves, we not only feel guilty but we become even more stressed when we think about all that we should or could be doing. Though this may be a sticking place for many of us, it is vitally important to take time for ourselves. Adding ourselves to the balancing act on a consistent basis is challenging and we may not get much support from those around us.

If we cannot find the motivation within ourselves to begin to make some changes and take some time for ourselves, remember that our behavior speaks louder than in our words. A mother who does not take time to do what she enjoys may be telling her children: "I'm yours to use, you don't have to be considerate of me or of anyone else for that matter. What you want is more important," "You are not competent to do things for yourself. I have to do it for you," or "Women are placed here to meet every expectation of men and children, not to have lives of their own." None of these attitudes will serve children well in the larger world, but when mothers sacrifice everything for their children these are precisely the messages they send.

New Rule: There is more to a mother's life than mothering. She is also an individual with her own needs, interests, and pleasures.

June 2

Old Rule: A good father works hard and brings home the money.

No other aspect of parenting is undergoing such radical redefinition as the role of fathers. As late as 30 years ago, we defined good fathering as bringing home a living that allowed the family to be comfortable and safe from financial problems while allowing the mother to stay home with the children. With respect to his children, a good father backed mother in her decisions about the children and became the ultimate arbitrator of discipline when mother was forced to rely on "Wait until your father comes home!"

Ideas about fathering have changed drastically. We no longer believe that good fathering stops with being a provider. Although we have gone through a period in which some believed that fathering is unnecessary, we are realizing that fathers are essential to the emotional well being of their children.

As a culture, we are coming to appreciate the role of the father in the day-to-day rearing of his children. We have come to appreciate that fathers play a vital role in the children's self-image and that children who have supportive active fathers are more likely to view themselves as capable and have higher self-esteem. For reasons that we do not fully understand, this is particularly true for girls. We also know that children who have actively involved fathers have a greater sense of safety and stability, even if parents are not married. They are more likely to have a sense of security and rootedness that is so essential for their emotional well-being.

Fathering, even if the marriage ends, does not end with financial support. Indeed, financial support is the bare minimum. What is really important to children is a father who ultimately cares for, supports, and nurtures their sense of themselves as worthy and important to him. They need a father who tells his children by his behavior that they are worthy of his time and energy. By giving of himself, he provides his children with instruction about the world from his unique perspective. In short, fathering is vital to the well-being of children and ultimately to the well-being of our civilization.

New Rule: Being a father is a very important role. Positive, responsible, nurturing fathering is vital to the welfare of children.

June 3 &4

Old Rule: We are not happy when others succeed.

Even though we do not like to admit it, this is an example of a destructive, unspoken rule that operates in a number of families. We practice this rule when we congratulate someone on their success, but disparage and criticize them behind their back. Witnessing this behavior, our children pick up the habit of discounting and criticizing others when they succeed. At its core, this rule is based on envy, feelings of low self-esteem, and a belief in scarcity.

Those who live by this rule believe that if someone else is successful it diminishes the chances that they will be successful. Somehow they have accepted the totally illogical notion that success is limited and scarce. Irrationally, they believe that there is only so much success in the world and that if someone else is successful then there is less for them. In reality, there is more than enough achievement and success to go around. One person's success does not diminish our chances of being successful, but a belief in scarcity prevents us from seeing this.

Such reactions are also based on envy. Comparing ourselves with others, we fall short in our own estimation. In order to feel just a bit better we devalue the accomplishments of others. Such envy has its roots in low self-esteem, the belief that no matter what we do, have, or achieve, it is never quite good enough and that someone else is doing better. We model this painful, energy draining, non-productive habit of comparing for our children, passing this destructive pattern to the next generation just as it was probably passed down to us.

The only way that we can break this pattern is to stop the comparisons. When we compare ourselves to others, we can always find someone who is doing better than we are and allow ourselves to become envious. We can also find someone who is doing worse than we are and feel a false sense of superiority. Both habits are energy depleting, destructive, and a complete waste of time. If we spend our time and mental energy comparing, envying, and being unhappy when we perceive that others are getting our share of the success in the world, we have little time for actually working toward our own goals. Cut it out! Stop it! This pattern is wasting your time and damaging your children.

Whenever you find yourself comparing yourself to others and falling into the habit of envy, stop and refocus on what you are doing. What you can do to achieve your own goals? When your children are comparing themselves to others, try to refocus them on what they do well, what they can do for themselves, and take the focus off of the "they" who tend to rule our lives. Soon the absurdity of comparing self to others will be evident. You will begin to enjoy freedom from this destructive pattern. As you find that you have more time and energy to work toward your own goals, you will find that self-criticism decreases and self-esteem rises. You might also find that your relationships with others begin to improve as you stop comparing yourself either negatively or positively to them. You will probably find that you can relate more openly with others when you are neither envious nor critical of them. Focusing on yourself and your own achievements allows you to be genuinely happy when others succeed.

New Rule: We do not waste time comparing ourselves to others and envying their successes. In our family we focus on our own goals and successes.

June 5

Old Rule: We are better than…

While it is quite natural and healthy to take pride in one's family and one's achievements, the belief that one is better than others because of wealth, education, occupation, religion, or any other standards of achievement or position runs the risk of teaching our children arrogant superiority and self-righteousness.

When we conduct ourselves in this manner and teach our children to view themselves as superior and to view others as inferior, we not only make the world a more painful and less charitable place to live, but we also handicap our children. In modeling this behavior for them, we impair their ability to respond with empathy to others who may not have their advantages.

The ability to be empathetic is another aspect of emotional intelligence so vital in all human relationships. This does not mean that we must condone behavior outside of our value system or that we do not hold others accountable when they have violated the rules of civilized society; rather, it is an ability to see the other's point of view. Arrogance and feelings of superiority hinder relationships. They also hinder the ability to solve problems in relationships.

Empathy and a willingness to withhold judgment allows us to understand others and to solve problems constructively. This ability is a valuable skill, best acquired from loving and empathetic parents who do not pass judgment on others, but who, instead, seek to understand.

New Rule: We seek to teach our children to be accepting of others and to see others not as superiors or inferiors but rather as unique fellow human beings.

June 6 & 7

Old Rule: A woman's primary responsibility is caring for and nurturing others. A good woman puts the needs of others before her own.

A surprising and revealing discussion recently took place in one of my classes. All of the participants were high achieving young women with bright futures. The majority came from loving, supportive families. The discussion centered on whether they would prefer to have boys or girls when they became parents. All 15 of them stated that they would prefer to have boys "because girls were too hard to raise!"

While I think some of these feelings stemmed from knowing the difficulties they experienced with their parents during their recently ended adolescence, I also think that these feelings come from the current cultural messages women receive.

In today's culture women are supposed to do it all. Successful women are supposed to have well paying careers, marry, and when they have children, they are expected to return to full time employment soon after the birth. Increasingly, they have little choice about returning to work. Much of the pressure to maximize their earning power by returning to full-time work is coming from their husbands, as well as themselves and their employers.

Furthermore, they are expected to be nurturing, involved parents, maintain an orderly, comfortable home, serve nutritious meals, and also be available to their spouses as lovers and companions. They are expected to do all of this with minimal or no assistance from anyone, including their spouse. Many women have come to believe that they should be achieving all of this while having few needs of their own. "Doing it all" has come at the price of personal time and leisure.

These young women know they will face all of these pressures. As a result, they often feel confused and powerless. They do not know how or what they wish to pass on to their daughters and, therefore, have enormous ambivalence about having them at all.

They also expressed a sense of vulnerability and an inability to protect their daughters. They tended to see the world as a dangerous place for girls. They cited incidences of physical and sexual assault, pressure to use alcohol and other drugs, pressure to have sex before they felt ready, and sexual harassment at work and school. They also feared being left to rear children on their own. Each of them felt victimized at some point. They felt powerless to protect themselves and, therefore, powerless to protect a daughter.

These young women are not unique. It is a dangerous world for women. We see daily evidence of this in the media. Likewise, it does seem at times that increased opportunities for young women yielded even more dramatically increased expectations. We ask young women to do it all in order to be considered successful.

We need to give our daughters guidance and teach them that it is not selfish to have personal needs and that women cannot be all things to the people around them any more than men can. If they attempt to do this, they run the risk of becoming exhausted, frustrated, and feeling they are not successfully fulfilling any role. We need to teach them that it is not a step backward into the bad old days of minimal opportunities and female financial dependence to ask for help, to say "no" to unreasonable expectations, and to take time out for themselves. We can teach this to them formally with our words, but also more powerfully by our own actions and willingness as mothers to be assertive and to take time for ourselves.

We also need to teach them that popularity with males should not come at the price of engaging in self-destructive behavior such as premature sexuality and substance use. They need to know that they are not solely responsible for the success of a relationship. They need to realize that having no relationship is better than an abusive one. They need to know that sexual harassment is not okay anywhere and that taking it meekly and hoping it will go away if one is nice will only make the situation worse. In short, they need to know that to take care of yourself and to protect yourself is not unfeminine.

It is difficult to be a girl and a young woman, but parents can make it easier by having reasonable expectations and teaching them to care for themselves in addition to caring for others.

New Rule: I am aware of the enormous pressures on my daughter to fulfill many different roles. I will help her to prepare for becoming an adult by teaching her to respect her own needs, say "no" without guilt, and protect herself.

June 8

Old Rule: What will the neighbors think?

At one time I lived in a small, rural community. Having been reared in a big city, I was completely unprepared for the interest these folks, though usually well-intended, took in their neighbors. I was not happy there and did not feel at all sad when I left, but I did learn three things. First, the neighbors will think what they will think. I cannot control them. Second, when someone else becomes more interesting, they will focus their interest and opinions on the next person. Last, I am not all that interesting. Most people are either too busy either living their own lives or too concerned about what others think of them to bother thinking about me for too long. Worrying about "What will they think?" is not only boring, it is a waste of time!

Still many of us are quite preoccupied with what the neighbors, our family, our parents, the people at church, or the people at work will think if...

We run most of the important decisions in our lives through the "What will they think?" filter. Seeking the approval or at least avoiding the disapproval of others claims a great deal of emotional and mental energy. We lose sight of what we think as well as our personal power to "they." Being a slave to the "What will they think?" rule, we do not take risks, voice anything but the most bland, non-controversial opinions, and generally constrict our lives down to an increasingly narrow sphere.

Unfortunately, we pass this anxiety and self-consciousness along to our children. When we teach our children the extreme importance of the approval of others, we rob them of their individuality and power to think for themselves. We force them into the blandness of not upsetting anyone and adapting to prevailing attitudes and behaviors with few thoughts of their own.

New Rule: I will teach my children both by word and example the significance of being true to self and that what others think is far less important than what I think of me.

June 9

Old Rule: What you wear, what you drive, where you live, and what you have defines you.

Status symbols are not new. In the 19th century the wealthy had their draperies made with extra material to lie in a heap on the floor because it was a sign that they could afford to be extravagant with the cloth. Households were decorated with antiques from Europe, signifying the owner's wealth and the ability to travel to obtain expensive treasures.

Weight, like now, was also considered a matter of status. Being large meant that one had enough money to eat well. Thinness was a sign of poverty. Having browned skin, a tan, was a sign that one labored in the fields. Pale skin, unexposed to the sun, was a sign that one did not have to do such work.

While status symbols change over time, the purpose does not. The purpose is to let others know one's superiority and lofty identity by surrounding one's self with status-enhancing possessions. The advertising industry uses the desire to have the latest status producing objects to sell us billions of dollars worth of ever-changing products.

To place one's faith in such symbols and to define one's position among others on the basis of such illusory, changing, and superficial things is to engage in self-deception. It is also a great waste of time and resources.

When we live our lives pursuing the latest status symbol we also teach our children these dubious values. Do we want them to believe that their value and the value of others is contingent on trendy possessions or on the content of their character? It is our choice.

New Rule: It is my responsibility to teach my children the true value and importance of possessions.

June 10

Old Rule: Marriage doesn't last.

Recently, I talked with a young friend about her life with her divorced parents. During this discussion she stated flatly, "Well, when I have kids, I'm going to let them see their dad!"

This startling comment reveals several assumptions. First, she assumes she will marry and have children. However, she also assumes that this marriage will have insurmountable problems and will end in divorce. Therefore, she will face custody and visitation problems, and her children will be forced to deal with the same issues she found so painful in her childhood.

The divorce rate in the United States has remained fairly constant since 1984. Approximately, one in two marriages will end in divorce. People who marry for the second time are more likely to divorce than those who marry once. Therefore, there are an enormous number of children who have experienced divorce and many who have experienced their parents' divorce, remarriage, and divorce more than once. Many of these children grow up believing that marriage probably won't work.

Divorce is a painful situation, not only for parents but also for their children. Some children seem to adjust well, while others have a very difficult time. The reality is that unless there is abuse and violence, most children would prefer that their parents remain together.

Adults have a responsibility to be honest with children about the level of commitment and just plain hard work that is involved

211

in making a marriage successful. Being happily married requires a willingness to share one's life, to be flexible, to communicate openly, and to learn to resolve problems effectively. Making a marriage work often means that we make drastic changes in how we relate to others. We also have the obligation to be hopeful with our children and tell them that even if our marriage ends in divorce that a loving marriage relationship is possible for them.

New Rule: Marriage requires work and commitment. Successful marriages are not created magically, but they are possible.

June 11

Old Rule: Divorcing is not an option. We do not get divorces in this family. You made your bed. You lie in it.

When families believe that marriage is for a lifetime and that couples should not divorce for any reason, marriage becomes a life sentence to be endured, not a joyful union between two loving adults. Divorce is painful for everyone touched by it and certainly, like marriage, should not be entered into lightly. However, when a couple finds that their relationship produces only loneliness and emotional pain to themselves and those around them including their children, it is best to end the relationship.

This decision is uniquely private. Other family members should not make this decision, even when they believe that divorce is outside of the family value system. When the partners feel that they have made a mistake or that what was once an alive and satisfying relationship is no longer viable, then it is their right to end it. Staying in the marriage, lying in your bed just because you made it, not only punishes the couple but ultimately their children.

New Rule: It is up to the couple to decide when a marriage is no longer alive and should be allowed to die by divorce. No one else has a right to make that decision.

June 12

Old Rule: Children are tough! They forget easily. Hurt feelings are a normal part of growing up. You don't have to be concerned about their feelings.

While waiting for a flight from a busy metropolitan airport, I noticed a family saying good-bye to their grandmother. There were two children, a boy about 8 and a little girl about 2. Grandmother was extravagant in her good-byes to the little girl, waving bye-bye and blowing kisses. The boy repeatedly said, "Good-bye Grandma." However, in her efforts to get just a few more minutes with the little girl, she did not respond to him. Indeed, she did not notice him until he brought the baby to the departing line for her to kiss and hug one more time. Only when she finished saying good-bye to the little girl did she acknowledge him with a pat on the head, said goodbye, and returned her attentions to the little girl. She even missed his "I love you, Grandma."

This child's self-esteem will likely survive having a grandmother who dotes on his baby sister. However, parents and grandparents should bear in mind how important our love and approval is to children and how much they look to us to mirror their importance and worth. We need to keep in mind the power we have to influence our children's self-image and regard their feelings with as much consideration as we would those of our adult friends.

New Rule: Children's feelings are fragile. We need to be as considerate of their feelings and handle them with at least the same care we employ with adults.

June 13

Old Rule: Don't get angry. Nice people don't get angry.

Anger is a normal human emotion. We are born with it. A crying hungry infant is actually expressing anger resulting from an unmet need. However, in many families anger is denied and suppressed under the guise of niceness or religious belief. In still other families one person is abusively angry, while the rest of the family, knowing the danger and pain of such rage, decides that anger is a "bad" emotion that hurts others.

In truth, it is impossible to be in a relationship with another human being and never become angry. Additionally, unexpressed anger does not simply go away. Suppressed anger builds and finds expression in whining, self-pity, revenge, physical illness, depression, or episodes of out of control rage followed by remorse and guilt.

Appropriately expressed anger passes, just as other feelings pass. Anger expressed in a timely manner and directed at the source of the difficulty or channeled in an appropriate direction is manageable and does not injure others. The nicest people get angry, but they express their feelings responsibly.

New Rule: By reclaiming my ability to express anger, I can teach my children to express their own feelings appropriately. Anger does not destroy my relationships with others. Instead, my relationships are enriched when I am honest about my feelings.

June 14

Old Rule: You are our perfect child! You can't possibly have any problems!

Some years ago, a young woman came to me for counseling. She was her family's perfect child. While her siblings struggled through high school and wasted several semesters in college only to drop out, she excelled and was on her way to a prestigious college. When her siblings were rebellious and troublesome, she consoled her parents and attempted to counsel her brother and sister when they got into trouble. She was the perfect child and everyone in the family loved her.

There was only one problem. She was buckling under the weight of being the loving, achieving, and helpful child. When she experienced hurt, worry, doubt, and fear, no one was there for her. Indeed, the family did not even accept the possibility that she was having difficulty. She attempted to hide her difficulties, feeling that there were already too many problems in the family. She did not want to add to anyone's burden. Eventually, she could not hide her depression and the resulting feelings of loneliness and desperation.

It is damaging to label our children as "the perfect one," "the slow one," "the problem one," "the smart one," "the athletic one," etc. They will likely live up or live down to our expectations and may loose who they are in the process. In a functional family, that is a family that successfully cares for and meets the needs of each member, each person in the family is accepted for who they are, for their liabilities as well as their strengths. Members of the family do not play a role or attempt to live up or live down to a label, but feel accepted and loved for themselves. Furthermore, each member of the family is allowed to have their bad days as well as their good ones and their problems as well as their triumphs.

Human beings, adults as well as children, are not perfectible nor are we totally defective. We are not the perfect children or the problem children of God, but instead God's human children.

New Rule: We cherish and accept each of our children, not for the role they play, but for their unique contribution to the family.

June 15

Old Rule: You can't possibly be … don't dream too big.

Searching for something to say, adults often ask children, "What do you want to be when you grow up?" The reply can vary from the very fanciful to the mundane and may change from day to day. It is normal for children to try on different careers without knowing much about what they actually entail. Adults tend to indulge or ignore early childhood fantasies, but as children grow older and adults begin to take their replies more seriously they are often told," You can't possibly be that, that is silly," or "You'll probably just be a …" Thus adults shame children into scaling back their aspirations and their dreams very early in life. They are taught to think small. No wonder by the time they reach adolescence and young adulthood they have limited their aspirations. They had early training to do just that.

Often these messages come from adults who believe, "In this family we don't have such lofty aspirations. We aren't capable of such important careers. Those are for other people." Having been given this message in their own childhood, they continue to live by it, limiting their own aspirations and passing these beliefs on to their children. Many times parents believe that if they point them toward "more realistic" goals that their children will not be disappointed and will focus their energies on what might be attainable. What a tragic waste!

How much better it would be if parents encouraged their children to dream, to have lofty goals, and to try on any career that suits their fancy. The world will take care of limiting unrealistic aspirations. We can always find those who tell us that we are "not

217

good enough to do that." Children may also decide for themselves that they do not want to do the work necessary to achieve their goals and switch to other options. This is a natural process, but we, their parents, need to encourage them to dream big. Maybe, just maybe, they are talented enough and willing to put forth the effort to achieve those splendid goals.

New Rule: It is my job to encourage my children to explore many career options, not to discourage them from extraordinary career ambitions. The world and they will take care of that.

June 16

Old Rule: Don't expect to be happy in your work.

We live in a time of unprecedented freedom and opportunity. We are blessed with the freedom to choose from any number of ways of earning a living and even to change our occupation as we please.

Yet in some families there is a persistent message that work is not meant to be satisfying and enjoyable. Indeed, many of us believe that enjoying one's work is not only not possible, but not even important. As a result, people give little thought to what they really want to do and take employment only to make money. Considering the time and effort invested into work, no wonder they are miserable, dread going to work, and do an inferior job! Working year in and year out at a job that one hates is not only miserable, it makes no sense given the opportunities available to most of us.

It is vitally important that we choose and help our children to choose a vocation that will be enjoyable and meaningful as well as financially rewarding. Since we spend so much of our time and energy working, it is important for our mental and physical health that our choices are a "good fit," that we find satisfaction and even fun in our work. Of course, not every day will be pleasurable and satisfying. We may go through weeks or months of frustration and workplace difficulty, but if on balance it is not rewarding, work can be a self-imposed prison sentence.

Parents play a powerful role in children's attitude about the world of work. We need to help them to learn that working can incorporate meaningfulness, satisfaction, and even fun in addition to a paycheck.

New Rule: Choosing one's work is important. Choices should be made based not just on financial reward, but also emotional satisfaction.

June 17

Old Rule: You have to be really sick to take a day off.

A colleague and I were discussing flu shots. She confessed that she had not gotten one because getting the flu was a welcome way to get a few days off work. I thought I was the only one who engaged in this crazy thinking! I thought I was the only one who saw illness, being <u>really</u> sick, as the only excuse to take a day off.

Many workers take pride in never missing a day and working while sick. Nurses and others medical personnel even take pride in not taking time to go to the bathroom or to eat on their shift. Workplace martyrdom is rampant. These workplace martyrs are the extreme opposite of those who take time off from work at the slightest excuse. Like any extreme behavior, it is out of healthy balance.

Do we really believe that taking a "mental health day," a day when we are not ill but want to relax or have fun, will result in the collapse of our workplace and financial disaster? Do we believe that if we let our kids take a day off from school to play with us that their academic careers will be seriously damaged?

Living in balance between two extremes, in this case between irresponsibility and over-working, is healthy, sane, and rewarding. Mental and physical health is found in such balance. So take a day off to play and maybe take the kids with you. All of you will return to your responsibilities refreshed and with pleasant memories of a day well spent.

New Rule: By my example, I help my children to achieve a healthy balance between work and play.

June 18

Old Rule: Your work defines you.

Work is important. Sigmund Freud believed that the primary developmental task of an adult is the ability to love and to work. When people first meet what one does for a living is the most frequently asked question. In many ways, occupation identifies us and we identify with our occupation. Difficulties arise, however, when we over-identify with work and allow it to become our total focus.

This over-identification is a symptom of work addiction. Work addicts are seldom content unless they are working. Indeed, they are usually quite uncomfortable if they are not working. Like all addictions, the function of work addiction is to use something outside of self to defend against uncomfortable feelings. Because there are so many cultural rewards for being dedicated to work, work addiction is somewhat different from other addictions. In addition to financial reward, there are many pay-offs, including bolstering sagging self-esteem and avoiding relationships in which one feels inadequate.

People who over work are out of balance. They have few friends, only work relationships. They avoid non-work social occasions because they believe they must always be productive. There is some controversy about whether or not work addicts are more successful or more productive than non-work addicts, but we do know work addicts neglect their families in favor of work. As they grow older they often find that their families have structured them out of the picture and have gone on without them. As the addict's working life ends, sometimes not at their initiation, they may find they are depressed and alone. As they examine their lives, they often wish that they had managed things differently. As Chief Justice of the United States Supreme Court William Renquist said in a graduation speech, "Take time for family and friends. Remember that it is true that no one comes to the end of their life and says 'I wish I had spent more time at the office."

Perhaps one of the most important things we can model for our children is healthy balance. This balance needs to be maintained in many areas of life, but one of the most important is the balance between working and spending time with family.

Old Rule: Achieving a balance between work and other areas of life is an ongoing challenge. I know the value of my relationship with my family and teaching my children about maintaining a healthy balance between work and family.

June 19 and 20

Old Rule: We have to move and the kids will just have to adjust. Kids are resilient. They'll be okay.

Moving is stressful for everyone, adults and children alike. Studies show that almost everyone who moves goes through a period of disorientation and depression, even if the move is viewed as a positive change. Children are particularly affected. Children are creatures of habit. Change upsets them and moving can really upset them. If we move our children, it is important to prepare them and handle the move in such a way that we minimize the upset and stress. This is not only good for them, but good for us because the more calm they are, the less stressed we will feel.

Sylvia Rimm, PH.D. a child psychologist interviewed on the "Today Show" (June 6, 2000), offered several helpful suggestions when moving children. First, realize that it is a difficult and stressful time that can be upsetting for children. The older the child, the more difficult the move.

Second, tell the children about the move as soon you know, but avoid burdening children with "We might be moving." Companies sometimes propose moves to employees that never come about and it is best not mention these to children. However, if children overhear or sense that a move is in the offing, be honest with them.

Third, explore the new community with your children. This can be done with tourism brochures, pre-move visits if possible, or over the Internet. Once moved, visiting stores, museums, parks, restaurants, and tourist attractions in the new community is fun and gives the whole family a chance to get to know the area.

Fourth, determine where your children will be in the school curriculum. Even if one moves in the summer, visit the school and the school principal to determine if your children will be ahead of or behind in the curriculum and help the children to catch up if necessary. A school visit is very important, for just as adults have a new work place, children have a new work place to which they must adjust.

Fifth, help them to make new friends while maintaining some contact with old friends. E-mail and the telephone can be great helps in the process of letting go slowly of old relationships or at least getting accustomed to the change in these relationships. It is important to respect children's feelings. Just as you miss your old friends and sometimes long for the comfortable familiarity of these relationships, even young children have the same feelings and miss their old playmates.

Sixth, avoid moving teenagers! Adolescence is a difficult time for everyone and we often compound the problems if we move, especially if the teenager is thriving in their current environment. Teenagers are frequently quite attached to their friends and their activities and may find that the kids in the new school are not particularly accepting of the new kid in school. As a counselor, I have heard many young people trace their difficulties with deviant behavior and depression back to an adolescent move that did not go well, when a deviant peer group was the only one that would accept them.

If adults must move, maybe the adolescent can stay behind with a family member or friend, especially to finish the last year of high school. Sometimes one parent will remain with the children while the other parent moves to the new location. While not ideal for the couple or even the parent relationship given the importance of the teenager's attachment to their peer group, it may be a wise to consider this course. If this is not possible, be prepared to handle a storm of feelings including anger and sadness and to do the hard work of helping the adolescent find a new peer group and ways to fit into the new situation.

Finally, Dr. Rimm states that when we must move and the children refuse, parents must ultimately be parents and be firm about the reality of the move. However, it is also important that we respect the children's feelings and know that the work of moving is more than unpacking the boxes.

New Rule: When we must move our children, it is important that we adequately prepare them and help them to adjust to their new home.

June 21

Old Rule: Adoptive parents are not real parents.

We don't say it, but many of us who have <u>not</u> adopted a child believe that giving birth to a child is the only way to become a "real" parent. However, we also know that pregnancy and birth are just a tiny part of being a parent. Being a parent is about caring about the well-being of children enough to devote much of one's life to them.

However, most adoptive parents have faced intrusive questions that imply they are not real parents, just sort of long-term baby-sitters. The media attention on children finding their birth families has the unfortunate effect of exacerbating those feelings that somehow adoptive parents are merely caretakers until children become adults and can find and rejoin their "real" families.

Sometimes the problem comes from relatives and friends who have not accepted the adoption and introduce the child as "the adopted child." Parents need to confront this behavior and insist that the adult change this behavior, at least in front of you and your child. This is your child. The circumstance of their birth is no one else's business.

Adoptive families face unique challenges, but avoiding those who would imply that your family is not "real" helps minimize these difficulties. After all, you are a parent and have enough to worry about without making adoption a big deal.

New Rule: Adoptive parents are real parents just like other parents.

June 22

Old Rule: We are so busy! Finding time for family is nearly impossible!

Indeed our lives are busy! We work, often commuting for long distances, take care of our homes, attend to extended families, and run errands. Family time can get lost in the shuffle. Several weeks can go by before we realize we haven't spent five consecutive minutes talking with our children other than to give them directions or correct them. Then we feel guilty about one more thing that we need to do, but haven't found the time. Stop feeling guilty and re-examine your values and where you are spending your time.

According to Stephen Covey, author of <u>Seven Habits of Highly Effective Families,</u> often adults who complain about being too busy spend more than 10 hours a week watching television. Actually, I think that this is an underestimation. I believe that many adults spend a lot more time than this watching television and that often parents who complain about not having enough time to help children with homework or to attend school functions are in front of the television.

Television is a way to relax and sometimes it can even inform, but sitcoms filled with adolescent and bathroom humor, soap operas with repetitive, ridiculous plots, and over- hyped sporting events are poor substitutes for relationships with ones children. At this point you might be saying that television is the only way you have to relax, the only form of enjoyment that you permit yourself. As a recovering television addict who can still overdose on television rather that relate to the live persons in my life, I empathize. However, consider that children do not need or even want us to spend an extra 10 hours a week with them. They would be tired of us long before we would be weary of them! All they need or want is one or two hours per week when we talk with them and do things that they enjoy. That is all! Give it a try, just for a few weeks, and see what happens. You may initially go through television "withdrawal symptoms," but stay with it and see if your real life children are not more interesting and rewarding than television.

New Rule: Television can be entertaining and exciting, but is no substitute for a relationship with my children.

June 23

Old Rule: When something goes wrong, blame someone else.

The blame game, everybody plays it! Governments, corporations, families, and individuals play it. When something goes wrong, it seems that our first instinct is to find out who is at fault and take the focus off of self. It is a normal developmental stage for small children to blame someone else, even an imaginary friend, for their misbehavior. A child I know had an imaginary sister who did all sorts of mischievous things that my little friend would never dream of doing. However, when blaming becomes a pattern that extends into adulthood, it is not only irresponsible, but also destructive.

We like to think of ourselves as responsible people who take care of our families and live up to our financial obligations and work responsibilities, but whenever we engage in the blame game we are being irresponsible and teaching our children, by our example, to be irresponsible.

It takes courage when something goes wrong not to blame someone else, unfavorable circumstances, or forces beyond our control, but to say, "Yes, I did it. I made a mistake." When we are at fault this act of taking responsibility is a powerful lesson to our children. Taking responsibility is characteristic of a person of integrity and action. When something goes wrong such people do not waste their time trying to figure out whom to blame. Instead, they assess their part in the problem and admit it. They have courage and personal power. Wouldn't you like to be associated with such a courageous human being, to hire such a person, to have them as a mate or a friend? Isn't this responsible behavior what we need to teach our children by example and design?

New Rule: When something goes wrong, we focus on fixing the problem by first taking responsibility for our actions. This is a productive way for adults to live and a valuable lesson for children to learn.

June 24

Old Rule: A good person takes care of others.

As a counselor, teacher, and interested observer of our human condition, I have come to believe that most healthy, productive living is found somewhere in the middle between two extremes, the *via media* or middle road. A good example of this middle road is the position we take between taking responsibility for our own actions and taking responsibility for the actions of others, thus enabling them to be irresponsible.

Parents are responsible for taking care of their children. Children are born dependent on this care and we continue to feel the need to care for them and to protect them from harm or disturbing events long after they are no longer dependent on us for their total physical care. This is our job, but when we do not allow them to take responsibility for their own behavior and to suffer the consequence of their actions, we are hurting them with our enabling. We have gotten off of this middle path between blaming them for things over which they have no control and protecting them from the consequences of their behavior. The middle way allows each of us to maintain accountability for our own behavior while not accepting blame for that which we cannot control. This is an important part of maturation and emotional growth.

When children are young and things get broken or they are involved in an altercation with another child they should not be allowed to blame it solely on the other child, but encouraged to look at their part in the problem. As they go through school and grades are not what they should be, they should not be allowed to fall back on "The teacher doesn't like me," or "So and so talks to me all the time." They should learn to take responsibility for their part of the problem. As they become adolescents and are caught drinking or using drugs, the excuse "Everybody I know does it" simply does not wash with responsible parents. They are choosing to use mood-altering chemicals and need to be held accountable. As one can plainly see, the issues become more important as children get older and it becomes progressively more crucial that we hold them accountable for their behavior.

If we choose not to hold our children accountable and to enable them by not letting them suffer the consequences of their behavior, we run the risk of allowing a life long pattern of excuse making, blaming, and irresponsibility to develop.

New Rule: It is important that I teach my children to take responsibility for their actions. I do this by setting an example of taking responsibility for my behavior and holding them accountable for theirs.

June 25

Old Rule: I've had a hard day. I need a drink!

Even those who were reared in a home with parental alcohol abuse find that when stress mounts, we are tempted to seek the instant relief of alcohol. Like our parents who initially used alcohol to medicate uncomfortable feelings such as anxiety and frustration, alcohol does what we want it to do and we feel better. While we will not initially experience serious consequences from using alcohol to medicate our feelings, we may begin to develop the same problems as our parents.

One of the first consequences is failure to deal constructively with stress. We tell ourselves that we are entitled to ease our tensions. We have a few drinks. Alcohol does what it is intended to do and the tension goes away - for a while. Inevitably, feelings of frustration and apprehension return. We have not dealt constructively with our difficulties. We have only numbed our feelings and postponed facing the problem.

Living responsibly demands that we examine what we use to medicate uncomfortable feelings, especially when we are tempted to justify the over use of alcohol with "I've had a bad day." Alcohol does not cure stress; at best it postpones it and at worst it increases it.

New Rule: I will closely examine my assumptions that entitle me to use alcohol to medicate stress. I choose to teach my children healthy and productive ways of dealing with tension and other uncomfortable feelings by practicing them myself.

June 26

Old Rule: It is okay for me to take these pills. The doctor gives them to me.

Abuse of tranquilizers and painkillers is epidemic in our culture. We seem to have the notion that if we feel uncomfortable, anxious, or in mild pain, we should treat these symptoms with medication. We feel that other methods of remedying these feelings or symptoms take too long or are not as effective. We justify taking frequent doses of these medicines by asserting that it is okay because a doctor prescribed them.

The use of tranquilizers and prescription pain medications does not remedy the cause of our problems. They only numb the symptoms for a short period of time and if we are to have ongoing relief, we must take more medicine. Addiction to prescription medicine often begins in just this manner.

Taking pills to soothe our nerves or numb our problems not only does not work, it sends a powerful message to our children: "If you are uncomfortable or anxious, take a pill. If you do not want to deal with something unpleasant or annoying, take a pill. If you are having difficulty with others, don't try to solve the problem, take a pill."

Drug use among adolescents and even pre-adolescents is a serious problem. Instead of blaming street drug dealers, many of us need look no further than our own use of prescription drugs. Many kids get their first drugs from family medicine cabinets. Incredibly, many kids were given their first tranquilizers by their parents when they were upset or anxious.

We need to examine our own attitudes and use of mood altering prescription medications and model for our children positive, productive ways of handling stress, anxiety, and minor pain.

New Rule: My attitudes and actions concerning mood-altering drugs, including prescription medications, are powerful messages to my children concerning the appropriate use of such drugs. I use these powerful medicines judiciously and responsibly.

Note: Although anti-depressants and other medications used to treat serious mental health problems are dispensed by prescription and do alter the functioning of the brain, they are not drugs of abuse and one does not become addicted to them. If you have any questions about the medications prescribed for you, talk with your doctor or avail yourself of the vast quantities of drug information available through your library, Internet, or your pharmacy. It is your body! Inform yourself!

June 27

Old Rule: We have rights! We need to stand up for our rights!

Of course, we all have rights. We have rights as human beings. We have laws that guarantee our rights as American citizens. Over the past few years, almost everyone has become quite interested in asserting their rights against intrusion or infringement by others. Groups and individuals file lawsuits every day believing that their rights have been violated.

One of the most recent groups to be empowered are children. Of course, adults should protect children and adolescents from sexual and physical abuse or exploitation by employers, but children may hear all of this talk about their rights and miss the point completely. Rights are about boundaries. Boundaries are the invisible fences between people. Our rights protect these boundaries and just as I have rights within my own boundaries, you have rights that begin and end at your boundaries. When I violate your boundaries, whether it is physically, sexually, emotionally, or intellectually, I have violated your rights.

We have tended to focus so much attention on our rights that we have lost sight of the rights of others. Our world is very crowded and becoming more so every day. In order to maintain our civilization, we must learn not only to guard our rights but also to respect the rights of others. It is appropriate to teach our children to be assertive and that they have a right to be treated with dignity and respect. We also have the responsibility to teach them that others have a right to be treated with the same respect.

New Rule: As I teach my children about the rights they have and how to carefully guard those rights, I will also teach them to respect the rights of others. The Golden Rule, "Do onto others as you would have them do onto you," is still a good motto by which to live.

June 28

Old Rule: If you can't succeed in any other way - cheat!

Recently, I listened to a colleague talk about her college experience. She shared that she had experienced difficulty in a class and had cheated on the final exam in order to pass the class. What was surprising about this conversation was that she, even with the hindsight of many years, felt that cheating was justified, since it enabled her to get her degree. She experienced no apparent guilt about her actions.

Some of the most powerful lessons we teach our children involve honesty, or the lack of it. Children watch and listen to us in their efforts to learn about how to deal with the larger world. When we teach them by our example that it is okay to cheat if they cannot pass any other way, it is no wonder they are willing to take this easier way toward reaching their goals. We not only tell them it is okay, we in essence say to them, "Do not fail. Succeed by any means necessary."

These beliefs have enormous consequences for our children and for our society at large. Do we really want our children to grow up believing that cheating is okay as long as they ultimately succeed?

New Rule: I teach my children that cheating is never permissible, even when it means they may fail. I want them to know that there is more disgrace in dishonesty than in honest failure.

June 29

Old Rule: Get what you need. If you can't do it honestly then lie.

Most parents would not consciously teach their children to lie in order to get what they want or need, but there are many cultural messages to children to do just that and they are listening. Movies and television are full of examples of people lying to others in order to get something or to get out of something. Perhaps the must disturbing images are the ones where trusting people are duped by the lies and charm of the hero. The trusting person is often portrayed as stupid and gullible while the liar is portrayed as smart and capable. There is seldom any penalty for having fooled the trusting person.

Additionally, our public officials lie and suffer few penalties. They often lie to get elected and to remain in office. It is expected and in many ways condoned when we say, "Everybody is doing it. This is what public officials do. What can you expect?"

Our children also learn from us when we lie to get out of something or to get our way. Like all teaching by example, this is a much more potent lesson than the one in which we <u>tell</u> them not to lie.

When our children hear us talk with others, in our professional and our business dealings, we are passing on our values to them. We are telling them how to deal with the larger word outside of their home. We are telling them how to do business, how to get things accomplished, and how to deal with others. Which values do we wish to pass on, the values that say, "Getting what you want by lying is a personal failure and that you loose more than you gain when you lie" or "If you need to lie to get what you want or need, it is okay. Everybody does, especially the smart people?" The choice is ours.

New Rule: We try to confront the images that say it is smart to lie and teach our children that winning through lying is a hollow victory.

June 30

Old Rule: Parents certainly deserve the respect of their children, but children do not deserve the respect of their parents.

Complaints about children's lack of respect toward their parents have been around since the beginning of parent/child relationships. However, the notion that children deserve the respect of their parents is fairly new. Respecting our children does not mean that parents should not parent. Parents do, indeed, have the right and responsibility to protect, discipline, and guide their children.

Respecting children involves several important aspects of being a parent. Children have certain rights by virtue of being human beings, even small, immature human beings who are dependent upon their parents for their survival. Children have a right to the respect of their own bodies. They have a right to decide who touches them and if they must be touched against their will, for instance in the course of medical treatment, they have a right to information about what is being done to them. In the most dysfunctional families, sexual and physical abuse occurs out of the basic belief that children have no rights with respect to their own bodies.

Children have other rights. Children are not just short adults. Children think and feel differently from experienced adults. Their physical capacities are obviously different. For instance, you would not expect a one year old to tie their shoes. It is essential to respect children's developmental stages. Aside from the physical developmental stages that we readily acknowledge and take into consideration, we need to respect that children's brains do not function like adult brains. Children are concrete thinkers. Therefore, explanations need to be simple and factual until they reach early to middle adolescence when they can begin to understand abstract reasoning.

Children experience feelings differently. Their feelings are intense and immediate. Their emotional needs are different. They have fears that adults might consider irrational. They may fear the dark, the shadows in the closet and under the bed, or new situations. We need to respond to their fears with explanations and patience, not ridicule and shame. Ridicule and shame do not make fears go away, but children will stop telling parents about them. Thus, they are left to handle their fears by themselves. In short, children have the right to have their developmental stages respected. This includes not only their physical development, but also their emotional and intellectual development.

New Rule: I expect my children will respect me as their parent and I am willing to respect my children.

July 1

Old Rule: Fathering is not important.

Our beliefs about fathering have changed radically in the past 30 years. Yet, in some families, the male contributes the sperm and feels that his part has ended. He has nothing more to do with the child. In many other families, the father disappears leaving the child rearing to the mother. He may go on to impregnate the next woman, perhaps repeating this pattern several times. Other fathers believe that if they provide financial support even though they are absent, they have done an adequate job of fathering.

Still other fathers, who are physically present and may see their children frequently if not daily, are emotionally absent. They provide the money to buy the material things children need and believe they have done their duty. Except for showing up sporadically at school functions or athletic events and an occasional "mind you mother," they are largely absent. They may live with their children, but disappear into the television, computer, chores, hobbies, or sports. They are emotionally absent, checked-out. These families are living by the old rule that states that fathering is about providing material things and being the disciplinarian of last resort and this is all that is necessary. Fortunately, this brand of fathering is not only becoming less acceptable, but also less prevalent.

In reality this form of fathering not only cheats the children it also cheats fathers, who have the responsibility of providing while experiencing none of the rewards of nurturing children intellectually, emotionally, and spiritually.

Children need a father's consistent, loving support in order to build healthy self-esteem and a positive self-image. This is true even if the child's parents are not married. Fathering does not end when the marriage ends. Rearing children does not mean providing just financial support. Scientific research suggests that children who grow up without a supportive father have lower self-esteem and experience more difficulty as adolescents and young adults.

Men who view being an emotionally present father as being a burden are missing out on the fun and rewards of being a parent. Women have known this all along; it is time that men knew it. Come on guys! Get in the game! It is fun and your kids are waiting!

New Rule: Fathering is vitally important, rewarding, and fun. It is worth the effort.

July 2

Old Rule: Clean your plate! There are starving children in Africa!

Fighting over eating is a constant in some families. Somehow, children and parents become locked in a power struggle over food. Mealtime is a battleground where parents feel frustrated and angry while children feel criticized, yet powerful. After all, parents cannot actually force children to eat.

This battle of wills is taking place in a country that is over fed, yet undernourished, where obesity even among small children is increasing. Left to eat as they choose, children eat differently from adults. Pre-schoolers have cycles of eating very little and then a great deal. These cycles may last a few weeks, a few days, or even a day. Their bodies are not hungry three times a day on a predictable schedule and when they are full, they quit. This is far healthier than eating because someone insists that it is time to eat or you have not eaten enough. Young children usually eat a limited variety of foods. While we want them to learn to eat a variety of healthy food, they will normally like and eagerly eat just a few things and these few things usually change over time. So while we may frequently introduce new foods, insisting that they eat a full portion causes needless battles.

Many children are learning to prefer high fat, high carbohydrate foods like hamburgers, fried chicken pieces, pizza, and sugared drinks. These foods should be limited, just as desserts should be offered only if children eat the earlier part of the meal. However, keep the food rules simple and above all enforceable. Attempts to absolutely control children's eating will only lead to frustration and conflict. Above all, resist the urge to use guilt to induce eating or cleaning their plate. They know that starving children in Africa will not receive what they do not eat and that this is an attempt to control them.

Children will not suddenly change and put an end to battles over food; only the adults can do this by changing how we react. Why not encourage your children to eat healthy foods by offering them frequently and in small portions, allowing them to say when they have eaten enough? This is not to say that pre-schoolers should eat on demand. Parents are not short order cooks. Meal times and snack times should be scheduled at the convenience of both parents and children. Continual grazing is not a good idea either, but sane reasonable expectations around food will not only end the food war but may help your children become healthier adults.

New Rule: In our home, we have simple enforceable policies about eating and food. We do not encourage over-eating through manipulation and guilt. We acknowledge that children's normal eating habits are different from that of adults and respect that children need to be taught about and offered a healthy, sensible selection of foods.

July 3

Old Rule: I'm busy. Go watch TV.

Recently, the American Academy of Pediatrics announced their belief that while there is much that is objectionable, television does have educational value. However, television viewing <u>should never</u> be used as a baby-sitter! The cheapest, most convenient, and most effective baby-sitter ever invented by anyone, anywhere that gives hard-working parents a few minutes to talk with each other without interruption or allows them to cook a meal without the distracting presence of a preschooler and parents are never supposed to use it?! Yeah! Right!

Parents know that television is a mixed blessing. On the one hand are good children's programs that teach while entertaining. On the other hand there is junk, that mesmerizes them and keeps them from more active, imaginative, and interactive play. We know that we need to interfere with excessive television watching, but let us not through the baby out with the bath water. Children are educated and entertained by some programs and are probably not harmed by small doses of junk.

Like most things in life, particularly in child rearing, reason and mental health are found in the middle ground. In this case the middle ground is allowing some television viewing, yes even babysitting, but prohibiting excessive viewing, especially of junk programming. In our television addicted culture we some times forget that life is not to be experienced as a spectator, but rather to be lived in reality. We need to encourage our children to turn off the box and experience life.

New Rule: Our children do watch television, but we also insist that they entertain themselves in other ways in addition to TV.

July 4

Old Rule: It doesn't matter. We can't really change anything, anyhow.

Cynicism, especially cynicism about our government, is at an all time high. I hear this cynicism expressed quite frequently among younger people. They are not interested in their government because they believe that all elected public officials are corrupt and self-interested. They believe that ordinary citizens cannot make a difference; therefore, they do not vote or take an active interest in their government. They are cynical and because of this cynicism they are quite ignorant of the facts.

It is true that we do have problems in the United States, big problems. Our government is often overly bureaucratic, sometimes corrupt, driven by money and self-interest, and often unresponsive to the needs of ordinary citizens. Still, we have the most freedom of any country that exists or has ever existed in history. The United States has waiting lists for immigration from every part of the world. No other country has so many people from other countries that are willing to break the law and risk their lives in order to come there and live.

While it is true that our government is unlikely to respond to the wishes, ideas, or complaints of one individual, people have always banded together to change things. We have seen this from the beginning of our history, including the anti-slavery, the civil rights, and anti-child labor movements, as well as workplace safety and environmental movements. The list could go on and on. We also have among the most free and fair elections in the world.

When we are cynical and say that it doesn't matter, we are not only wrong, but also excusing our laziness and inaction. This cynicism says more about our ignorance and unwillingness to be involved than it does about our government. The danger is that we sometimes get exactly the government that we, in our complacency and ignorance, deserve.

New Rule: On this Independence Day, I will examine the sources and effects of my own cynicism and tell my children the truth about their country and the freedoms we enjoy.

July 5

Old Rule: We are young; we don't have to worry about making a will.

Parents are often too busy dealing with today to consider what might happen to their children if they were to die. We don't like to think about it, but the unthinkable can and does happen: parents of dependent children die every day. In some cases children, lose both of their parents at one time. This can be devastating not just emotionally, but financially, even if the family has few financial assets.

If both patents die and there is no will, children are thrown into a legal limbo. The courts must decide what is in the best interest of the children. This may or may not be what you would consider in their best interest, but if you do not prepare in advance for this eventuality, the court has no other choice. The court must name a legal guardian to rear your children. Anyone can step forward and ask for the job and the court must decide who wins custody. While you might not think that someone who does not truly wish to love and rear your children would step forward, remember that your children will be eligible for Social Security benefits at least until they turn 18 or, if they chose to go to college, 22. They will also inherit any assets that you have, including life insurance policies. We don't like to believe this, but money may be a powerful incentive to some persons who may not have the best interests of your children at heart.

In reality, you know your family or other prospective guardians much better than a judge. You know who will be able to cope with grieving children. You know with whom your children are the most comfortable and who will rear them with the values and religious beliefs that you want them to have.

Making these decisions is the responsibility of every parent! If you have not already done so, see a lawyer, soon, and take care of business.

New Rule: I have made out a will and I have named a willing person as my children's guardian. This is part of my responsibility as a parent.

July 6

Old Rule: Possessions can make you happy.

Most of us say that we do not believe this rule, but our behavior, which always speaks louder than our words, says otherwise. Indeed, we are encouraged by our culture to indulge an insatiable appetite for more and more things.

Huge shopping malls, virtual palaces dedicated to obtaining things, are a part of every major American city. Our homes are becoming grander and larger, as magazines and television show us how the wealthy live. We are encouraged through advertising to buy everything from clothes and shoes (with the brand label on the outside) to perfume and cars. All of this is sends the message that having more things, especially more fashionable, expensive things will make us happy. Children get these messages loudly and clearly. They learn not just from advertising and their peers, but also from their parents when we indulge in the belief that a grander home, a new car, or a new boat will make us blissfully happy.

Yet, we all know in our hearts, even as we are buying the latest clothes or the newest car that it is not going to work. Even if it does, the fix will be temporary. Accumulating things doesn't fix anything, just ask all of the divorced couples who believed that redecorating or a new fine home would repair a troubled marriage.

It is difficult to teach children that happiness comes from loving relationships with others, using your talents and creative abilities, and giving back to your community some of what you have been given. It is especially difficult when we are countering the messages from the media and the rest of the culture. However, if we do not teach them what will actually bring them happiness, they will be drowning in possessions, wondering why they are not happy, purchasing yet more things to make themselves happy, and feeling the despair that comes from being emotionally bankrupt.

We need to teach our children with our example and our words about those things that have brought us true contentment and joy. It is fun to have new and plentiful stuff, but we all know that none of it will bring lasting happiness.

New Rule: Having more and better possessions will not bring happiness. I try to teach my children about those things that will make them truly happy.

July 7

Old Rule: Women are fragile and less competent than men and need to be protected.

This is a myth promulgated by male-dominated cultures that value male physical strength and the ability to make war. In truth, women are strong. They have always been strong. Women actually do most of the work that gets done in this world, from primitive cultures where men only hunt and the women take care of most everything else, to our own culture where women go to work, return home, then start their second job as the primary caretaker of the home and the children.

Women are emotionally strong. It is women who must bare the burden of going on and rearing children and providing for themselves and their families when men abandon them or are killed in war. They may not be allowed in battle, but it is women who must figure out how to survive and help their children survive whether it is in Eastern Europe, in the chaos of the Middle East,

247

in the neighborhoods of a large city, or in small town poverty. Historically, women have rebuilt their lives and the lives of their families after great disasters both natural and man-made. They have made homes and rebuilt the fabric of civilization after great migrations of people, whether as refugees from another country or across the plains to settle in the wilderness. Women keep families together, doing whatever needs to be done to provide for and educate their children when men find the responsibilities of family too burdensome and leave. Women are strong and capable. We need to teach our children that while women may lack the muscle mass of men (this is really all that we are talking about in terms of strength differences) women have what it takes to help their children as well as the men in their lives survive.

Remarkably, as we come to the beginning of the 21st century, we are still telling girls and boys that girls are weak, not as competent as boys, and must align themselves with successful, strong men in order to succeed. The media still puts out this powerful message. We need to stop indoctrinating little girls with the myth in our homes and in our media that they are not strong, need to be protected, and that they are not as competent as men. We need to tell them the truth that they must learn to use their abilities to their fullest in order to care for themselves and that, while relationships are wonderful and can bring much happiness, when they are based on the myth, "I am not strong and need a man to take care of me," they are doomed to bitter failure.

New Rule: I tell my children the truth that women are capable, competent, and strong, and they always have been.

July 8

Old Rules: Boys are tough. They don't need to be protected.

Silence, independence, and toughness are highly prized male virtues. A successful male is one that needs no one, is silent about his feelings, and is physically strong and capable of withstanding any pressure or tragedy without the assistance of others. He is a perfectly contained, independent unit who takes care of business.

We teach these things to little boys early in their lives. We teach them to be independent, to rely only on themselves, to be silent when they are hurt, and to get even when they are angry. In athletic competition we tell them to be tough and that it is manly to play while injured. We tell them the worst thing they can do is to show vulnerability and reach out for help, even within their own families. We push male children out on their own and expect that they will successfully navigate the complexities of this world. Because of the devaluing of fathering and the unwillingness of many men to assume and maintain the father role, they are often expected to do this without a father to guide them.

Small wonder that young men are turning to violence, find their primary support in deviant groups of other young men like themselves, and are committing suicide and murder at an alarming rate.

Our young men are in great danger; they are not as tough as we have thought they are. They need us. They need fathers and mothers to help them handle their emotions and to guide them through the complexities of our culture. They need us to help them find an identity, a purpose, and to fulfill their potential. Young men need much more protection and support than we are giving them. The survival of our culture depends upon whether or not we are willing to nurture and teach our young men or push them out into the world to be tough and take care of themselves.

New Rule: Boys need protection, and guidance as they grow into men. It is crucial to their survival that we provide them with the safety of a haven in which they do not need to be tough and self-sufficient.

July 9

Old Rule: Showing feelings is a sign of weakness.

All too often the problem of adolescent male violence is front-page news. Boys are committing appalling violent crimes. Many seem to have a complete disregard for the consequences of their actions to themselves and others. Enraged, they act out their anger in a violent attack on those they believe have wronged them. What has gone wrong that so many boys act out in such horrendous ways, destroying not only the lives of their victims but also themselves?

According to research psychologist William Pollack of the Harvard Medical School, we rear boys to be silent and tough, but to take action. Such rearing may be at the heart of the problem. In our culture we still teach boys that to show their feelings, especially sadness, is not masculine, and some parents feel that giving boys too much physical affection and emotional support will result in, let's be honest, a feminized male.

Therefore, we tell our boys to be a "man" and not cry. We do not give them as much physical affection and support as girls. According to Dr. Pollack, we shame them for showing any feelings except anger. Add to this mix the frequently ungrieved loss of an absent father and we have a situation that makes it difficult for boys to handle adversity. Many of the boys who commit violent crimes are actually depressed, but rather than crying and admitting to feeling sad, they act in the only acceptable way - with anger. As Dr. Pollack states, "For some boys who are not allowed tears, they will cry with their fists or they will cry with bullets."

We need to change how we rear boys, just as we have changed how we rear girls. We need to give boys permission to express feelings of hurt and sadness and give them more physical affection. Such things will not make them feminine, but may save their lives.

New Rule: We are rearing our sons with warmth and affection and permission to express their feelings without shame.

July 10

Old Rule: It is normal for kids to laugh at and tease each other.

Growing up is difficult. It can be especially difficult and painful for the child who is laughed at and teased by other kids for being different. Often parents take such behavior for granted. We seldom attempt to stop it, feeling that it is just a part of childhood and kids will survive and outgrow it.

In the course of normal intellectual and emotional development, children have difficulty putting themselves in the place of another. In other words, they have not developed a sense of empathy that tells them that teasing hurts the other person. When adults do not say anything about such behavior and feel that "kids will be kids," teasing and ridicule is more likely to occur. Parents are responsible for their children's moral as well as their physical and intellectual development. When we tease and make fun of others or let teasing and ridicule go without comment on television, in the movies, or between siblings and friends, we are condoning these behaviors with our silence.

While such behavior has always been a part of childhood, we can make life easier for children and teach valuable moral lessons when we ask our children "How do you think you would feel like if someone did or said that to you?" If we do not actively teach empathy, our children will have difficulty developing this important character trait. Being able to put ourselves in the place of others, to see the world from the point of view of another, is a valuable interpersonal tool and a sign of the emotional intelligence so vital to success as children become adults.

New Rule: When my children tease and laugh at others, I do not remain silent. I use these times to help my children learn empathy and compassion for others.

July 11

Old Rule: Be careful what you pray for. You just might get it.

We repeat this rule in jest, but seldom stop to analyze what it really means with respect to our understanding of God's relationship to human beings and, more importantly, what we are teaching our children about this relationship.

When we say to be careful what we pray for we are implying that God is a trickster, ready to give us what we said we wanted, but with consequences we do not want. Therefore, we need to get it right. We need to pray in just the right words or this not very compassionate God will play a trick on us. In other words, we must be very careful in our prayers least we say the wrong thing and end up with a catastrophe and feeling very foolish.

We are our children's first and most important teachers with respect to faith and their relationship with God. When we teach them that God is out to get them, to give them what they do not intend if they do not pray correctly, we put a barrier between them and God. We teach them to fear God in ways we do not intend. We take away the concept of a loving God who is always ready to hear our prayers when they are sincerely offered no matter what the actual words. We also take away the concept of the loving Father who wants the best for His human children, especially His youngest children.

New Rule: As my children's earliest teacher about faith and their relationship with God, I am careful to foster that relationship in such a way that my children will never fear to pray and will not be afraid to go to God with their deepest desires and concerns.

July 12

Old Rule: You don't need to worry about what you say around children. It's just like water off of a duck's back.

I was interviewing a prospective student for the therapeutic massage school where I was the school counselor. I asked the candidate if she had ever experienced difficulty learning. She replied that she probably has mild attention deficit disorder and that as a child her 4th grade teacher had told her mother, in her presence, that she was "stupid" and "would probably never amount to much." Far from rolling off, every syllable sunk deep into this little girl's heart, effecting her beliefs about her abilities from that moment into adulthood. That teacher, who either did not care or believed that this child would not take in this comment, planted the seeds of self-doubt and feelings of inferiority.

To children, adults are wise and all knowing. They absorb what adults say about them as literal truth, especially when authority figures like teachers, doctors, ministers, and parents are talking. We need to be very careful when we talk about our children with others, especially when the conversation deals with potentially negative information. We also need to defend our children when thoughtless, ignorant adults are unfairly critical of them. How powerful it would have been for this child if her mother, rather than being intimidated by the teacher, would have countered with,

"My child is not stupid and she is far too young for you to predict her future. What are you going to do to help her learn?"

New Rule: I am aware that my children hear and absorb what adults say about them and I will protect and defend them against thoughtless, ignorant critics.

July 13

Old Rule: You don't need to explain medical procedures to children. They won't really understand, and it will just upset them and waste time. Just do it and get it over with!

As a nurse, I always avoided pediatrics, because it interfered with my neurotic need to be loved by my patients. Having a 2-year-old terrified at the very sight of me was more than I could handle. But as a parent I have spent a lot of time in emergency rooms, hospitals, and pediatricians' offices. While my children generally received good physical care, the emotional care was sometimes less than satisfactory. I am also guilty of not attending to my children's emotional needs by too often adopting a "just get it over with" attitude.

In nursing school, we were taught to tell adult patients what we were about to do to them. Failure to do this is considered a violation of the patient's personal boundaries as well as their right to information about their care. This takes time, but it is necessary. Why don't we do this for our youngest patients?

It takes very little time to explain to children what the doctor or nurse is about to do and it helps children to prepare themselves for what is coming. Parents can do this both before visiting the medical facility and during any procedures. Remember to keep explanations brief and simple, but honest. If it is going to hurt, tell them! They have a right to know.

We can also ask doctors, nurses, and lab technicians to slow down and give explanations. They know this is appropriate, but sometimes they get too focused on getting the job done and forget about the little patient.

If we take time to explain what is about to happen when our children must be treated, not only will they feel less frightened and violated, but they will also trust parents and caregivers more and may be less anxious and more cooperative in the future.

New Rule: Children, like adults, deserve truthful explanations about their medical care. As a parent it is my responsibility to see that my children get those explanations.

July 14

Old Rule: A healthy baby is a fat baby.

This rule is a hold over from the time when children who were underweight usually died and parents very much wanted fat babies who, therefore, might survive. Today, we have a population that is overweight and becoming more so every year. Unfortunately, this also includes our babies and children. According to the Office of the United States Surgeon General, about 13% of children ages 6 to 11 years are obese, as are 14% of adolescents, ages 12 to 19 years. It is important to keep in mind that an obese child is not one with a few extra pounds, but a child who weighs at least 10% too much for their height and body type. Obesity usually begins between ages 5 and 6, but it can develop earlier. Studies show that a child who is obese between the ages of 10 and 13 has an 80% chance of being obese as an adult.

We are all aware of the health risks associated with being overweight, but perhaps the most devastating to children is the resulting decreased self-esteem and depression. Children are cruel to other children. They can be especially cruel to overweight children. These problems only increase as children grow older and find less and less acceptance by their peers and even other adults. This may not be fair, but it is a reality.

How can we help our children to achieve and maintain a healthy weight? First, let them know that our love and appreciation is not contingent on their weight. There are many things about them that are far more important than their weight. Second, adopt sensible eating habits ourselves, overweight families have overweight children. Children learn from us how, what, and when to eat. If we clean up our own act, our children are much more likely to follow our lead. Next, avoid the widely available, processed, high calorie, fried, sugary, and carbohydrate loaded foods. If we do not have them in our home, children, especially young children, are less likely to eat and develop a preference for them. Fourth, increase physical activity - do it as a family or as an individual, but do it!

Lastly, attend to the emotional issues surrounding eating. Do not use food as a reward or comfort for children. Many troubled, depressed children consider food their only friend and refuge. If there are substantial problems in the family, attend to them and don't allow your children to medicate their feelings with food. If you find that you must make substantial changes in the way that your family handles food, make the necessary changes one at a time. Dramatic changes all at once will only bring hostility and resistance. Do it slowly and deliberately, but do it.

New Rule: In our family, we strive to have a healthy, sane relationship to food and eating in order to maintain physical and emotional health and well being.

July 15 and 16

Old Rule: Don't talk back to me!

We encourage them to talk and dote on their every new word when they are small, but when children get older we sometimes wish that they had not learned to talk at all. Most parents encounter talking back, insolence, defiance, and sassiness at some time while rearing their children. As children grow older, if a pattern of respectful speech has not been established, such talk can degenerate into the abusive language that we hear adolescent children use on the television talk shows. Clearly, we do not want this situation to develop in our homes.

In the April, 1999 "Dr. Mom" column in *Parenting* magazine, the author offers some helpful insight into teaching respectful speech. "Dr. Mom" states that children often begin to use their new found language talents to get attention or to test their arguing skills. Other times disrespectful language can be a way of dominating others. Children will sometimes use their words to make people, including their parents, angry or sad. This new found sense of power to influence the feelings of others is the source of many defiant comments. Not all rude speech, however, should be considered an act of defiance. Children and adults are generally more respectful outside the home than inside the home where they are more relaxed and feel safer. Also do not confuse insolence with the normal grumbling or even anger at parental authority and limit setting. Children need to be able to express displeasure with parental authority even as they grudgingly obey. Such behavior is normal and children should be taught to express normal human anger appropriately.

Serious insolence should not, however, be overlooked. The article offers some suggestions for preventing and dealing with such behavior. Children will act toward others as they are treated or see parents deal with others. The "Golden Rule" applies. When we speak disrespectfully to them and to others or when we disparage others, we teach them that this is appropriate speech. Children learn by example. When we provide a negative example, we get this behavior in return. Conversely, when children are respectful and courteous, give positive reinforcement for the speech that you would like to hear more often. Human beings tend to respond to praise by increasing a behavior, rather than decreasing a behavior in response to criticism or increasing a behavior in response to silence. In other words, tell your children when they have done well.

As was mentioned previously, do not confuse insolence with being assertive by having an overly broad definition of "back talk." We want children to learn to be assertive and not stifle their emotions, opinions, and preferences. Once again the "middle way" is helpful. We need to teach children to express themselves appropriately without hurting others or being disrespectful. When a child is being insolent, one tool is to say, "I do not talk to you in that tone of voice, and I will not allow you to talk to me that way." (Use this statement only when it is true. Otherwise you leave yourself open to all manner of unpleasant arguments.)

Unfortunately, the media, especially television, plays a powerful role in shaping children's behavior. In the media, children and adolescents are often insolent smart-alecks whose rude one-liners are greeted with laughter by audiences. Frequently, the children who are portrayed as heroes are disdainful of adults and able, by their cleverness, to circumvent adults who are often portrayed as bumbling and stupid. Talk show guests often use sarcastic, rude, and crude language with each other and the audience, all in the name of entertainment. Even the most careful parent cannot completely screen out such material, but we can interject our own values and opinions, and engage the child in formulating and expressing their thoughts about the appropriateness of such material when it does appear.

Even though we cannot completely do away with back talk by our children, we can teach them to respect others and to express themselves appropriately.

New Rule: Respectful language is something we both expect to give and to get in our home.

July 17

Old Rule: Don't ask why.

When we are teaching our children about manners it is sometimes difficult to explain to them what to do with their natural curiosity about others. For instance, if they see someone who has an obvious difference, we do not want them to stare or to ask questions aloud that might be embarrassing to the person as well as ourselves, so we tell them to be quiet. In a sense, by hushing them, we say to them that to inquire about differences is not permissible and that to have a difference is shameful and should not be discussed. In short, we say to them "Don't ask." Neither the adult nor the child is comfortable with this solution.

Recently, I heard a story that illustrates a different way to handle the problem. A child and a mother were eating in a restaurant when the child commented on the fact that the hands of the lady at the next table were shaking. The mother told him to be quiet and the child looked ashamed, but was quiet. The lady at the next table, hearing the remark and the mother's reaction, got up at the end of her meal and asked the mother if she could talk to the child. The mother reluctantly agreed and the lady told the child that her hands shook due to a disease called multiple sclerosis. She explained that it is a disease of the nervous system, but nothing for him to be afraid of. This simple act illustrates how to give children information in a way that encourages them to ask questions, while fostering compassion for others.

The next time your children stare and ask "why" or stare and do not ask "why" but you know there are questions, try a simple explanation either at the moment or at an opportune time. You will not only encourage your children's intellectual curiosity, but will likely increase their compassion and understanding for others.

New Rule: I encourage my children to ask "why" when they observe differences in others and, therefore, to learn about those differences rather than to fear them.

July 18

Old Rule: Be careful of those people. They are all…

Child development researchers believe that children are born with two fears: the fear of sudden loud noises and the fear of falling. They learn all of their other fears from living in the world, our world. As the Rogers and Hammerstein song from "South Pacific" says, "You've got to be taught to hate and fear. It's got to be drummed in your dear little ear. You've got to be carefully taught."

When we pass our fears and prejudices on to our children, for prejudice is largely based on fear, we do them a grave disservice. When we teach them to hate and fear others based on skin color, religious preferences, country of origin, or any one of the other characteristics that separates human beings from one another, we impair their ability to live successfully in the world.

When we teach them that all members of a particular group behave in a particular way or have particular characteristics (Have you ever noted that these assigned characteristics are never positive?) we perpetuate and pass on misinformation. If you disagree, think about what is said about all members of <u>your</u> group. Do these stereotypes actually apply to all members of the group or to you? Would you rather be judged as an individual member of the group or by some supposed characteristic of the total group?

It is a cliché that our world is getting smaller, but it is true. Few people can live in isolation or only with members of one group. The planet is simply too crowded to get away from those who are not members of our group. We must learn to live together. If we do not, we face an increasing incidence of the violence and misery as we have seen in various parts of the world due to ethnic and religious hatred and perceived differences. These differences are not even visible to outsiders, but are enough to murder the children of the group one dislikes and views as inferior or even less than human.

In order to prepare our children to live successfully, we must teach them not to fear and hate those who are different from them, but to learn about differences and to be tolerant of those who are different. We can light a candle of knowledge in our own homes in a world too often darkened with ignorance and its resulting fear.

New Rule: In order to help prepare my children to be successful, I will teach them not to fear differences in others and replace prejudice and fear with knowledge.

July 19

Old Rule: All women are… All men are…

In these days of political correctness, we may be more aware of sexual stereotypes and a bit more careful about where and when we mention them, but they are still part of our thinking and still as mistaken and destructive as ever.

As an instructor in marriage and family courses, I continue to hear stereotypes about the supposed attributes of the sexes. Like racial and ethnic prejudices, these stereotypes are negative and generalized to the entire sex. They usually include such things as: "All men are jerks and abusers and not to be trusted."; "Men don't communicate."; "Men will leave if the going gets difficult."; "All women just want to get married."; "Girls are more trouble to raise than boys."; "Women talk too much and want to communicate about everything."; or "Women are too emotional. They think with their feelings."

We have all heard them and they are true - for some members of each sex. The problem arises when we generalize and teach our children that you can expect these objectionable characteristics from every member of the sex. Because of the negative stereotypes about female competency, I think girls and women have probably suffered more historically from such stereotyping and sex-linked shame. However, men also suffer due to these beliefs, especially the stereotype that all men are sexual predators, potentially abusive, cannot be trusted, and will leave if problems arise. To treat all men as abusers is no more accurate than to treat all women as incompetent.

When we are tempted to use these stereotypes around our children or when they hear them, let us remember how powerful these can be in determining the thoughts and behaviors of those who are just learning about gender differences. Instead, let us try to teach our children to deal with each other as individuals who are male or female, just as we teach them to deal with people as individuals regardless of race, ethnicity, or religion.

New Rule: I do not pass on sexual stereotypes as a way of teaching children about themselves and relating to members of the opposite sex.

July 20

Old Rule: Be quiet now. I'm watching TV.

Television addiction is rampant in our culture. Many of us watch hours of TV every week and permit our children to do the same. Television may accompany family activities from morning until bedtime. We zone out in front of the tube, tuning out things around us, letting our children do the same. Then, remarkably, we become angry when they do not seem to hear us. In fact, we have taught them to do this.

Television has revolutionized how we live. It brings into our homes news, special events, information, and exposure to people all over the world. It informs and enriches our lives. However, it is a double-edged sword, for much of the programming deadens our minds and promotes violence, predatory sex, dishonesty as a legitimate expedient, and rampant striving for more and more things. It may also diminish our relationship with our children and other family members because they so seldom receive our undivided attention; they get only what the TV does not absorb.

There is a legitimate place for TV watching in our lives. It is interesting and fun to watch sitcoms, dramas, and sporting events. It gives us valuable information, as well as entertainment and relaxation. However, like most things, healthy functioning is found in the balanced middle ground. Most of us probably need to turn it off more often and talk with our children and our spouse, spending more time really listening to them. Listening is the greatest compliment we can give to those we love. We also might find other ways to stimulate our minds and model this behavior to our children. Simply telling them to turn off the TV and go out and play or read a book is not enough, we need to set the example.

In short, in order to break our children's addiction and non-healthy use of TV, we need to break our own addiction to it.

New Rule: In our family we watch and enjoy television, but we also turn it off and take time to talk with one another, read, exercise, and have fun in many other ways.

July 21

Old Rule: Nice people do not know too much about sex.

We are sexual beings! Our sex immediately identifies us. Indeed, it was probably the first statement made about us! Whether we are sexually active or not, we continue to be sexual until the day we cease to breathe. This is reality. To deny this simple fact is to engage in unreality, but most of us feel inadequate or at least apprehensive when we approach the subject of sexuality with our children.

As adults who enter into sexual relationships, it is appropriate that we know about our own sexual functioning as well as that of our partner. It is our right and responsibility to inform ourselves through reading and other sources. It is our right to talk about sexual matters and to ask questions.

Sexual expression is a joyful and pleasurable part of adulthood. Not to know about sex or to operate on half-truths and mistaken notions is not only sad but also dangerous. In our lack of knowledge we can inflict pain on those with whom we are the most intimate. Sexuality is important! We need to know about it! As we learn more about our own sexuality and become comfortable in that knowledge, only then can we teach our children about their sexuality and how to use this powerful, wonderful gift in a responsible manner.

New Rule: I acknowledge that I am sexual. I can learn about and explore my own sexuality. It is the nice thing to do for myself and for those I love. Only by learning about and accepting my sexuality can I teach my children to honor and enjoy their own.

July 22

Old Rule: You only get one chance to do it right, so don't mess it up.

This would seem like a good place to stop and take a break. Today, July 22, is my birthday and as a present to myself and you, I want to reassure all of us that we have many chances to be good parents. There are many opportunities to do the right thing and to be a loving and positive force in our children's lives.

Of course, we will make mistakes. Sometimes they will be big ones and we will find it necessary to ask our children's forgiveness. Sometimes we will believe we are doing the right thing only to realize that we have made an error in judgment. We may learn that we did not have all the information and, if we had more information we would have acted differently. While all of this is true in human relationships in general, it is intensified in the parent-child relationship. We are human beings. We mess up on a regular basis!

The good news is that children do not need perfect parents. They can survive and even thrive despite parental mistakes. So, if you are feeling overwhelmed by this book, (Heaven forbid! My goal is to make parenting easier, not more difficult.) or by parenting in general, remember that what children really need is consistent loving concern for their well-being and respect for their individuality. That is it. If we are concerned for their welfare and treasure them as individuals, we cannot go too far wrong. We will be successful parents with successful children.

Relax! Enjoy being a parent. I know you do not believe me if you have small children, but this period of having your children in your home is really quite brief. Take pleasure from it while it is here.

New Rule: We try to relax and enjoy our children. They do not need perfect parents, only generous amounts of love and respect.

July 23

Old Rule: Feeling bad? Buy yourself something!

The bumper sticker reads, "When the Going Gets Tough, the Tough Go Shopping." We chuckle but, in reality, many of us believe it. Consequently, when we feel angry, sad, hurt, or lonely we go to the mall to buy something to help us feel better. Like all compulsive or addictive behaviors, buying works and we do feel better - for a while.

It is important to learn to treat ourselves well and to value ourselves enough to purchase some of the things we want, as well as those things we need. However, the belief that buying will fix uncomfortable feelings not only leads to financial disaster, it also means that we never confront the reasons for those feelings. By our attitudes and actions, we pass this legacy down to our children. They will also come to view buying as a panacea for uncomfortable feelings and situations.

Recovery from compulsive spending dictates that we no longer use buying or shopping to numb sadness, anger, or loneliness. Instead, we can decide to face the causes of our uncomfortable feelings and find more productive ways of handling them. In doing so, we help our children to learn productive ways of dealing with their own unpleasant feelings.

New Rule: It is important to be honest with myself about the reasons why I spend money. Buying myself something when I feel hurt or angry only postpones the problem while creating new ones. I look at the sources of my difficulties rather than buying more things. Furthermore, I teach my children that new things do not resolve difficulties and uncomfortable feelings.

July 24

Old Rule: "No" does not mean "no," it means "maybe."

We have all been there. We said "no", but the child keeps on asking. "Pleeese", they say in that whiney voice like fingernails on a chalkboard. We say "no" again. The nagging continues. We become angry and say "no," as the whining and nagging escalates. Finally, we give in and say, "Oh all right, but just this once." Having achieved their goal, the child walks away satisfied. We feel angry with the child for the nagging and with ourselves for being such a spineless wimp. We promise ourselves that this is the last time we are going to give in like this. Deep down we know we were manipulated.

Parents are the only ones who can end this drama. Children are not going to change their behavior. It works for them. It is a little trouble, but it works. It is a great game and they get what they want. We are the ones who are unhappy and must end the game if such behavior is ever going to stop. Actually, we are the ones who are keeping the behavior going by our reinforcement of the nagging. The children have come to know, because we taught them by giving in, if they whine and nag long enough, "no" will become "maybe" and "maybe" will become "yes."

It will be difficult, especially if we have reinforced this behavior for some time, but if we are ever to put an end to the nagging and manipulating, we must stand our ground. When we say "no," we must stick to it. We might start by talking with our children about what we have realized and our intention to change. They will test us to see if we are truly serious. We might devise some consequences if the whining and nagging do not cease, like withholding a favorite privilege. All of this will take conscious effort, but we created the problem by not following through with what we say. Consequently, we are the ones who must solve it. Our children are just being children and taking advantage of our wishy-washiness. Thus we are responsible for the solution.

New Rule: When I say "no," I mean "no."

July 25

Old Rule: My children fight all of the time! It drives me crazy and worries me. Sometimes I think they hate each other.

Sibling rivalry dates back to the very beginning of human history, back to when Cain slew Able, but it still drives parents crazy. We want them to get along, to share with each other, or at the very least to stop picking at each other and give us a little peace. It is like a game with them. Put them in a room together for too long and they will start bothering each other, doing what they know will get a response from the other. The bickering is petty, loud, and bothersome to you, but not to them. They seem to rather like it. Why else would they do it so often? What is worse, they often want us to take sides in the battle.

Such interaction is probably normal. It is certainly usual. After all, they are vying for attention and possessions within the same household. While parents may not see these things as scarce resources, children do and they want their share and then some.

While sibling conflict and rivalry is normal, we need to be careful not to contribute to the problems with our own behavior. Contributing to the problem might take the form of referring to the children by their supposed role within the family, such as the pretty one, the smart one, the talented one, or the problem one. Try to view each child as an individual with a unique set of attributes both positive and negative.

Although we do not like to admit it, most parents do have a favorite child, the child we find most appealing or the easiest to discipline, but it is important that we not view one child as the persistent victim and the other as the victimizer. Chances are that the child who is the constant victim is doing something, although it might not be obvious, to keep the battle going and to draw you as the parent into it, and play your role in the drama as the rescuer. Try not to take sides during an argument. This is difficult, especially if one child is much younger.

Set clear rules and consequences concerning physical fighting and separate them if possible when the bickering is bothering you. Allow them to settle their own battles without you and suggest that they bring the big, ongoing conflicts to family meetings. (See Oct. 5 & 6) Do not insist that they play only with each other or that older children include younger children all of the time. Allow them to have separate friends and play experiences. Give their relationship some space.

Lastly, try not to worry too much about it. Sibling rivalry is normal and will resolve over time, if we keep our perspective about it. I know this is not good news for the parents of pre-schoolers, but as they grow and spend less time with each other and more with their friends there are fewer opportunities to argue and your home will be a bit more peaceful.

New Rule: Rivalry among siblings is normal behavior. We attempt to handle it calmly and know, like wet diapers and stranger anxiety, it will pass.

July 26

Old Rule: Don't mess up! You only get one chance to do it right!

I listened to an interview with twin brothers who are successful engineers and scientists. As boys, they were constantly experimenting or building something. They had many failures and small disasters, but their parents always encouraged them to think about what went wrong and to start over in a different direction. Obviously, their parents' strategy was sound for their sons grew up to be independent critical thinkers.

As a college instructor, I find that one of the most difficult things to teach is the ability to look a situation, gather information, find novel ways to approach a problem, and to logically analyze the results. Indeed, research indicates that it is quite difficult to teach critical thinking to college students. I believe it might be a skill that develops earlier. Trying to learn to think analytically and arrive at alternative solutions to problems may be like trying to learn to speak after the crucial window of opportunity in the young child's life has past. Their skills will never be as fully developed as compared to those who learned during that window of time.

What can parents do to foster development of children's thinking and problem solving skills? We can begin by creating opportunities to learn from doing and creating. This may include creating art with blank materials instead of coloring books or making their own creations out of interlocking building blocks rather than following the instructions of exact models of someone else's work.

There are many opportunities; we need to be aware of them. Certainly, we need to limit the television and video game time that stunts rather than enhances thinking skills. We also need to talk with them. Ask their opinions, rather than constantly giving them directions and our opinions. Ask them "What do you think might happen if you do this or why do you think this happened?" Teach them to be observant, ask them what they see, hear, and smell. Make it fun, make it part of your usual conversation with them.

This is not formal, sit-down, and be quiet education. This is moving, on-the-go education. Involvement does not end when children go to school. Do not rely on your children's school to continue in this vein. Our current methods of education are often fact-oriented and do not focus on critical thinking. The continuing development of such skills may depend largely on parents.

New Rule: It is important that our children learn to think critically. We can help them learn these skills in the home we create and the conversations we have with them.

July 27

Old Rule: I will be happy when…

What is your ending to this sentence? I will be happy when I loose weight, when I have the right job, when I have more money, when I get married, when my spouse changes, when I have another child, when my children behave, when my children are grown, when I have a better house, when I live in a different place. While the endings are many and varied, the basic belief is always the same. Something outside myself, something not yet in my life, frequently something over which I have little or no control, will bring me happiness. Likewise, the result is the same: failure to live in the present, to enjoy today, and to take action toward making our lives better.

While we hope there will be good things in our future and our dreams will come true, today is all we have. Today is our only guaranteed chance to be happy. Today is the chance we have to teach our children gratitude for what they have and to take action concerning today's challenges.

It is important to accept and teach our children that genuine happiness comes not from having our wishes magically fulfilled. Instead, it comes from an inner sense of who we are in relationship to our fellow human beings and having a sense of the meaning in our lives. Lasting happiness and peace comes from inside, from acceptance of ourselves and compassion and tolerance for others. We can teach our children these simple truths only by accepting and living them ourselves.

New Rule: I refuse to postpone being happy until the right circumstances occur. I will cultivate an attitude of happiness and gratitude for today. By adopting this attitude, I can help my children not only strive to reach their personal goals but to also enjoy the journey.

July 28

Old Rule: If only…

This rule, a cousin to "I will be happy when…" allows us to postpone happiness and to live not in the present, but somewhere in the future. We fantasize that "if only" something in our lives would change, then we could be happy. Often we apply this rule to another person. If only my spouse would get sober, if only I could find the right mate, if only someone/my parents would love me, if only my boss or my spouse would appreciate my efforts, if only my children were better behaved, smarter, or more talented. The list is endless! The common element in all "if onlies" is a focus on the behavior and attitudes of others, while ignoring our own power and responsibilities. By adopting this pattern of thinking, we pass it along to our children and teach them these destructive mental habits.

Letting go of the "if only" habit means accepting that we cannot change or control the behavior of another person, not even those we love and who love us and honestly seek to please us. The only person whose attitudes and behavior we can control is our own. While there is implicit responsibility in this belief, there is also great freedom. By accepting this truth we are free to accept and cherish others, as they are, not attempting to change them into what we believe they need to be. By this acceptance, we can use our energies to focus on ourselves, nurturing important and satisfying relationships that are available to us today while letting go of the fantasy that painful relationships will magically improve without our taking action.

New Rule: I choose to let go of the "if onlies." I will not postpone my life waiting for another to change and by my example I teach my children to do the same.

July 29

Old Rule: We are not as good as others.

One pattern of thought that I saw frequently in those who came to me seeking counseling, especially for depression, is the tendency to constantly compare themselves to others. They compare their attractiveness, material possessions, achievements, and anything else that is important to them to those around them. They engage in a persistent mental "one up - one down" game. While they sometimes find that they are better than others, they frequently find themselves lacking in important areas and feel badly as a result.

This mental torture, which creates so much suffering among its practitioners, is a habit learned from and reinforced by parents who do this themselves and pass it on to their children. Practicing this constant comparing not only creates needless suffering, but it also saps mental energy and time that could be used for creative pursuits, achieving ones goals, and enjoying relationships.

I have noted that those who are the most successful and feel the most content with themselves and their lives are those who spend little time and energy comparing themselves to others. Their only barometer of how they are doing is whether or not they are happy with themselves. If they decide that they are not pleased, they attempt to change the things that they are capable of changing and let go of that which they do not have the power to change.

The next time you find that you are comparing yourself to someone else, stop those thoughts. Instead, compare yourself only to yourself. See what happens when you refuse to suffer in this way. You may find that you are happier and have more mental energy to accomplish those things that are truly important to you.

I also encourage you to pass this gift on to your children. When they compare themselves to others, talk with them about stopping this habit and focusing only on themselves and how they are doing with their own goals, not how others are doing with theirs. There is great freedom in refusing to compare ourselves to others. Claim this freedom for yourself and your children.

New Rule: In this family, we do not compare ourselves to others. Comparing oneself is a destructive habit that causes suffering and wastes time. We choose not to do it.

July 30

Old Rule: We are better than others.

This rule, which is somewhat the opposite of the "we are not as good as others," results from the same comparing mindset. It also causes great suffering.

Such comparisons generally reflect what is important or valued in the family. If moral correctness is valued, then we believe others who do not hold our moral values are inferior to us. If money and material possessions are important, then we view as inferior those who do not have as much. If education and achievement are valued, then we see ourselves as superior to those who are less educated and have achieved less than ourselves. The list can go on and on and may include ethnic and racial background, regions of the country, social standing in the community, even the social standing of one's ancestors.

All of this results in a false sense of superiority, created solely by human beings to distance themselves from others and to make themselves feel better. This destructive pattern also saps a good deal of creative mental energy.

In reality, most of the world's religions and moral philosophers teach that as humans we are all children of a divine creator, we are all equal in the eyes of that creator, and, therefore, we should love and care for each other.

This is not to say that we must agree with or condone all of the behavior of our fellow humans. However, accepting that we are all equal is not only the first step in learning to love others, it is also the first step toward decreased suffering and genuine peace. If you examine the history of conflict in our world, you realize that much of it begins with the belief that one group is better, more valuable, and consequently more deserving than another group. We can only change this attitude one person and one family at a time.

New Rule: I teach my children the fundamental truth that we are not better than or superior to others. I teach them that all humans are created equal and, therefore, worthy of respect.

July 31

New Rule: I am going to have my kids young and grow up with them.

I hear this statement often, usually from those who have either not had children or whose parents did not spend much time having fun with them. While I think they are saying they want to enjoy their children, this statement concerns me.

Parenting is an adult occupation. It requires adult perspective, knowledge, and patience. Being a young adult, in one's late teens and early twenties, is a time to take advantage of opportunities and complete important developmental tasks before moving on to the next stage of life. The foundation for a career needs to be laid, emotional and financial independence from parents needs to be accomplished, and mate selection does not need to be hurried, but thoughtfully considered as the other two tasks are accomplished.

Being a young adult is also a time to have fun, the kind of fun unique to being single or newly married. It is also a time to explore the world beyond where one was reared and to seek out new experiences. Young adulthood is a time of exploration, growth, and increasing independence. It is a special time that does not need to be short-circuited by early marriage and/or child rearing.

Children are wonderful when one is ready. They can be enjoyed when parents are in their late twenties, thirties, and even forties. There is no rush, so enjoy being a young adult. If you already have a child and are in your late teens or early twenties, you might want to postpone a second child until you have a chance to grow and experience some of the benefits of being at this stage of life. I know from experience that you do not have to have your children close in age for them to be friends as they grow up or for you to have a fulfilling family life.

New Rule: I know it is important to be mature myself before I have children. I can enjoy my children at any age. Having fun with children is a matter of attitude, not a matter of age.

August 1

Old Rule: Here, dear, let me do that for you.

When parents of adolescents gather, the subject soon turns to their children: their refusal to help around the house, their lack of willingness to do things for themselves, and the fear they might never be able to manage on their own. While this has been an issue between adults and adolescent children forever, the extreme of this situation has its roots in early childhood when we do virtually everything for them, believing that we are being good parents. We consider ourselves to be attentive and loving, wanting our children to enjoy their childhood and "stay children." In reality, by stepping in and doing everything for them, much of which they are capable of learning to do for themselves, we are discouraging them from learning and sending the message, "You can't do it. I can. I'll do it for you."

Aside from squeezing into small places and playing computer games, there is not one task that an adult cannot do better than a child. Adults can perform tasks quicker and better with less mess.

Therefore, adults get into the habit of doing things themselves rather than teaching their children, just because it is faster and easier. The job is done better than and in less time than it would take to teach and allow the child to do the task.

As our children's first teachers, we have the power to instill confidence or self-doubt, to encourage or discourage learning, and to foster competence or helplessness. We foster confidence and competency by teaching our children and then standing back and allowing them to practice, make mistakes, make a mess, and learn from their mistakes. This is especially true of preschool and primary school age children when they are eager to learn and practice their new skills, the same skills they need to learn in order to function independently. This period of learning and practicing is necessary even if it means that beds are not made perfectly, counter tops are a bit sticky, rooms are not perfectly tidy, cars are not uniformly clean, and other household tasks are not up to adult performance.

New Rule: I do not rob my children of the joy and pride of learning new tasks by doing them myself. I teach my children and give them time to practice what they have learned. I try to keep in mind that increased competency and self-confidence is my goal, not perfection.

August 2

Old Rule: Children belong to their parents.

At first, this rule sounds loving and responsible, but in truth it is the root of child abuse. It says, in effect, "Your body belongs to me. You have no right to privacy. I can abuse you sexually and use you for my own gratification. I can vent my out-of-control anger on you. I can beat you and call it discipline. Your mind belongs to me. I can call you names. I can tell you how to think. Your spirit belongs to me. I can demand perfection of you and berate you when you cannot attain my impossible standards. I can tell you that I know the only true relationship with God and if you do not accept my way, you will not only loose me, but will be eternally damned."

Children are entrusted to their parents for a short time to teach, nurture, affirm, and love. Having a child does not entail ownership, but rather an abiding respect for the individuality and uniqueness of that child. While parents have responsibility for their children, they do not own them. No human being belongs to another.

New Rule: Children belong to themselves, not their parents. Children need guidance and loving support to find their own path in life. They also need parents who are wise enough, and unselfish enough to let go and let them be who they are and love them at the same time.

August 3

Old Rule: Children should take care of their parents.

This is one of the unspoken rules that operates in dysfunctional families, where wounded or emotionally immature parents do not look to other adults to meet their emotional needs, but instead to their children. Such parents include the mother who has babies so she will have someone to love her, the emotionally wounded and depressed parent who uses their children as confidantes and emotional caretakers, the drug and alcohol addicted parent whose children must take care of them or listen to their drunken rambling for hours, the lonely, isolated, and angry divorced parent who uses their children to ventilate the hurt and anger they have for the former spouse, or the overwhelmed parent who gives the younger siblings to the older ones to rear.

This is emotional abuse and children emerge from such homes feeling inadequate and lacking self-esteem. They want very much to please their parents and make the parents' lives better, but they are being asked to do an impossible task. Children cannot heal the emotional life of an adult; no matter how hard they try. If such healing is to occur, the adult must take responsibility.

This role reversal can also set up a life long pattern of neglecting self in order to please others and attempting to earn love by taking care of others. The consequences are painful and potentially disastrous when young adults, feeling that they have failed to adequately care for their parents and heal their pain, enter into a series of relationships in which they attempt to fix others in order to earn love. They usually come away from these relationships feeling victimized and inadequate. Until they become aware of the pattern and heal themselves, they will continue to seek out others who need help, attempting to fix them and earn their love and loyalty.

We can end this painful cycle in our own families by taking responsibility for our own healing and not looking to our children to heal our emotional wounds. We need to let our children be children and focus on our care of them. They deserve parents who take responsibility for themselves.

New Rule: It is not the duty or responsibility of children to heal their parents and to make them happy. In a functional family, children do not take care of their parents, but are, instead, cared for by emotionally mature and competent adults.

August 4

Old Rule: A good father is a provider who backs mother in matters of discipline, plays with the kids occasionally, and stays out of the way.

This is truly an outdated rule. Fathers are no longer the only provider in the family. In most families, neither parent can provide total support. As a result, fathers are expected to help care for the children and assist in maintaining the household.

Most fathers no longer feel they are fulfilling their total responsibilities when they provide financial support and are the last arbitrator of discipline. Thus fathers are discovering some of the difficulties of rearing children that mothers have traditionally encountered. They may experience doubts and uncertainties about what exactly is a good parent and what do children really need.

With little help from past generations, fathers are re-inventing themselves. They are learning that they play a crucial role in the emotional development of their children. Fathers are learning that they are needed in ways that their own fathers never thought possible. Their presence and approval is vitally important to the self-esteem of their growing children. Their dependability offers a sense of safety and essential predictability. Their way of being in the world, their knowledge of how to get on outside the home (different than a mother's way) offers their children many lessons in dealing with the complexities of the adult world.

Being a father requires dedication and courage, a willingness to be emotionally as well as physically present, and a willingness to learn. A man does not take on being a father; he acquires it, he grows into it, he becomes it. This process is not without some confusion and pain, but the rewards, like anything else that requires devotion and effort, are immense.

New Rule: Becoming a father is important, vital, rewarding work.

August 5

Old Rule: I was only teasing.

When an adult teases a child, it can quickly escalate into a form of emotional abuse. Persistent teasing is a way of ventilating anger and criticism without seeming to be angry. It is also a way of controlling children. Few children can match wits with an adult and even fewer have permission within the family to tease them.

In reality, teasing is a vicious, self-esteem destroying, sneaky way to relate to children or to anyone for that matter. Be honest with yourself. When you are teasing another, whether it is an adult or a child, you are not just being funny at someone else's expense, you are expressing a criticism that you do not feel comfortable voicing directly. So, you say it teasingly. When the other person is hurt or takes offense, then you can always hide behind the socially acceptable "I was only teasing." You can further control the situation by insisting that the injured party is "too sensitive and should develop a tougher skin" or "doesn't have a sense of humor."

Children learn to tease from their families as well as from their peers. A child who is teased at home will not use their teasing skills on their parents, but instead on their siblings and peers. Most of us can recall the pain of being teased at school or by playmates who used this dysfunctional method to communicate anger and frustration, or to feel superior to others.

Parents cannot completely control their children's exposure to or use of teasing. However, we do have the power to refrain from using this painful and damaging method of expressing anger and criticism ourselves. When we hear them teasing others, we can talk with our children about the painful effects of teasing. Refraining from teasing might just make home and school more pleasant and emotionally safer places to be.

New Rule: In our home we do not hide anger and criticism under the guise of being humorous and "only teasing."

August 6

New Rule: If you can't win any other way, use sarcasm.

The root of the word "sarcasm" is a Greek word meaning "to bite in rage." Sarcasm, no matter how clever, is meant to wound and humiliate another. As such it has <u>no</u> place in any loving relationship, especially with children!

The ability to use sarcasm, some of us have an absolute gift for it, is an advanced cognitive skill that we develop in adolescence. Adolescents love to use this newfound ability and its close cousin, ridicule, on each other. It is one of the things that makes adolescence so difficult. Adults continue to use this skill in order to humiliate and best an opponent. Children do not have these advanced cognitive skills and are, therefore, no match for these words. They are just injured by them. Even after they develop these skills, a sarcastic parent or teacher will not usually permit this skill at wounding with the subtle put-down to be used on them.

When parents speak to children in the contemptuous mocking tone that characterizes sarcasm, those words hurt! They are meant to hurt! They destroy children's self-esteem! I believe that deep down the sarcastic, mocking parent intends to do just that - to wound and belittle the child, in order to enhance their own fragile self-esteem by humiliating and keeping their children subservient.

The next time you hear a sarcastic comment, no matter how witty, remember you are hearing the product of a weak and fragile sense of self-worth who must be cruel to those who cannot defend themselves in order to feel superior.

New Rule: Sarcasm has no place in a loving relationship, especially family and child/parent relationships.

August 7 and 8

Old Rule: Never say, "I'm sorry." It is a sign of weakness.

We all know people who will not admit fault and apologize for their behavior no matter how strong the evidence of their wrongdoing. Would you consider these people strong? Probably not. You might consider them stubborn, self-absorbed, in denial, or lacking in self-confidence, but not strong. In their refusal to admit a mistake and ask forgiveness, you might even consider them weak.

The willingness to admit when one is at fault and to express regret is a sign of self-knowledge, confidence, and personal strength, just the opposite of weakness. When we are able to admit that we have committed an error and to ask for forgiveness, our relationships become stronger and we gain the respect of others.

When I was about 7, my father was supposed to pick me up from school for a doctor's appointment. He forgot and after waiting for some time, I walked home a distance of about five miles. (This was before schools were so conscientious about letting children leave school without a parent present.) When my father arrived home, having remembered the appointment, his genuine, heartfelt apology to me was not a sign of his weakness, but a sign of his love and concern for me. He loved me enough to apologize for his error and to ask my forgiveness. My forgiveness mattered more to him, than his pride over admitting a mistake and appearing flawed to his child.

Unwillingness to admit an error and ask forgiveness when we have wronged a member of our family is false pride and self-delusion. Realistically, who knows our imperfections and shortcomings better than our families, including our children? Therefore, to delude ourselves into believing that we never err and have no need to apologize or to feel that to apologize would somehow give others power over us is ultimately a sign of weakness and a symptom of lack of self-confidence.

When we admit to others that we have erred in our relationship with them, those relationships become stronger. This is true whether that relationship is with our spouse, our extended family, our co-workers, our friends, or our children. We also increase, rather than diminish, the respect others have for us. We usually admit to error out of a sense of self-confidence, not an unrealistic desire to be seen by others as infallible and perfect. Admitting to our fallibility, models for our children the reality that honorable, strong, and confident people admit to error and ask forgiveness.

When we have erred in our relationship with our children or with other significant persons, as we certainly will, we gain power and respect when we admit our faults and say those difficult, but magical words, "I'm sorry, I made a mistake. Please forgive me."

New Rule: We try to teach our children to readily admit fault when they are wrong by doing so ourselves, most especially when we must say to them, "I'm sorry, please forgive me".

August 9

Old Rule: Oh, I'm so sorry. I'm so stupid.

We have all met these folks; perhaps we even live with them. Everything is their responsibility. They apologize for everything that goes wrong, even if it is not their fault. Humble and self-effacing, they inform everyone of how inadequate and incompetent they are.

They sound modest, but actually they are playing a game in which they apologize for everything, even for the air they breathe and the space they take up on the earth. Your part in this game is to reassure them that they are not stupid and incompetent, and, indeed, they have many talents they themselves do not appreciate, but others do. The goal of the game is to get their "self-esteem fix."

The people who play this game are lacking in self-esteem and seek to alleviate this painful condition by getting crumbs of affirmation and approval from others. They seek to get a bit of self-worth by manipulating others into giving them reassurance. Of course, these good feelings do not last and one must find another player and go through the apologizing, putting one's self down, and obtaining reassurance game one more time.

I am intimately familiar with this painful game. I played it for years. Occasionally, I am embarrassed to admit, I revert back to it when I am feeling unsure and inadequate. It does not work anymore for me because I can no longer delude myself into believing that I am modest when I am being manipulative.

Emotionally healthy people quickly tire of this game and will avoid the player. Emotionally unhealthy people play this game and create dysfunctional relationships. Children see their parents play the game and learn to play themselves. These children also begin to doubt themselves. They see that their parents do not feel good about themselves and begin to internalize this view, believing, "If my parents are so terribly defective, then I must also be defective."

If we experience difficulty with our sense of worth and self-confidence, we pass this along to our children just as it was probably given to us. This family game is passed through the generations. The only way to break this painful cycle is to stop playing the manipulation game. (I hope you can no longer play it once I have revealed that others are aware of the real goal of this behavior). The second step is to develop a healthy, realistic sense of self. Many of us need the help of a trained professional to assist us with this difficult task. However, it is worth the financial and emotional expense of visiting a counselor in order to end this destructive family legacy. Do it, if not for yourself, then for your children.

New Rule: I refuse to teach my children to apologize and put themselves down in order to receive compliments and reassurance. Instead, I will strive to develop a healthy, realistic sense of self-worth and pass it on to my children.

August 10

Old Rule: If you want to be desirable to men, "dumb down."

When I talk with young female college students, many of whom are capable and bright, I am amazed and saddened at how many of them live by this rule. They hide their intelligence and capability. They do not share their thoughts and opinions. They do not seek out leadership positions, and they do not assert themselves in relationships with men. Even after all of the progress toward gender equality, they continue to "dumb down." They hide who they really are in order to be attractive and acceptable to men.

Where are they continuing to learn this stuff? I think from us - adult women who continue to be overly modest about our abilities and accomplishments, differential to men, and who believe that the worst thing that can happen to us and to our daughters is to be unacceptable or undesirable to men. If you believe this a harsh exaggeration just recall how much money is spent in our culture and to what lengths women will still go to meet prevailing standards of attractiveness. Also, listen to the vitriolic attacks made against women who are successful. Smart, well-educated, and competent women are often greeted with ambivalence in our culture. We admire them, but often disapprove of them. Viciously attacked as being too aggressive and angry and often referred to as "bitchy," such women pay a high price for their success. All of this criticism has not been lost on young women. They see clearly that being a smart, capable woman is not always desirable.

What is the consequence of this behavior? Obviously, when young women hide their competences, they do not use and develop them. Thus, they and our culture, in general, do not benefit fully from their abilities. What is less apparent are the difficulties that "dumbing down" can cause in their relationships with men, especially husbands. Even the best "dumb down" player cannot stay this way forever. Once married she will often decide that she no longer needs to hide who she is. She will begin to assert herself, much to the dismay and shock of her young husband who thought he had married a deferential, "nice" girl only to find out that she has opinions and competencies she wishes to use. The first years of marriage are difficult enough without starting with such deception! Wouldn't it be better to teach our girls not to hide who they are in the first place?

It is difficult for parents to counteract such potent cultural messages. The guidance of fathers seems to be especially important in this area. By examining our own attitudes and giving them our support for using their abilities, we can help them find the strength to be all that they can.

New Rule: While I know that there is still great pressure in our culture for girls to hide their competencies, I will support my daughters in finding the strength and confidence not to "dumb down," but instead, to celebrate and be who they truly are.

August 11

Old Rule: We are better than others.

I have often focused in this book about the importance of fostering healthy self-esteem in our children. However, as in most situations, emotional health is found in the middle road. In other words, I believe it is a mistake to tell children that they or their family are superior to others.

Each of us has talents and abilities that may be above the average. Likewise, each of us has liabilities and areas in which we are less talented than others. Granted, some people seem to be blessed with an overabundance of gifts such as superior intellect or athletic talent, while others always seem to struggle. (Very often what seems to be an abundance of talent is actually the result of focus and hard work over a long period of time.)

Our children need to understand that others, who may not seem to be as gifted as themselves, are worthy of respect. They need to develop compassion, not just tolerance, for those who may not be as talented or fortunate. For instance, it is a temptation in our culture, which values outstanding athletic performance, for the athletically talented person to become arrogant and believe they are not only superior to others, but do not need to abide by the rules of decency and fair play that apply to others. In this belief are the seeds of self-destruction, as well as harm to those around them.

In a culture where we seem to equate having money with worth, some believe that having money and material possessions makes one or one's family superior to others who are less fortunate. While we may not verbalize it, we probably all hold this belief to a certain extent and we pass it on to our children in our attitudes and actions. This is true whether or not we have many material blessings.

In order to teach our children to regard themselves as valuable and talented and to regard others as equals, we must first examine ourselves and decide if we need an attitude adjustment. When we begin to change our own attitudes about others and our relative superiority or inferiority to them, then we can teach our children to have a healthy regard for themselves and respect for others.

New Rule: Our family is neither superior nor inferior to others. We have regard and respect for ourselves and for the talents, abilities, and circumstances of others.

August 12 and 13

Old Rule: Those people are different from us. We don't associate with those people.

We do not have to look very far to realize that human beings have a very long way to go in our ability and willingness to accept and live peacefully with those who are different from ourselves.

The past twenty years in Eastern Europe and the Middle East have demonstrated graphically that despite two world wars and numerous other conflicts, human beings are quite prepared not only to distrust and avoid those who are different from ourselves, but also take their lives and property.

Least we become too smug, we have only to read the headlines about violence done to others in the United States because of their difference from another's racial or ethnic group. Attending a National Multicultural Institute Conference helped me to realize that, while such acts may be illegal and publicly denounced, racial and ethnic discrimination, humiliation, and prejudice are still a fact of life for many people in the United States. Many parents must still teach their children to manage and survive their encounters with the dominant white culture.

This continues despite the fact that as a country we are becoming more and more diverse. By 2050, it is projected that whites will no longer be an absolute majority. In reality there will be no majority! Whites will be the largest minority with Blacks, Latinos, and Asians together compromising the majority of the U.S. population. This will be a dramatic shift for majority, as well as minority, populations. We must prepare our children to deal with the realities of this situation, lest we descend into the ethnic, racial, and religious conflicts we have seen in many parts of the world.

We must prepare our children to live peacefully and tolerantly with others. Whether or not they do so with an attitude of tolerance, they will frequently encounter those who are different from themselves. We cannot escape this fact and for many of us this will be difficult. It is challenging, as the bumper sticker suggests, to "PracticeTolerance."

How do we begin? Perhaps the first steps lie in acknowledging that we as individuals and as a country have a long way to go. We can affirm for our children that diverse does not mean "bad" but only different, and that no one group has an exclusive hold on virtue. We can also attempt to practice what virtually all of the world's great religions espouse: respect for the dignity and value of all humans.

This is a very tall order. For most of us it represents a conscious and dramatic shift in how we think about and relate to others. If we do not begin to make those changes, our children, navigating in an increasingly diverse culture, will be forced to deal with the results of our unwillingness to accept and accommodate this reality.

Gay Moore M.Ed. RNC

We need to learn to manage diversity and differences, not just to survive as a species without doing pointless violence to one another, but also because a life that embraces diversity is rich and fulfilling. Conversely, the person who avoids the unfamiliar and different is impoverished. While living in such a way as to encounter and learn about the racial, ethnic, and religious diversity is more difficult and stressful, to live otherwise is too confining and promotes unnecessary intellectual and spiritual poverty. This is a valuable lesson for our children. Our human diversity, while often challenging, is neither frightening nor undesirable, but rather an opportunity to live an immeasurably enriched life.

New Rule: Diversity among human beings is a reality. We teach our children to accept and learn from those who are different from themselves.

August 14

Old Rule: Now don't act your color.

At a recent multi-cultural conference, we were asked to share some of the childhood messages we received concerning our own group and cultural differences. An African-American woman shared that she was told as a child by her mother when they went out that she was "not to act her color," meaning that she was not to behave like the negative stereotypes that whites have about blacks. As an adult, she continues to hear women of color say this to their children.

This is a striking example of what is called "internalized oppression." Internalized oppression occurs when a member of one group takes in and actually agrees with the negative opinions of a more dominant and favored group. The shocking part is not so much that older people have heard this, but that younger people continue to say this to their children.

Another example of internalized oppression was illustrated by a study done some years ago in which African-American children were shown two dolls, one black and one white. They were asked to identify the pretty doll, the good doll, the smart doll, etc. and then the bad doll, the ugly doll, the stupid doll. Overwhelmingly, the children attributed the positive characteristics of prettiness, smartness, and goodness to the white doll and the negative characteristics to the black doll. This study was first done over 40 years ago, but when it was replicated in the 1990's, the results were very much the same! Clearly, we have much to do as parents and as a culture.

It is essential that parents of color carefully examine and identify where they have internalized oppression in their attitudes and beliefs about themselves and their group. It is also essential to talk with their children about such beliefs and the lies that they perpetuate when they hear such statements made by others.

New Rule: I am aware of the insidious messages of internalized oppression and work to root them out in order to prevent my children from internalizing these damaging, life-destroying messages.

August 15

Old Rule: I am just one person. One person certainly cannot change things.

Racism, classism, prejudice, and discrimination. As Americans we do not like to admit that such things continue to exist. We do not like to look too closely, especially when we are members of the predominate group with the unearned power and privilege we enjoy as a result of being a part of this group. When we do look and see injustice, we tend to feel powerless, so it is just easier and less painful not to look too closely.

However, we do need to look and we can act. We need not feel powerless or helpless, for we do have power. The African-American contralto Marion Anderson, who was refused permission to sing in the Daughters of the American Revolution Hall and with the assistance of Eleanor Roosevelt sang on the steps of the Lincoln Memorial, said, "There are many persons ready to do what is right because in their hearts they know it is right. But they hesitate, waiting for the other fellow to make the first move - and he, in turn, waits for you. The minute a person whose word means a great deal dares to take the open-hearted and courageous way, many others follow."

Obviously, we do not have the power of Eleanor Roosevelt, but we do have power with our acquaintances and certainly within our home to do the right thing. To paraphrase Eldridge Cleaver, we can refuse to be part of the problem and, instead, participate in the solution. When we talk with our children, we can be a light of knowledge and tolerance in an ignorant and intolerant world. We do have choices and we can make a difference!

New Rule: "We can embrace our diversity, find strength in it, and prosper together, or we can focus on our differences and try to restrict access to resources by members of ethnic and racial groups different from ours and limit prosperity for all." Andrew Young, former Congressman and United States Ambassador to the United Nations (1996)

August 16

Old Rule: Money cannot be managed.

This powerful, unspoken rule resides in families where it seems there should be enough money, but there isn't. There is money for a new boat or fashionable outfit, but not for toothpaste. Having learned this rule as children, we find ourselves frustrated and confused about money. We make enough money to take care of ourselves, but somehow we loose track of how we spend it and experience chronic financial difficulties. We spend unwisely and impulsively, enter into elaborate balancing acts with our checking accounts and credit cards, or play "I'll get mine before you get yours" games with our spouse. We make resolutions and budgets to manage our money only to sabotage ourselves. The old habits win out and we are left feeling ashamed and frustrated.

In order to stop this painful, self-defeating cycle, we must first examine our parental messages concerning money, as well as our financial history. We must also take the risk to seek advice and counsel concerning our financial attitudes and actions. Only then can we begin to manage our money successfully and teach effective money management to our children.

New Rule: I am honest with others and myself about how I handle my money. I have learned to manage money and can teach successful money management to my children.

August 17

Old Rule: My children had better not lie to me or I'll give them the beating of their lives.

At some time, every parent must deal with a child who lies, cheats, or even steals. Such events are a normal part of childhood. Even though we do not like to think of our children as sneaky or dishonest, we know that every child will try it at least once or twice.

Small children may not clearly understand the line between facts and make believe. Later, they may know better, but lie to get out of something or to enhance themselves in the eyes of their friends. Rather than overreacting, parents might treat such behavior as a teachable moment. When a child is caught lying, rather than ranting, raving, and threatening, try giving them a consequence for the initial behavior and an additional consequence for lying. Parents might also talk with the child who is lying to self-enhance about the futility of trying to be liked for what they have or do and how foolish they will feel when their friends find out they lied.

Cheating by school age children can result from learning problems or too much pressure to achieve. Often young children do not see behaviors such as copying homework as dishonest. They need to be educated about the ethics of cheating. When they cheat, children need to be held accountable. They need to own up to it, even if it means that they fail a test, get an "F" for their homework, or loose a "win" for their team. In order to avoid cheating, parents can moderate the pressure to achieve and praise their children for doing their best rather than achievement.

Often young children do not understand the concept of stealing. It is important not to overreact when a toddler takes something that does not belong to them, but instead explain and make them return the object. Later, children may steal as a result of peer pressure or the need to "look cool." This is serious behavior and once again, while we do not want to overreact, we do not want such behavior to continue. Stolen items should be returned with restitution and an apology as well as consequences for the behavior.

When dealing with these upsetting behaviors, it is important for parents to remain calm, but firm while issuing and maintaining consequences. Of course, the best teacher of honesty is our behavior. When we attempt to be impeccably honest in our behavior, we can then demand honesty from our children.

New Rule: I realize that my behavior is the most potent example. However, when my children are dishonest, I try to remain calm, give them appropriate consequences for their behavior, and teach them the value of honesty.

August 18

Old Rule: Hurry or I'm going to leave you. See that policeman over there? If you don't behave, he is going to come and arrest you and take you away.

In our efforts to discipline our children we sometimes say the most ridiculous things, especially when we are in public. We just want them to hurry up or behave so we can get our shopping done or the chores completed. So we tell them we are leaving them, that a police officer will come and take them to jail, or that something else equally undesirable will happen to them if they do not do as we ask.

This form of discipline not only makes us look silly, it does not work. It doesn't take long for even the smallest child to figure out that these are idle threats. Most children are sophisticated enough to know that the police don't take small children to jail for annoying their parents. Moreover, we do not want them to fear the police. We want them to go to a police officer if they are lost or in trouble.

During the month of October, I will focus on discipline, but I challenge you to prepare to make changes in the way you discipline your children by resolving to be reality based in your discipline methods. Begin by discarding idle threats and issue only those consequences that you are willing and capable of maintaining.

New Rule: It is important that discipline be clear and based in reality. Meaningless threats do not work and are a waste of my energy.

August 19

Old Rule: The school will teach my children about sex.

We may not say it and we don't like to admit it, but often we think it: most of us are extremely uncomfortable teaching our children about sex and reproduction. Even 30 plus years after the sexual revolution, most parents dread "the talk" and will postpone it, secretly hoping that the day will never come. Although we may have mixed feelings about sex education in the schools, many of us are quite relieved that someone else is doing the job. It may be surprising, but enough of my young college students continue to tell me that they learned about sex from school and their friends to convince me that little has changed. Parents are still leaving sex education to other sources.

Just as we teach children to avoid talking to strangers, to protect themselves when they are home alone, and eventually to drive responsibly, it is our responsibility to teach them about sexuality.

Good instruction not only teaches them about the facts of reproduction, but also conveys sexual values. As parents we want our children to know the physiological mechanisms of sex, in addition to a set of values that protects them from the pain of pre-mature sexual activity. We want them to know that it is okay to say "no" and not permit themselves to be used for someone else's gratification. We also want them to know that it is not okay to use someone else for their gratification or ego enhancement. Imparting sexual information as well as values takes more than just one "talk." It means being alert to the many small opportunities, teachable moments, to give them this vital information.

Teaching children about sexuality has always been the responsibility of parents. Historically, most of us have shirked that responsibility, but this doesn't mean that we cannot begin to fulfill this important task and teach our children not only the mechanics of sexuality, but also sexual values.

New rule: It is my responsibility to teach my children about sexuality and sexual values.

August 20

Old Rule: When is a penis not a penis and a vagina does not exist?

Although inundated by sexually explicit TV shows and sexual innuendoes, we are still a shy, inhibited culture when it comes to talking with our children about sex and sexuality.

We would never dream of neglecting to tell our children the proper name and function for their legs or arms. We would never lie to our children and avoid answering questions about the functions of their ears or stomach. We would never insist that they call their nose by some cute euphemistic word. Yet we avoid talking with our children about sex and reproduction. Feeling embarrassed or ill equipped to answer; we may pass off their questions, giving them the unspoken, but clear message that we don't talk about such things. We give their body parts cute names like "wiener" and "wee wee" and we never mention to little girls that they have a vagina. When we give silly names to body parts, we send the message to our children that those parts are different from other body parts and are somehow so shameful that we cannot even talk about them using straight-forward language.

It is part of a parent's responsibility to provide sane, accurate information to their children about their bodies including their sexual functioning. I am not suggesting that we give every 2-year-old a lecture on sexual anatomy or a 6-year-old a full explanation of sexual intercourse and reproduction complete with diagrams as one young female student received from her physician mother. What I am encouraging is the use of appropriate names for body parts, to talk openly about where babies are carried in the female body and how they exit, and to provide a simple explanation of conception as soon as the child can understand or asks.

In our sexually ambivalent culture, be prepared for a bit of opposition from relatives, perhaps from teachers and other caregivers, and maybe even from your own spouse. You may even have to deal with the embarrassment of having, as a former neighbor did, your bright, talkative 4-year-old inform the dinner guests that "Daddy has a big penis, but my baby brother has a little one!"

However, demystifying sexuality and the body when children are young will serve both you and your children well as they grow and feel comfortable enough to come to you with questions about sexuality.

New Rule: I will overcome my own embarrassment about sexuality and teach my children about their own bodies. In doing so, I will open the door for them to ask questions concerning their sexuality.

August 21 & 22

Old Rule: Sex outside of marriage will condemn you to hell.

This old rule has recently enjoyed resurgence with some parents and religious leaders in an attempt to stem the rising tide of adolescent sexuality. However, just as it was a bad idea to scare adolescents into not having sex 40 years ago, it is a bad idea today.

While it is true that children as young as 11 and 12 are sexually active and our rates of adolescent pregnancy and sexually transmitted diseases are frighteningly high, the fear approach seldom works and often produces unintended results.

Statistically, it is true that adolescents reared in a religious environment with strong prohibitions against sex out of marriage are more likely to postpone sexual intercourse. Even if they do not wait until marriage, they are more likely to have sex in the context of a committed relationship and have fewer sexual partners. However, when we try to regulate adolescent behavior with the fear of separation from God or eternal consignment to hell, we not only interfere with their relationship with God, we set up a situation in which they feel that if they have already had sex that they are going to hell. So they might as well continue whenever and with whomever they please. This situation tends to lower their self-esteem, especially in girls, and may lead to the same risky behavior we sought to avoid.

Silence on the subject does not work either. I have had many clients and students tell me their parents never talked with them about sex. They became sexually active, armed with nothing but hormones and curiosity, in order to find out the big secret. They often experienced life-altering consequences as a result of their parents' lapse of responsibility.

What does seem to work in promoting abstinence and sexual responsibility is an approach that is open and non-judgmental. Using this approach, parents and others who have influence with children tell them the truth about sexuality. Such adults acknowledge even to girls, that their bodies might be saying, "yes" to sex, even as their minds are saying "no." They tell them the truth about birth control and pregnancy. Advisors and parents should also learn the facts about sexually transmitted diseases, for pregnancy may not be the most damaging consequence of sexual intercourse. They see to it that kids are armed with the truth, including STD prevention information.

We also need to tell kids that sex is a powerful thing not to be taken lightly. It is okay to say "no," and being sexually active does not mean that you must say "yes" to anyone who indicates a desire for sex. This includes boys, as they often feel pressured into sex by girls. We must also foster self-esteem, especially in girls, so that they do not see their self-worth reflected in their desirability to boys. It is important to teach them that it is not appropriate to manipulate another and use someone else's body for their own gratification.

We also need to let them know that sex in a committed, loving relationship can be exciting and fulfilling and that waiting may be in their best interest.

Kids respect those who tell them the truth and eventually disregard those who purposely mislead or frighten them. They tend to listen to those who attempt to understand their point of view and tune out those who lecture and pass judgment. We all know this. It has not been that long since we were there. Even if this approach does not work completely as we intend, at least we will have planted the ideas and the channels of communication are more likely to remain open as children grow into young adults.

New rule: I am honest with my children about sexuality. Frightening them does not work. My desire is to keep the channels of communication open so that I might help them deal with their sexuality.

August 23

Old Rule: I can't help it. This is just the way I am. It is the way I was raised.

Whenever I heard these words from clients, my reaction was a cross between frustration and despair. I knew I was faced with someone who was terrified of examining themselves and how their behavior affects others. They were even more terrified of change. This form of resistance is extremely difficult to overcome.

When we retreat into our fear of change and fail to look at ourselves honestly, we cannot heal and grow. In this way dysfunction and pain is handed down from generation to generation. This stance is also the catalyst for many divorces, when one partner realizes that the other is saying in effect, "I am not willing to accept any responsibility for the problems in this relationship or for working to make things better, either take me as I am or leave." It always amazes me how shocked they are when the other spouse takes them seriously and gives up on the relationship.

When we are willing to face our fears and do the hard work of changing our attitudes and behavior, we can make positive changes in our families. Rather than adopt the passive, irresponsible stance that says, "That is just the way I am and I can't help it," if we are willing to accept responsibility for who we are and what we do, we can begin to alter outmoded, destructive patterns of relating to our children and spouse. When we are willing to do this difficult work then marriages can heal and become richer and more fulfilling. If parents are willing to face themselves and life, in general, courageously and honestly, then children will learn the habit of self-honesty and develop relationship skills that will serve them well as they begin careers and create their own families.

New Rule: I am capable of change when it will benefit my marriage, my family, and myself. I have the courage to grow.

August 24 & 25

Old Rule: You can't change your life. This is just the way we are; so accept it.

I have seen it happen many times. A client begins to look at their lives - how and why they do what they do and the resulting painful, destructive outcomes. Their family begins to sense a change in them, changes in the way they react to the family system or a change in the role they have played in that system. Such change causes anxiety and fear in the family. Family members begin to feel challenged to look at themselves and the way they react or play out their own roles. This is frightening and potentially painful.

The family begins to try to stop the process by stopping the first person from changing. This is not a conscious process. They will tell you that they want their family member to get well or sober, but the fear is overwhelming.

One of the ways families stop progress and pull the family member back into their place in the system is by telling them, "You can't really change, this is just the way life is, things are not so bad, and the therapist is influencing you in the wrong direction." At this point the client is in a difficult position. They can either risk losing the family by moving ahead and attempting to break the old dysfunctional patterns or they can stop themselves by adhering to the old family rules. If they take the latter road, the family stays in its comfortable, known misery and children are reared with the same old rules with the same painful results. If they continue to change, they face increased resistance and perhaps hostility from family members.

I have been a client myself, as well as a therapist. I know that one can change how one lives. I know it can get better and we can live healthier and more productive lives. However, this process involves hard work. The therapist has no magic wand to pass over clients that will effortlessly and painlessly change the old patterns. The best a therapist can do is point the way and offer suggestions and support along the journey. It takes work to make the journey of self-discovery and change.

This work is risky, for family members will sometimes leave you. Although most come back, this is an enormous gamble. For this reason, I have great respect for the courage of those who choose to make this journey of change and compassion for those who find it too difficult and frightening. When I have wanted to stop my own process of recovery and change, I have often found the bit of strength that I needed by reminding myself that one of the reasons I wanted my family to be different was so that my children could grow up and not have to experience the same difficulties I have. If you want to rear your own children differently from the way that you were reared, I encourage you to do the work of change.

This work can begin with a therapist or member of the clergy, a parenting class, or a 12-step group. I recommend a group or at least one-to-one therapy since few of us can effectively go through this process of self-examination and change alone. We tend to get too bogged down and loose our way. We need others to give us feedback and support along the way.

Life, your life, and consequently your children's lives can change. It can get better. We can do it differently. All it takes is time, courage, hard work, and others to help us along the way.

New Rule: By changing how I live, I can create a healthier, more satisfying, and productive life for my children and myself.

August 26

Old Rule: We are good people. There is nothing wrong with our family.

Not long ago I saw a television news story about a family in our area. The mother was standing on her porch being interviewed because yet another one of her sons had been arrested for a serious crime. Her husband had served a term in prison. Several of her other sons were either serving or had served prison terms. She concluded this interview by stating that they were "good people."

Although amusing this family situation is also tragic. Obviously, this is failed parenting at its most extreme. This mother actually believed that she knew how to parent! Even though they might be well intended, these two people obviously didn't know anything about how to successfully rear a family. Despite an abundance of evidence to the contrary, this woman continued to believe that she and her husband had done a good job of parenting!

Becoming a biological parent does not mean that we know how to parent. It does not come naturally like the sexual act that produced the child. We learn to parent from our own parents and from the wider culture in which we live. Sometimes what we learn is dead wrong and damaging to our children.

Children are in large measure a product of the homes in which they are reared. It is true that parents are not the only influence that children experience. Even good parenting sometimes fails to counteract powerful cultural patterns, but the way we react to our culture is largely determined by the way in which we were parented. This is also true of our genetic predispositions, which we are only just beginning to understand. We do know, however, that our parenting heavily influences the manner in which genetic predispositions are expressed.

Parenting is an important job, not to be taken lightly. It is important not just for individual children, but also for the larger culture. If our culture is to be productive and healthy, it will be because families are productive and healthy. There is no shame in not knowing how to parent. The beginning of knowledge is to admit that we do not know and to be open to learning. We fail when we do not know, but are too ashamed, too proud, or too arrogant to admit that we do not have the slightest idea about how to be a good parent. This is true ignorance and will lead ultimately to tragedy.

New Rule: I know that I do not know everything there is to know about how to be an effective parent. While I will never be a perfect parent, I am open to learning new ways to help me to be a better one.

August 27

Old Rule: My kids never listen to me! They either tune me out or argue with me.

When my older son was 4 I was convinced there was something wrong with his hearing. He did not seem to hear me when I talked to him. Since he had had ear infections, this seemed a logical conclusion. I took him to his pediatrician, who after an examination and audiology test issued a diagnosis – "mother deafness."

My child is surely not the only one with this annoying disease. Therefore, we need to find out what causes it. While a constant dialogue of "do this, don't do that" may be a principle cause, children also tune out criticism. No one likes to be criticized, but kids do not usually have the freedom to tell a parent to "stop." So they do the next best thing to protect themselves from a critical barrage, they tune it out. They don't hear it. Idle threats and inconsistent discipline also contribute to the problem. Continual screaming will also cause children to tune out. We get louder and louder and they seem to get better and better at not hearing.

Just as I did, most of us have some remedial work to do with respect to parent deafness. Children will only change their behavior when we change our way of communicating with them. It might be helpful to first examine our communication style. Do we yell, scream, or make angry, meaningless threats? Are we constantly nagging and critical? Are our only conversations with our children commands to start or stop doing something?

After analyzing your style, turn the tables on the children. First, get their attention by making eye contact. It is hard for even children who are quite afflicted with mother deafness to ignore you if you are looking straight into their eyes. If you usually yell, get quiet. If you threaten, make sure it is something that you are willing to do if their behavior does not change. If you are nagging and critical, try telling them how much you appreciate what they do. Praise works wonders for their sense of hearing. If you are constantly telling them to start and stop some behavior, try having a little fun with them. They might be inclined to listen to you initially because they will think you have gone crazy and may keep listening because it is more pleasant to do so. Give it a try, especially if you relate to a diagnosis of "mother deafness." It is likely that what you are doing is not working so what have you got to lose?

New Rule: It is important to learn to communicate effectively with my children. If what I am doing causes them to tune me out, I will learn other ways to help them tune me in.

August 28 and 29

Old Rule: My children never talk to me.

It is hard to believe when children are toddlers and chatter constantly and all you want is a little peace and quiet that by early adolescence the conversation will stop. At this point parents, wanting to know what is happening in their children's lives at school and elsewhere, find themselves asking scores of questions with minimal, non-committal responses.

Some of this is normal. School age children and certainly adolescents are in the process of breaking away from parents. They have their own lives that they want to keep to themselves. They do not want Mom and Dad to know everything. They are becoming individuals, but this often leaves parents feeling like police interrogators with very reluctant suspects.

Perhaps our children would talk more if we took down some of the barriers to communication or if parents of younger children avoided putting them there in the first place.

For instance, we may attempt to control the situation by telling them what to do or giving long lectures with our version of the solution to their difficulties without ever asking their opinions. On the other hand, we may ask question after question thus putting the adolescent bent on privacy on the defensive. Worse yet, we may become sarcastic or belittle the child's concerns. Ridicule and sarcasm have no place in a loving relationship, especially with children who do not have the cognitive skills to reply in kind, nor do they have permission from the bullying sarcastic parent.

Parents may also attempt to distract or minimize the child's concerns with a "you'll get over it message." This also protects the parent from their own uncomfortable feelings and they can avoid seeing their child in distress. Counselors and therapists are often guilty of attempting to use our skills to analyze and interpret the child's behavior to them. We would probably do well to keep our psychological analysis to ourselves when it comes to our families.

Most parents are guilty of at least a few of these communication mistakes, but we can take down the barriers.

First of all, <u>listen</u>. Do not listen formulating your reply, but really listen to what the child is saying. (We might also try listening to our spouse as well. It might help unblock the communication in this relationship, too.)

Second, listen for the feelings behind what your child is telling you and connect with those feelings. The worst thing we can do in communicating with anyone, including children, is to tell them "You shouldn't feel that way" or "You know you don't feel that way." Avoid passing judgment on their feelings. Accept that children feel just as they say they feel, regardless if you feel the same way or not.

Third, help the children learn to think for themselves. Suggest alternatives; help them explore consequences and outcomes for their plan of action. We want them to learn to think independently, but they will not be able to do this magically when they become adults. They must learn to do this as children and teens. We can be of help by listening to their ideas and helping them to think them through.

Last, follow up. Check back with the child. See how things have worked out. This shows interest in the things that interest the child and keeps the communication flowing.

Remember, even the most loving and concerned parent will occasionally obstruct communication with their children. No one communicates perfectly. Children want more privacy as they get older, but taking away the blocks to communication and using some simple skills can keep the lines of communication open when it really counts. When they are troubled and need to talk with someone, they will know that you are trustworthy and willing to listen.

New Rule: We try to keep the lines of communication open with our children by avoiding those communications habits that hinder it.

August 30

Old Rule: Don't you talk back to me!

Whether we call it "talking back," "being mouthy," or "being sassy," children will occasionally voice their point of view in a negative, disrespectful, argumentative way. Parents will typically react with, "Don't you talk to me that way!" and the fight is on.

When parents permit their children to talk to them in a disrespectful manner without any consequences, children learn to be verbally abusive and rude. This will not serve them well as they go into the larger world. They must change their way of dealing with others or they will be doomed to failure in school, work, and social interactions. Most people will not tolerate this behavior without negative consequences.

More often, parents reprimand their children for such behavior, assigning some consequence even if it is a tongue lashing. Something that might work is a reminder to the child, "I don't talk to you that way and expect that you will not talk to me that way." Of course, we have to be certain that we do not talk to them in an abusive and disrespectful manner for this to work.

However, the focus today is on letting children express their opinions. Old authoritarian methods of child rearing say, "Children should be seen and not heard." This is no longer appropriate and workable. We want to assist children to think for themselves and verbalize their thoughts and opinions so that they will be able to do so outside of our homes. We want them to be able to disagree respectfully with others, including us. This is the challenge, allowing them to speak their minds and offer their thoughts, even when they collide with our opinions and values.

I have heard many people say that the only safe opinions in their home when they were teenagers were ones that agreed with the parents. Opinions that differed from the parents were ridiculed or punished in some other way. They did not, however, change their opinions to conform to their parents. They stopped talking to them. They stopped coming to them for advice and help in working through difficulties. They stopped communicating. This is the unintended consequence of not allowing children to speak their mind: silence.

New Rule: While I insist that my children speak respectfully to me, I allow them to express their opinions and thoughts without ridicule or punishment.

August 31

Old Rule: There are losses and hurts in life from which it is impossible to recover.

Sometimes living hurts. Life is filled with losses, some of them devastatingly painful. We lose relationships with others through abandonment, death, and changes in life circumstances. We suffer loss of opportunity, loss of youthful vitality and promise, and eventually loss of health. Tragedy and pain are real and inevitable, as is the grief we feel when we lose that which is important to us. However, even in the midst of tragic and painful circumstances, human beings have within them a marvelous capacity to grieve and heal.

In some families, however, there are hurts and losses that are never healed. The pain of loss remains an open wound. Family members may actively cultivate the wounds, never permitting them to heal. The pain of these unhealed wounds poisons today's relationships saying, in effect, "Because we have suffered this loss, we will never be happy again and those who care about us are permanently sad, too." To re-embrace life and experience joy is labeled as betrayal, lack of concern, or selfishness, thus the pleasures of the present are either lost or ignored.

We can grieve losses and move beyond them to enjoy the relationships and possibilities that remain and embrace new ones. While we never forget the loss, we can permit ourselves to heal and model this emotionally healthy process for our children.

New Rule: I want to show my children how to grieve the losses we all experience and move beyond them to find renewed happiness and purpose in life.

September 1

Old Rule: Life is to be survived, not enjoyed.

We blame the Puritans for this rule, but evidence suggests that the Puritans actually had fun and enjoyed their lives. However, many families view enjoying life as unnecessary, believing, instead, that life is intended for hard work, doing one's duty, and taking one's commitments and responsibilities quite seriously.

All of these are laudable virtues, but to focus entirely on commitment, work, responsibility, and duty is to miss half of life. All of the world's great religions view life as a gift, a wonderful gift. What are we to do with such a marvelous gift? Frown and act serious and put off taking pleasure in it until all work is done and all responsibilities and duties are fulfilled. Of course not. Gifts are to be enjoyed and this marvelous and gracious gift is to be enjoyed above all others.

Relax, enjoy the life that has been given to you, and take pleasure from the lives of those around you. Luxuriate in the endless abundance of nature and the commonplace joys that surround us every day. Learn to stop and indulge in the small pleasures of life and add a few big ones for good measure.

If you have been living by this old family rule so long that you have no idea what would bring you pleasure, start with what you think you might like. If this does not work move on to the next most likely thing. There is no scarcity and you won't use up your quota of enjoyment by experimenting. Cultivate the acquaintance of those people you might have previously dismissed as frivolous and irresponsible. Chances are they know how to have fun and even though their lives might be a bit out of balance toward the pleasure side, you need them to help you bring yours into balance.

Lastly, learn to laugh at the small stuff. Learn the difference between what is important and what can wait. Develop balance between irresponsibility and viewing everything as terribly important. Once again, mental and emotional health lies in the balance between two extremes. (I worked in a trauma intensive care unit at one point in my career. I have seen life and death situations and most of things we take seriously are not!)

The ability to derive joy from life is one of the finest inheritances we can give our children, but we cannot give it to them until we give it to ourselves. So get out there and enjoy yourself.

New Rule: In our family we appreciate the gift of life and every day we find moments to take pleasure in this gift.

September 2

Old Rule: Don't take risks. Huddle together! It is a dangerous world out there!

Fear is a sensible, rational reaction to a perceived threat and granted there is much to fear in our world. We are bombarded daily with information concerning threats to our children and ourselves. Sometimes it seems the only sensible thing to do is to withdraw into the safety of our family and home and bolt the door, keeping the unsafe world at bay.

While few families actually retreat totally into their homes, many retreat emotionally and intellectually. They withdraw from those outside the family, avoiding relationships that require trusting another. They withdraw from the world, avoiding new experiences and new places. They withdraw intellectually, not allowing their children or themselves to learn about different ideas and beliefs. Fearing that which is different from themselves, they huddle together. Fear is contagious. It is particularly contagious from parent to child.

However, such isolation is debilitating to children. It is impossible to completely avoid the outside world, but it is possible to fear it so much that we do not take risks and do not learn how to deal with new people, ideas, and situations. Therefore, children do not develop competency in dealing with those that are different from themselves. Furthermore, they do not learn about the pleasures and challenges that are beyond one's family and the familiar.

While it is vital that we teach our children caution, discretion, and critical thinking, we must also teach them to take risks and to learn about and be a part of the world around them. Only then can they feel competent and effective in whatever path they choose out in the world beyond their family.

New Rule: We teach our children to explore the world around them, not to fear it. We teach them to take manageable risks.

September 3

Old Rule: They are our relatives and we have to love them.

There is a myth that states because we happen to be related to someone, especially if that person is older than us, we must be blind to all of his or her faults. Even if they behave badly, we must not say what is obvious. There is a corollary to the myth that says we should not speak to that person about our feelings concerning their behavior. It is usually permissible, however, to complain to everyone else about that person, but only if you are an adult.

We tend to pass this myth onto our children, admonishing them not to voice their negative feeling about relatives, especially older ones, even to us. We may at times deny their perception about the reality of the family situation and the behavior of others. This subtle form of the "Don't talk" rule not only causes children to question their own reality and to feel guilty about their feelings of anger and distaste for a relative, but it also keeps them from talking with their parents about their concerns and their feelings.

Negative feelings about relatives are a normal part of family life. To deny them and tell children, "Don't talk that way about our relatives." passes up a wonderful opportunity to teach our children about accepting people, tolerating the idiosyncrasies of others, and respecting others. It also teaches children to attend to and value their feelings and opinions. This skill may some day keep them from being victimized by someone they are supposed to trust and not speak ill of.

New Rule: We allow our children to express their negative feelings and perceptions about older family members to us. We

325

take this opportunity to teach them valuable lessons about living successfully with others, while paying attention to their feelings of wariness and discomfort.

September 4

Old Rule: Don't speak ill of the dead.

Human beings are endowed with a wonderful capacity to forget the bad and recall the good. Fortunately, memories of misery and hurt in past relationships dull and fade with time, especially for emotionally healthy people. There is, however, a difference between letting go and forgiving those who may have wronged you, knowing that the relationship is truly over and that one must move on for one's own sake, and making myths about those whose behavior was less than exemplary.

One of the characteristics of a dysfunctional family is the habit of making myths when reality is uncomfortable or embarrassing. Many of the myths that families concoct surround the dead. We are all familiar with these myths, the difficult, irascible, spouse that the wife complained bitterly about for 30 years becomes "my beloved husband", while the bitter, mean, departed grandmother becomes saintly. In reality this behavior stems from an old superstition that if one spoke ill of them, the dead would return to haunt the one who disparages them. I doubt we still feel the need of such protection.

While it is good to forgive and develop objectivity and emotional distance from the difficulties of a past relationship, such myth making sets a hypocritical standard for our children. In such circumstances, children usually know the truth and the nature of their relationships, but are not allowed to speak the truth simply because the person has died.

Wouldn't it be a powerful lesson in human relationships and forgiveness if we acknowledge that there were problems in the relationship and at the same time let go of resentments, forgive, and let the past be the honest past?

New Rule: I let my children speak honestly to me about others, including those who have died. Along the way, I find opportunities to teach them about forgiveness and letting go.

September 5

Old Rule: Cleanliness is next to godliness.

My children used to flinch and run whenever I came at them with the washcloth, vainly attempting to keep faces and hands on busy little bodies clean. Most mothers spend a great deal of time, energy, and money attempting to keep children and their surroundings as clean as possible.

We read and hear reports about bacteria, food born illnesses, and the dangers of coming into contact with all varieties of germs. I even saw a study that preported to advise parents (let us face it

– mothers) which stall in public bathrooms is usually the cleanest. Manufacturers are eager to sell us household disinfectants and hand cleaners for our purses to keep children germ-free when we are out and about.

Just when we thought that we were doing the right thing, another study comes along that suggests that mothers are keeping their children too clean! This study contends that by making their environment too clean and free from contamination by germs we have contributed to the rise in allergies and asthma by not giving the immune system enough to do. We just cannot win!

Or can we? Want to know how to win this battle? Land in the middle! Once again the middle ground is where common sense and health, both physical and emotional, lie. All of these scientific studies are interesting and informative, but children will get dirty. It is part of the fun of being a child. Some dirt will not adversely affect their health, but your sanity may be affected if you try to keep them disinfected and germ-free. Cleanliness, like most things in life, is best practiced in moderation.

New Rule: I know it is impossible to keep my children germ-free, so I will use common sense and moderation in helping them stay clean.

September 6

Old Rule: Always be pleasant. If you haven't anything good to say, don't say anything at all.

We southerners have civility and pleasantness down to an art form. In the south we are noted for not saying anything about anyone that is unpleasant, at least not to his or her face. As the author Mary Hood says, "Even when we are being critical, we qualify our statements. For example, 'Aunt Mary burned the barn down. Bless her heart.' Or 'Grandpa exposed himself in the Piggly Wiggly again. God love him.' We couch our criticism of others in the most gentle and civil terms. It is one of the things that make life in the south so interesting and complicated.

However, in some families it is never okay for anyone to be unpleasant or the least bit critical of others. This is part of a conflict avoidance strategy that keeps unpleasant matters from being discussed in the family. However, these unspoken complaints and conflicts do not go away but continue, adding to the stress of family life. One cannot live with another and not have conflict. You cannot live without experiencing unpleasant situations that one needs to discuss. When children are reprimanded for bringing up unpleasant matters or when adults do the same in their relationships with each other, children learn there are subjects that are not okay to discuss. These are often the very subjects that should be talked about within families. When this rule is in force, conversations are limited to the most innocuous subjects, like weather, sports, recipes, and how cute the new baby is, while avoiding other more important, yet uncomfortable, subjects.

Artificial pleasantness in the face of conflicts and difficulties is no more functional than constant complaining and negativity. When we put the icing of pleasantness on the moldy cake of unspoken feelings and conflicts, we are not making them go away, we are just temporarily hiding them.

Children need both our willingness to listen to their concerns and criticisms and to hear us verbalize our own concerns and criticisms in a non-abusive manner. We need to model for them functional conflict resolution in which we voice our concerns, ask for specific changes in behavior, and resolve conflicts through discussion and negotiation.

New Rule: While we value harmonious, courteous relationships with others, this does not mean that conflicts that require action and resolution do not arise. When conflicts do arise, I teach my children, by my example, to handle them in a constructive manner.

September 7

Old Rule: Keep the peace.

Just in case you are wondering, "peace at all costs" families are not confined to the South. They can be found virtually everywhere, and they all look pretty much the same. These families are usually headed by someone who has experienced the pain of rage and violence in their home as a child. They have sworn to themselves that they will not create a home where people argue and get hurt by out of control anger. This is an understandable and desirable goal, but they go too far. In their fear and avoidance of anger, they prohibit all forms of disagreement. They mistakenly assume that what is not talked about is not there.

As a counselor, I usually know when I encountered someone from such a family when I ask them about their family and the reply is a tight lipped, "We are close." This usually means that there are many issues, hurts, and resentments that the family is not talking about. It also means there is great fear of conflict and what will happen if they begin to talk about how they really feel.

In the absence of talking about issues within the family, there is a feeling of being locked into a system with those one both loves and hates. One feels guilty about the anger, but also fears talking about it. If you try talking about it, other family members silence you in some manner. Children in these families feel the tension and fear within the family, while learning the dysfunctional techniques of conflict avoidance. They also tend to pass these detrimental ways of dealing with problems on to their own families.

The only way to change this pattern and teach our children a different way of dealing with this fear is to model more constructive problem solving in our homes and refuse to be hushed up by our extended family. If we have not experienced constructive ways to handle anger and conflict, we can learn to do so and pass these techniques on to our children (see November 2 - 7). This is the only way to turn the tension ridden "keep the peace" family into a truly peaceful haven for all family members.

New Rule: Accepting the fact that all families experience conflict, I will learn to handle conflict successfully so that I can model these life-enhancing skills to my children. I will teach them that anger is a normal emotion that can be expressed without hurting others.

September 8

Old Rule: Don't expect to be happily married.

While the media, religious instruction, school classes, and self-help books, as well as the relationships of other married people may provide some information, the most potent information our children receive about marriage comes from us - their parents.

What are we teaching them? Are we teaching them that conflicts arising in marriage can be resolved when both partners work together, or are we teaching them that one partner does all of the accommodating? Are we teaching them to honor their commitments or that when problems arise divorce is the best solution?

Are we telling them that the basis of marriage is fidelity and trust or that it is permissible to have affairs and what feels good at the moment is more important than building a lasting relationship? (In case you believe children do not know about affairs, let me assure you these secrets seldom remain secret and ultimately children do know the truth.)

Are we teaching them that conflicts are best resolved by screaming, crying, hitting, storming out, slamming doors, threats of divorce, and getting even, or are we modeling for them that conflicts can be resolved without doing injury to the other partner?

Are we teaching them that two parents are not important and that one partner can walk away and create a "new family" and simply forget or throw away the old one? Are we teaching them that if parents must divorce or if they were never married one does not divorce ones' children? Are we teaching them that caring for the children one creates is a life-long responsibility?

Are we teaching them that marriage is boring and stale and does not bring happiness or that marriage can be the most meaningful relationship of one's life, if one invests in it?

Just as in every other area of our lives, our beliefs and behavior concerning marriage are what we teach our children. What are we teaching today?

New Rule: I must look at my own attitudes and actions in order to teach my children how to have a lasting, successful, satisfying marriage.

September 9 and 10

Old Rule: Having a father is not important. Children reared by their mothers do just fine.

We have seen a dramatic rise in the number of children being reared in single parent homes. These children, reared mostly by their mothers, are the majority in many communities. Many of them have little or no contact with their fathers. They have never lived with their fathers or have been separated from their fathers through divorce or broken relationships. It is also not uncommon for children to have a series of stepfathers or live in "fathers" who come and go with little or no commitment to the children in the household. Such actions add to the belief many young people have that you cannot trust men to stay and that it is perfectly okay for men to have several "families" for which they have little or no commitment, involvement, and responsibility.

This sad commentary on fathering and the state of relationships between adults is presumed to have little negative effect on children as long as they have a stable relationship with their mother. Those who study children and families are beginning to discover that this is simply not true. While having a mother who is a continual presence in children's lives is important, having a father is equally important. Individual children reared without the presence of a father have survived and thrived, but social scientists and others are speaking out on the potentially devastating results of being reared without a relationship with a father.

According to the National Fatherhood Initiative, a non-profit, non-partisan, non-sectarian national civic organization founded in 1994 to confront the growing problem of father absence, 75 percent of children who live in single parent homes will experience poverty and its devastating effects before they turn 11 years old. Only 20 percent of children reared in two parent families will experience poverty. Children under the age of 6 with unmarried mothers are five times as likely to be poor as those living with married parents. More than half of all poor children under the age of 6 live only with their mothers.

Those children who grow up without a father have higher rates of suicide, lower intellectual and educational performance, and higher than average levels of mental illness. Children in single parent homes are at least twice as likely to become involved in drug and alcohol use. Violent criminals are overwhelmingly males who grew up without fathers. Various studies have found that up to 60 percent of rapists, 75 percent of adolescents charged with murder and 70 percent of long-term prison inmates grew up in fatherless homes. In fact, the chief predictor of crime in a community is the percentage of father absent households.

Girls, who live in single parent families, when compared to those living with both parents, are more likely to begin sexual activity at a younger age and become teenage parents.

A bleak picture, indeed. However, if you are a single parent, do not despair. There are many children from single parent homes who do well. However, it is likely that you and your children will experience greater stress than those families with two committed, responsible parents.

There is a reason why it takes a woman and a man to create a child, for it also takes a mother and a father to help rear a child. Fathering does matter!

New Rule: As an individual and as a citizen, it is important that I support responsible fatherhood.

September 11

Old Rule: You should have been a boy. You should have been a girl.

Early in my career, I worked as a nurse in the post-partum and newborn nursery departments of a large hospital. Having seen mothers who risked their lives to have babies, as well as diabetic mothers who risked their eyesight and their kidneys, or seeing parents face the emotional devastation of losing a child or having a severely handicapped child, I admit that I have little empathy or patience with those who are disappointed when they have a healthy baby, but not the sex they wanted.

When parents have a strong preference for one sex and have the other, children often grow up feeling that they are a mistake and a disappointment. This is true even if the parents do not directly express their desire to have a child of the opposite sex. Since boys continue to be more valued than girls in most cultures, this affects more girls than boys. In counseling, women often reveal they knew from earliest childhood that they were a disappointment and a mistake. No matter how good they were or how much they attempted to please their parents, they knew they were somehow inherently flawed. These feelings have a devastating effect on self-esteem and are very difficult to overcome no matter what their level of accomplishment. As a matter of fact, such people are often driven to succeed without knowing where the sense of having to earn approval from others, especially their parents, and even the right to exist comes from.

To parents who have such strong preferences, I want to say, "Grow up!" "Get in the real world! Talk with couples who are struggling with infertility, have lost children through miscarriage, or who have a severely handicapped child!" "Count your blessings!" "Get a life!"

New Rule: A child of either sex is a blessing. Every child is an opportunity for joy and fulfillment as a parent.

September 12

Old Rule: Don't worry too much about talking to your kids when they are young. The teenage years are when you really need to communicate with them.

When I teach marriage and family classes, we spend a lot of time talking about family communication. Many students relate that now that they have reached late adolescence their parents want to talk. Their parents want to know their thoughts and feelings about sex, relationships, and prospective career choices. All of a sudden parents are interested in what is happening. As one of my young male students, whose father was preoccupied with his own life for much of his childhood, said shaking his head in disbelief, "My dad wants to be my friend now. He wants to talk to me about everything."

By the time our children reach young adulthood it is usually too late for us to begin building a relationship. The time to communicate with our children is when they are small, when they really want to talk to us, not when they are adolescents and have many people to talk with.

Talking with children requires no complex skills. All you need is the willingness to take some time and the ability to listen without lecturing, passing judgment, and taking over with your point of view. Instead, share just as you would with a friend.

If you are having difficulty getting started, take your child out to eat, take a ride in the car with the audio system and the cell phone off, or take a walk and begin the conversation by commenting on something you see along the way. (It is best to make this a private time for you and one child.) Begin by sharing something that interests you. The child, especially if they are in elementary school, will usually take it from there. You will find that they are eager and willing to talk and you will learn so much.

Start talking now. Adolescence is too late! Build rapport and communication early so that when the difficult years of adolescence come you and your child will have the basis for continuing the dialogue.

New Rule: Learning to communicate with my children when they are young not only makes parenting much easier, but also a lot more fun.

September 13

Old Rule: Silence.

When some of us are displeased, we simply stop talking. We clam up and give those around us the silent treatment. We may mistakenly believe that the silent treatment is preferable to shouting and the verbal expression of anger. We arc wrong!

The silent treatment is actually a control game. When we are silent, we are attempting to gain control over others. Others are left guessing about what they have done wrong and/or what they can do to remedy the situation. This is particularly true of children. The silent treatment is not only an ineffective way of disciplining and communicating with children, it is also abusive. The younger the child the more abusive it is. Children often view the silent treatment as a withdrawal of love and will anxiously attempt to figure out what they have done and try to pull the parent back into relationship with them. When parents withdraw into silence, children often feel a sense of panic and insecurity. In truth, this panic may be precisely the reaction the parent is seeking. This dysfunctional manner of settling conflict is a powerful lesson to our children that may be carried down through the generations.

Occasionally it is necessary to tell someone, including children, with whom we are quite angry that we cannot talk now and must wait until we are less angry and more rational. Nonetheless, telling others what has caused us to be angry or hurt and to ask for what we need is a more effective, functional, and less destructive way to handle conflict. An angry raised voice is preferable to several days of the silent treatment. If we have the courage to tell others about what is on our minds and what we need, difficulties within the family have a fair chance of being resolved. Try it. The only thing we have to lose is our dysfunctional, destructive effort to control others.

New Rule: I do not use silence in an attempt to control the behavior of others, including my spouse and my children. I have the courage to talk about what I feel and what I need. If someone attempts to use silence to control me, I refuse to be manipulated into a frantic attempt to guess what is wrong and how to fix the problem. I will simply inform them that I would like to hear what the problem is, but that I am not responsible for knowing what I have not been told.

September 14

Old Rule: Keep the secret.

Family secrets, all families have them. The unplanned pregnancy that ended with a child being adopted out of the family, the alcoholic uncle who disappeared, the cousin who committed suicide, all of these secrets are painful and many feel they are best forgotten and never mentioned again.

Often we believe if we do not talk about these matters that they will be forgotten and will not affect the family, especially the children. However, such secrets do not go away, no matter how much we attempt to hide them. Mysteriously they linger, casting a shadow over the family even those who do not actually know them.

As a counselor, I listened as clients talked about learning information later in life that would have answered many questions for them while they were growing up. It would have helped them if they knew the truth because they always knew that something was wrong. Often what they believed was worse than the truth or they mistakenly believed that they were somehow at fault.

While I am certainly not advocating that small children be told all of the painful family history, I believe that as children grow into adolescents they can handle the truth about family problems and history, especially truths that may affect them. Such history might include substance dependence, mental illness, HIV-AIDS, the death of a sibling, or the reasons for rifts in the extended family.

When we are honest with our children, we teach them that human beings can cope with almost anything if they know the truth and have adequate support. In short, the truth will make you free, but first it might make you uncomfortable.

New Rule: As my children grow into young adulthood, I am honest with them about the unpleasant realities of human existence. I use my adult judgment about the timing of this information and help them to understand and cope with unpleasant and puzzling information. We do not keep secrets because they often hurt us more than the truth.

September 15 & 16

Old Rule: Parental alcohol and drug addiction has little effect on children as long as the home is kept intact and they have food, clothing, and shelter.

Because alcohol and drug abuse or addiction effects about 10 to 20 percent of the adult population at any given time, an enormous number of children are being reared in homes with parental substance abuse.

Most of us would agree about the adverse affects of parental substance use when children lack food, clothing, shelter, and medical care. However, there are other effects that are initially less obvious that are just as damaging to children. These effects have to do with the nature of mood-altering chemical use and the ability of the parent, who is under the influence, to parent effectively.

First of all, human beings use drugs and alcohol to alter how they feel, hence, the term "mood-altering chemical." Even alcohol is used primarily to alter the function of the brain, thus altering how we feel. Most mood altering chemicals numb feelings. We feel better under the influence because we do not experience unpleasant emotions. However, mood-altering drugs do not just numb unpleasant feelings. They numb all feelings. One who is under the influence is emotionally less available, thus children who are reared by those who are frequently under the influence are parented by adults who are emotionally numb and unavailable to them.

Second, all mood-altering chemicals lower inhibitions. One of the primary diagnostic criteria for substance abuse is doing something under the influence that one would not do while sober. Such lowering of inhibitions leads to a rise in child abuse, including physical, sexual, and emotional abuse. Those who are under the influence are less patient when their children misbehave. They say and do things that they may not if sober. Over 50 percent of childhood sexual abuse occurs when the perpetrator, usually someone known to the child, is under the influence of inhibition lowering drugs and alcohol.

Third, as the use of mood altering chemicals increases, the primary "love" relationship becomes the chemical, not the people and certainly not the children in one's life. Obtaining and using the chemical becomes more and more important as use increases and physical and emotional dependency develops. Parents who habitually use drugs and alcohol are neglectful. The more they use, the more neglectful they become. Emotional neglect starts early in the using career of the parent. As one of my former clients said, "What do you think it does for your self-esteem when you realize that the contents of a small brown bottle are far more important to your father than you are?"

As a counselor, I often heard those who are chemically dependent say, "My using doesn't affect anyone but me." This is denial in action. Such denial is one of the primary symptoms of chemical dependency. In reality, the abuse of mood-altering chemicals affects everyone who comes in contact with the abuser, especially their children.

New Rule: The abuse of mood-altering chemicals negatively affects everyone in the family, especially children who are helpless to prevent the effects of that use on themselves and their family.

September 17 & 18

Old Rule: Sure, I smoke a little pot. It doesn't hurt anyone. Besides, it is less dangerous than alcohol.

Using marijuana is so common in our culture that we almost view it as a normal part of adolescence and young adulthood. If the figures are to be believed, marijuana is easily available and widely used among many different segments of our culture. Indeed, the laws against marijuana use are practically unenforceable because its use enjoys such wide acceptance. Marijuana is so ubiquitous in schools and places of recreation that adolescents, including very young adolescents, have to make the decision not to use marijuana rather than to use it.

Among users, marijuana is considered a fairly innocuous way to relax and unwind, much less debilitating and dangerous than alcohol. Therefore, pot use among parents is fairly common. But is marijuana safe?

Marijuana is not one psychoactive chemical, like alcohol or cocaine, but many chemicals, well over 300, of which about 70 are psychoactive, that is they alter brain function. The marijuana currently being sold is about 20 times more potent than that sold in the 1960's and 70's. This is due in large measure to the scientific expertise of the illicit marijuana grower. It is a unique and complex drug. Yet, we actually know little about its effects on the brain, both short-term and long-term. Because it is illegal, produced and distributed in uncontrolled conditions, its quality and potency vary greatly. Therefore, the effects, both desirable and undesirable, vary.

What we do know is that using marijuana during pregnancy is dangerous to the developing child. Marijuana acts on the brain tissue of the user and it also acts on the immature neural tissue of the child. Its use during pregnancy, especially early pregnancy when the mother might not even know she is pregnant, has been implicated in learning and behavioral problems. These problems may not be apparent during infancy, but will surface as the child begins to interact with others and goes to school.

Marijuana is also a cancer-causing agent. Like tobacco smoke, it is irritating and hazardous to the respiratory system of users and those exposed to second hand smoke.

Like all other mood altering chemicals, marijuana numbs feelings, thus rendering the user emotionally unavailable to those around them, including their children. Because it does not produce the dramatic withdrawal symptoms of alcohol or narcotics, many do not view marijuana as physically addicting, but psychological dependence is certainly possible. Psychological dependence on marijuana has the same symptoms as psychological dependence on any mood-altering chemical: preoccupation with obtaining and using the chemical to the neglect of relationships and responsibilities. Those who are psychologically dependent use marijuana when confronted with problems or stressors. They fail to solve problems or grow emotionally. Instead, they simply "get high". Life problems stack up and go unresolved.

Marijuana use is illegal despite its wide spread use and acceptance. Using marijuana teaches children disrespect for the law and teaches them to break the law if they can avoid being caught.

Most users, if they were being honest, would be upset if their children began to use. Even those who are the most ardent concerning legalization have serious reservations about its use among children and adolescents. (This does not count those who think it is amusing to blow smoke into the face of a small child to see them get "high" or think that it is "cool" to use with their kids.)

Marijuana is not a simple drug. It is a complex drug with complex reactions. Perhaps it is an unnecessary complication to introduce into the lives of our children.

New Rule: Parental use of marijuana has a negative effect on the lives of children. Responsible parents who use marijuana usually decide that their children's well being must come before their use of this mood altering, psychologically addicting chemical.

September 19 & 20

Old Rule: Violence on television, video games, and in the movies has no effect on children.

Yeah, right! The media has an effect on everything else we do: what we eat, what music we listen to, what we wear. But it doesn't have an effect on behavior?! Give me a break! Even the military uses video games to train soldiers for the battlefield!

Reviewing a number of studies, the American Psychological Association concluded that media violence has a number of detrimental effects on children. First, it tends to desensitize them to violence. When human beings see repeated violent acts, their emotional reactions tend to become blunted. They do not react as strongly, even to the most horrifying events. Children who view recurring violence have been shown to have less sympathy for victims and tend to be less alert to violence. Paradoxically, children who are exposed to media violence tend to view the world as a frightening and dangerous place and to overestimate their chances of being exposed to violence in the actual world.

Second, children exposed to media violence tend to view aggression as a way to solve problems. The media tends to glorify and portray as heroes those who commit violent acts, but seldom depicts the resulting suffering, death, and incarceration. Therefore, children do not see the consequences of violent behavior accurately depicted; they only see that a problem was resolved by violence. Most portrayals of violent heroes in the media are male. As a result our boys are more at risk for acting-out aggressively than girls, but sadly girls are also getting the message and they are catching up.

Children in our culture are exposed to the media from early childhood, including television, in-home videos, and video games. Many children watch four or more hours of television daily. While this is too much exposure, it is a reality in many homes. Due to children's immature thinking, they have difficulty determining what is real from fantasy. (Look at the struggle that the average 6 or 7 year-old has with whether or not to believe in Santa Claus.) Children are often unable to accurately tell the difference between fantasy violence, which has few consequences, and actual violence with many consequences.

Earlier studies also found that viewing violence correlates with at least a temporary increase in aggressive behavior in children. What children see they want to try out. Since the media portrays this as somehow okay for adults, they are given at least temporary permission to do it themselves.

The media response to such data is that this is a parental problem and that while most of today's parents have seen violence in the media, they are not violent. The depiction of graphic media violence has increased, not only in so-called entertainment television, but also in television news programming which tends to show horrific incidences over and over to an increasingly desensitized audience. Indeed, most adults who view violence do not themselves act out violently, but most of today's parents were not exposed to the level of graphic violence that our children currently view.

Parents do have a responsibility to monitor their children's exposure to the media and most parents try, but parents have a lot of other things to do and are not always with their children. Even the most diligent parent cannot screen out the violent image that unexpectedly appears on the screen or what their children might see at other children's homes or with a sitter. As children grow, certainly after they reach school age, parents cannot be 24 - 7 monitors and should not have to be. The media has much of the responsibility for what they put into public view, just as cigarette manufacturers have some responsibility for the way they have marketed to young potential smokers.

What can we as parents do? Obviously, we must continue to monitor and limit exposure to media violence. Second, when our children are exposed, we can interject our own thoughts and values concerning such behavior and keep an open dialogue with our children about what they see and hear. Lastly, we can become active in the efforts to limit the amount of violence that the media produces. Write letters (sponsors and programmers really do attend to them) join organizations that are working to reduce violence, and let your voice be heard in defense of your children.

New Rule: Violence as depicted in the media does have a detrimental effect on children. As a parent it is my responsibility to protect them and, whenever possible, moderate its effects by expressing my feelings about such behavior.

September 21

Old Rule: Movies and television do not teach my children anything about sex and relationships.

Outside of their parents, the media is probably the most powerful purveyor to children of information about relationships and sexuality. Therefore, it is important that we look closely at the messages these powerful sources send.

By the time children reach school age they have watched hours upon hours of television and videos, including daytime dramas, "talk shows," and prime time television shows intended for adults. What are the consistent themes and messages of these shows? They often give the message that sex outside of marriage is usual, desirable, begins early in a relationship, and is free of consequences. Often those who are sexually active are quite young, giving the message that sex is a right of passage into adolescence. There is also a message, especially from the daytime dramas and "talk shows," that fidelity in a relationship probably does not exist, that divorce and serial marriage is the norm, and having children and lying about or not knowing who is father of one's child is not only usual but also dramatic and exciting.

In the media, desirable women are either depicted as large breasted, with small waists and hips and long flowing hair, such as the Disney heroines Pocahontas and Ariel, or tiny and childlike like Ally McBeal. Neither of these stereotypes is realistic and appropriate, but they influence young women and girls, as well as boys and men.

Men in the media are often portrayed as sexually predatory. "Media men" are frequently perpetual boys who do not take responsibility for their families and the children they create. For example, we see a parade of single mothers on the "talk shows" attempting to force some guy to take responsibility for his child. Although men are often portrayed as slightly stupid, they continue to be depicted as having more power than the women who are intent on forcing them into a committed relationship.

Just as we attempt to filter out and provide an opposing point of view to our children when they are exposed to violence in the media, parents have the responsibility to do the same concerning media sexual and relationship messages.

New Rule: Movies, television, and videos are powerful teachers for my children about relationships and sexuality. My voice also needs to be heard with respect to these important issues.

September 22

Old Rule: It is not necessary to teach children about sex. There is plenty of time when they are teenagers.

Several years ago there was a controversy in our town about the availability of library books explaining sexuality to those in early adolescence. The mother who started the controversy stated that her daughter, who was about 12, "would loose her virtue if she were to read any of these books."

Explaining sexuality to our children, giving them the right information at the right time, is one of the most difficult, yet important, tasks we have. We want to protect them from information they are not ready to have. We also want to convey our values about sexuality as well as knowledge. Most of us are hesitant to talk about sex with our children. We really do not want to face the fact that our children are interested in sex or even sexually active. The situation is genuinely uncomfortable for most parents. No wonder most of us put off having the "sex talk" for as long as possible.

Actually, the "sex talk" is not just one conversation. It is many conversations over the years starting with the simple facts about pregnancy and birth when a new baby comes into the family and continuing through to information about adult sexuality, contraception, and sexually transmitted diseases. Additionally, we feel the need to frame information in terms of sexual values and responsibility. It is impossible to do this all in one conversation.

We are kidding ourselves if we believe that even grade school children do not know about and discuss sex with their peers. We are also deluding ourselves if we believe that our children do not begin to explore their sexuality at an early age. Our culture is replete with sexuality and sexual messages. We use sex to sell everything from perfume to cars. Children see these messages and attend to them just as we do. The media gives many lessons in how to handle their sexual feelings. The culture's voice is very loud and will, if we remain silent, certainly have the most influence over their sexual behavior. Is this really what we want or do we want to be a major influence over the kind of information and sexual values our children hear? If it is the latter, we must overcome our denial and our remnants of shame and embarrassment, open our mouths, and teach them about the responsibilities and the gift of sexuality.

How did the controversy turn out? I am happy to say that common sense and the First Amendment prevailed and the books remained available to young adults.

New Rule: It is important that I teach my children about their sexuality and how to use it responsibly.

September 23

Old Rule: Don't be silly! There is nothing to be afraid of! Be quiet!

Childhood fears can be annoying to parents. We know with our rational, experienced adult mind what is to be feared and what is not to be feared. Children, on the other hand, with their inexperienced, immature intellect often have seemingly irrational fears. Their fears, as annoying and inconvenient as they might be, are nonetheless real.

There was a picture in the local newspaper of a young mother with a small boy about 18 months to 2 years. They are watching a large Canada goose. The mother and the little boy are obviously curious, as is the goose. The little boy, who looks frightened and apprehensive, is peering at the goose from the shelter of his mother's protecting arms.

Our children are in the business of exploring the world and some of it is frightening to them. They lack the experience and cognitive ability to determine what they should be wary of and what is safe. From our protecting embrace we have the opportunity to teach them about this world. Rather than angrily judging and ridiculing children's fears, it is far more productive to accept that a child sees a situation as frightening and attempt to allay those fears with reassurance and information. I know this does not always work and that some children are fearful of a great number of things, but to shame children about their fears does not mean that such fears go away. They are simply unexpressed and grow into bigger, more bothersome, worries.

When we are in a relationship with a person who accepts our feelings, we are more likely to trust them. This is true in relationships between parents and children as well as relationships between adults. When we respect our children's fears, we not only build trust in the relationship, but we also have a valuable opportunity to teach our children about courage. Courage is not the absence of fear, but rather being afraid and doing what needs to be done in spite of fear.

New Rule: I respect my children's feelings, including their seemingly silly, unfounded fears. I attempt to help them overcome their fears with reassurance and knowledge.

September 24

Old Rule: Don't make a fool of yourself! Behave! Be quiet! People will stare!

I was sitting in a doctor's office waiting room along with a number of others, including a young family with a delightful boy about 4 years old. He was looking at a "find the character in the scene" puzzle book and was attempting to show his parents his successful efforts. They ignored him for a while and then the father told him to be quiet in the waiting room. The child was annoying to no one but the father, who was obeying and passing on his own "be quiet in public" rule that his parents probably gave to him. Inadvertently, he was teaching the child to focus not on his own interests, but on the opinions of others. The father was giving his son a dose of shame about being conspicuous even in a positive way. While we want our children to learn to be respectful of the needs and rights of others, don't we also want them to feel free to enjoy life and express themselves?

Conversely, I was sitting in a fast food restaurant located next to a seniors' housing complex. The apartment residents frequented the restaurant and I had a chance to observe all manner of interesting interactions while staying at a nearby beach hotel. A 60's - 70's rock and roll radio station was playing and a man, who was probably over 80, was talking with others and dancing, rather stiffly, but dancing nonetheless to the music. He was obviously enjoying the day, quite unconcerned about the opinions of others and clearly not living by the "behave yourself, be quiet, others will stare" rule. Must we and our children wait until we are 80 to really enjoy ourselves or can we begin to be conspicuously joyful today?

New Rule: While it is important to teach my children to respect the rights of others, it is also important for them to be free to express themselves and not be imprisoned by worries about what others will think if they enjoy life and its many wonders and pleasures.

September 25

Old Rule: Don't be different.

Kaye Gibbons, in her 1998 novel <u>On the Occasion of My Last Afternoon,</u> describes the condition as "quick marrow," that is a "quest for avid living… a natural state of being, enjoyed by those who love life and want more from it than food, and shelter, and sleep. The earnest quest for peace of mind and heart mingled with the desire for titillation, the intrigues of romance, the questioning of why we are on this earth and how we got here, the drive to know why crazy uncles are kept in the attic and the need to know why maple leaves turn scarlet before oak."

A child who is born with a different way of viewing and experiencing the world is a challenge to parents. It is more difficult to rear a child who challenges conventional wisdom, who dreams about wider possibilities, who wants more from life than the ordinary, and is constantly asking "why?" It is also thrilling to have such a child. The challenge is to ground them in practical realities while nurturing their love of life, their curiosity, and their need to explore the mysterious and unique.

When faced with this challenge the worse thing we can do is shame the child for being different, for dreaming and wanting more and attempt to pull them down to the pedestrian and common place. In short, to be different than who they are. The best thing that we can do is accept this special child, to nurture their search for meaning and love of learning, to value their "quick marrow," even if we do not fully understand it. To do otherwise is to destroy the essence, the "marrow," of the child.

New Rule: I accept and cherish my child who sees the world through different eyes, who demands more from life than the ordinary, and who may soar to great heights with my loving support.

September 26

Old Rule: Why can't you be more like…?

Frequently parents use these words out of a sense of exasperation, hoping their children will follow the good example of other children.

However, in addition to sending a "you are not as good as…" message to the children, this rule teaches them to compare themselves to others. Begun in childhood, such comparing becomes a lifelong habit.

Some of us live our entire lives comparing ourselves to others: "She looks better than I do, but she is fatter than I am"; "He makes more money and has a better job than I do, but he is really messing up and going nowhere"; or "They have more money, a nicer, bigger, home and a better car than we do, but these people are living in a run down house in a not too good neighborhood." The comparisons positive or negative go on and on as we play a continual "one up, one down" game.

This comparing is a trap that robs us of time, energy, and creativity. We can always find someone who is doing better and someone who is doing worse on any subjective measure of life's supposed competitions, allowing us to feel artificially superior in some situations while feeling irrationally inferior in others. What would life be like if you freed yourself from this mental prison, if you stopped comparing yourself to others and judged yourself solely by your own standards, goals, and accomplishments? What freedom you would find! What a precious gift to give to our children - the gift of freedom from comparing!

New Rule: In our family we do not waste time and energy needlessly comparing ourselves to others. The only comparisons that matter are those we make measuring ourselves against ourselves. We live our life in accordance with what we have decided is important for us. What freedom!

September 27

Old Rule: You are just like…

I have battled my weight since early childhood. Concern about being fat is one of my earliest memories. My family was concerned about it too, for among the lectures about my weight, I can remember being told that I was "just like Great-grandmother Fisher." Grandmother Fisher was dead long before I was born, but I gather that she was a large woman. Although I believe that my family told me about her to comfort me, what I heard and came to believe as a result of this statement was, "I'm fat, I was born this way, I'm just like a fat grandmother and I will never be any different." How I disliked Grandma Fisher and her hateful, overweight genes that doomed me to a life of being fat!

We know that there is a genetic predisposition to be fat or to be thin, to be short or to be tall, and a great many other physical as well as personality traits, but are not "just like" anyone. To tell our children that they are doomed to be a certain way because of the objectionable traits (we seldom do this with more positive ones) of some relative is not only damaging and cruel, but also untrue.

357

These comparisons are particularly cruel when they come in the context of marital battles and divorce when the child is told, "You are just like your father or your mother." The unspoken message is "You have the same traits that I despise so much in your mother or father and I don't like you either."

Each of us is a truly unique combination of the genetic inheritance of both of our parents. Our genetic predispositions are influenced by a set of environmental circumstances and events that make us individuals. We are not "just like" anyone! Each of us has distinct liabilities and potentials. If our goal as parents is to rear children with high self-esteem and self-respect, we would do well to remember this when we are tempted to say to our children "You are just like…"

New Rule: I appreciate my children's individuality and know that no one is exactly like another. I attempt to treat my children as unique individuals with their own characteristics, talents, and possibilities.

September 28

Old Rule: I'm going to raise my kids just like my parents raised me. I turned out okay.

Many are fortunate enough to have had parents who were loving, attentive, and firm yet fair in their discipline approach. As they become parents themselves, they are able to use their own parents as role models for child rearing. Others are not so fortunate. They want to rear their children differently than they were reared. There are also those parents who have not closely examined how they were reared and blindly go about parenting pretty much as they were parented.

Whatever state we find ourselves, the reality is that child rearing has changed dramatically in the past 20 years. Our children must learn to live in a different world from the one we were reared and certainly different from that of our parents. Technology has altered the nature of our existence. There are many dangers to our children that our parents did not have to consider, but we must prepare our children to handle.

Today, some methods of discipline, especially physical discipline, are not only ineffective but considered abusive. Parents are more focused on teaching by disciplining rather than controlling by punishing. We are challenged to parent much differently than our parents, to find better ways to discipline and prepare our children for an increasingly complex world.

The next month's readings are dedicated to suggestions for effective discipline. The ideas come from a variety of sources and are certainly not an exhaustive list, but they do represent some methods that I and other "seasoned" parents have found to be helpful.

Remember all children are different and what is effective for one child may not be effective for another. What works at one time in a child's life may be ineffective and inappropriate at another stage of development. As in many things, the key to successful discipline is versatility and flexibility. Hopefully, you will find in October's readings some new tools for your discipline tool kit.

New Rule: Because the world has changed since my parents reared me, I need to find effective ways to discipline my children to help prepare them for today's increasingly complex world.

September 29 & 30

Old Rule: We are going to be perfect parents.

Entering "discipline month" would seem to be a good time to remind you about the trap of feeling that you must be a perfect parent.

In a 1993 "Sky" magazine article, Stephen Garber, Marraine Gerber and Robyn Spizman identified four myths about the possibility of becoming perfect parents. "The first myth is that there are such things as perfect parents." We tend to compare ourselves to others, especially those who seem to be having an easier time and whose children seem to have fewer problems than our own. Some parents do seem to have an easier time, but we do not see all that goes on behind closed doors. Actually, children don't need perfect parents; what they need is human parents who are willing to grow and adapt to the needs of their children. The fact that you are reading this book is evidence of your willingness to look at your parenting skills and perhaps learn some new ones. So take some of the pressure off yourselves, relax, and enjoy being parents.

The next myth is that "parents must be parents all of the time." It is true that once we are parents we cannot resign from the job. Being a parent factors into most of what we do, but we are also adult persons with interests and pleasures that have nothing to do with parenting and children. I am always concerned when I see those who do nothing but parent. Their lives are totally involved in caring for their family and an endless series of child-focused activities. They neglect their relationship with their spouse and they neglect themselves. They often end up resentful, exhausted, and estranged from their spouse. Such parents teach their children that being an adult is an endless dreary round of working, chores, and other family related responsibilities. Parents have a right to time for themselves, for adult fun, and for each other without feeling guilty. As a matter of fact, when we take time for what interests us, we usually return more relaxed and patient parents.

The third myth is that "there are perfect children." It should be obvious that just as there are no perfect parents, there are no perfect children! A "perfect person" by definition is one that never gives me any trouble and who always behaves just as I would have them behave. Such a perfect child never existed and never will!

The final myth is that "there is a direct cause and effect relationship between parenting effort and outcome." Some children come with problems that make them more difficult to parent than others. Each child comes with his own unique genetic make-up that will present parents with distinct challenges. Furthermore, what works well with one child may not work at all with another.

As they grow and develop, most children will engage in behaviors that will be difficult for their parents to handle. Other stages of development will be easier. Each stage brings with it its own characteristic opportunities and challenges. Some of these challenges we will feel equipped to handle, while with others we will not be as confident. Fortunately, there are many opportunities to be an effective parent. When we make a mistake, the important thing is that we learn from it. The most essential thing is not to allow the "prefect parent" myth to keep us from enjoying our children.

New Rule: I do not need to strive to be a perfect parent. Not only is this impossible, my children don't even need one.

October 1 & 2

Old Rule: Do you want a spanking? Do you want me to get my belt?

To spank or not to spank - a controversial issue as well as a parenting dilemma. Most of us were spanked, survived it, and might even say that most of the time we deserved it. Some of us are told we should spank our own children so that they will not grow up to be undisciplined hellions and criminals. Yet many of us are uncomfortable with the idea of hitting our children, especially when we tell them not to hit others. We do not want them to get the idea that if you are bigger and stronger you have the right to strike others.

The debate continues, but there are some things we do know about spanking. First of all, a spanking is an open hand on a clothed bottom, using an implement, such as a belt, ruler, hairbrush, or switch, is a beating. We are more likely to bruise or injure children using an implement rather than our hand. Second, spanking has diminishing returns. The more you use it, or threaten to use it, the less effective it becomes. Third, it is not effective at all with older children. Older children will take their punishment and go right on doing what they wish, only next time they will be sneakier.

All of this is not to say that we should not discipline our children. Discipline is an important part of our job as parents. We need to discipline our children not only for their sake, but also for the sake of our culture. Therefore, we need to find effective ways to discipline that teaches children that misbehavior has negative consequences.

What does work? All parents really want is a way of disciplining that either starts or stops a behavior in a timely manner without doing damage to their child or their relationship with that child. If nothing else works, spanking may succeed in stopping a child from misbehaving at that moment, especially if their safety is involved. However, there are many other options that might be even more effective.

Isolating a child or time-out may be effective, provided you are reasonable and consistent about the length of time. Withdrawing favorite things and privileges works well, especially as children get older. Reasoning with a small child does not usually work. They simply do not think like adults. Their brains and thought processes are not as mature as ours, but family meetings in which options for behavior and clearly established consequences for unacceptable behavior are discussed will work, even if there are only two in the family (See Oct. 5 & 6). Threats do not work. If we threaten and do not follow through, children will quickly learn that what we say is empty talk. They will learn to ignore us. Never issue a consequence unless you are willing to carry it out.

Love works. Children genuinely wish to please their parents. Yet, if we are overly demanding, unreasonable, critical and they feel they cannot please us, discipline becomes more difficult. Like adults, children want their own way. Most discipline problems result from tension between these two conflicting desires, wanting to please their parents and wanting to do what they please. Children usually do not misbehave just to drive us crazy or to hurt us. They misbehave because they want to do what they want to do.

Furthermore, what works with one child may not be effective with another. A parental frown, look of disapproval, and a mild rebuke may be enough for one child, while another may require frequent time-outs and withdrawing of privileges. We need to be sensitive to what works with each child and not apply the same methods to all children, just because our parents did it this way or it worked with an older child.

Parents also need to be in agreement concerning discipline. Do not engage in "easy parent- tough parent" games with your children's other parent. Discipline problems only get worse when the parents are not in agreement. Even if you feel that the other parent is being too strict or too lenient, it is far more confusing and destructive to undermine that parent than to back him up. If you disagree, then talk with the other parent and if the rules are changed then tell the children together. Do not add to your parenting stress and difficulties by teaching children to manipulate and play parents against each other.

Remember that the word discipline means, "to teach." We need to keep in mind what we are teaching our children, as we attempt to change their behavior. If nothing else works, spanking may stop children from doing something for the moment, but it should be our last resort, instead of our first option.

New Rule: Disciplining is an important part of being a parent. I have many tools at my disposal when I discipline my children. Spanking is only one of them.

October 3

Old Rule: Because I said so ………

All parents, especially when exhausted and frustrated, have fallen back on, "I'm your parent, do it because I said so." However, when parents consistently use these words in an attempt to discipline their children, they invite the very thing they wish to avoid: active or passive rebellion and an impaired ability to make sound decisions.

When children are ordered to do something, they do not learn to think for themselves. As a result, when children become adolescents and young adults, they may adopt one of two modes of making decisions. First, when a request is made, they rebel and refuse, even when to comply might be in their best interest. They may rebel either outright or silently. That is they may simply neglect to do what is asked of them, even if they have committed to it. They may procrastinate as long as they can, fail to complete the task, or botch it up. In short, they rebel either aggressively or passively. The results are the same. Others are angry with them and mistrustful of their promises.

The second consequence results from the unspoken parental message, "You are not capable of comprehending the problem, formulating a solution, and making a sound decision so I will do it for you." They carry this message into adulthood, assuming that they are not capable of making good decisions. Therefore, they allow others to make decisions for them or drift into decisions by default while reserving the right to criticize others when the results are not to their liking. It is also essential that we do not unintentionally create a situation in which they feel that the only

365

way to gain independence from us and make their own decisions is to rebel.

Giving our children the opportunity to ask "why" helps avoid these destructive behavior patterns. It teaches children to think for themselves. Good parenting means that we teach our children how to make decisions with minor consequence so that when decisions of lasting consequence arise they will be able to decide for themselves what is in their best interest.

New Rule: I teach my children to make decisions by allowing them to ask why and to use their growing intellectual abilities to govern their own behavior.

October 4

Old Rule: Scream! It is the only way to be heard.

We have all felt like screaming and most of us have done it. However, a number of us spend much of our lives screaming. As a result, our children have tuned us out and ceased to listen.

By its very nature, screaming is abusive. It assaults the ears of those around us. It is demeaning to the child and to the person doing the screaming. One does not yell kind, encouraging words. We yell cruel, abusive words. Yelling is not about calm rational problem solving or effective discipline, it is about irrational verbal assault. It says to everyone, "The situation is out of control and I am out of control as well."

Because screaming is abusive, children and others on the receiving end try to protect themselves from it and tune out the words as well as the message. After a while, screamers are not really heard, they are ignored. The only thing they communicate is that they are yelling and out of control. Screamers lose the respect of not only their own children, but also other adults. Screamers are perpetuating the very behavior they are seeking to stop - ignoring their wishes and continuing to misbehave. Yelling simply does not work and it makes a home an extremely unpleasant place to be.

By using screaming and yelling to communicate with family members, we are also teaching our children to do the same. Believing that this is the way to get the point across, they will yell at their friends and perhaps their teachers. Sooner or later, they will yell at us. We will, eventually, reap what we have sown.

If we are to change the pattern, we must first lower the volume. When we begin to speak in a firm lowered voice to our children, making eye contact with them and stating our thoughts and instructions clearly, they will be initially so astounded that they will likely do what is asked of them. Reserve a raised voice for when the situation is truly urgent or we are extremely angry. Then it will get everyone's attention. Give it a try! You have nothing to lose. It might work and rekindle the respect of everyone around you while saving your voice and energy.

New Rule: We do not yell and scream at one another in our home. We talk to each other with respect. When we are unhappy or angry at the behavior of another we express it decisively, but without screaming.

October 5 & 6

Old Rule: We don't resolve conflicts. Conflicts among members of the family just go on and on.

Each family, if we look closely, probably has several core areas of conflict that come up again and again. These might include keeping the house clean, household chores, respect for the property of others, or use of the telephone. Families may find that they have the same fight over and over, never resolving anything. Everyone walks around feeling resentful and determined to get his or her own way the next time. Parents usually hope the conflict will somehow magically go away. However, the problem does not go away and the same old fight disrupts the family one more time.

Obviously something is not working. There must be a better, more effective, way to resolve family conflicts. Well, there is good news and bad news on this front. The good news is that there is an effective way to settle conflicts. The bad news is that it requires doing things differently and taking risks, as well as work and commitment on the part of the family.

The solution is called family meetings and they really do work. This form of democracy in action may be a radical change for many families. However, such meetings are worth the required time and energy.

The format and rules are simple.

1) Family meeting time should be scheduled on a regular basis, usually once a week. The meeting time takes precedence over all other activities. The TV, telephone, and disc player are turned off,

as are any other distractions. This is an important time and should be treated as such.

2) All persons are equal within the context of meeting. All persons have a right to be heard and their thoughts and feelings respected. There is no name calling, arguing, lecturing, blaming or storming off during the meeting. However, anger and hurt can be expressed verbally. For example, "When _____ happened I was angry/hurt."

3) Any issue within the family is open for discussion, even those in which the children have an objection to the parents' actions.

4) Although the parents have the final say on important issues, for instance a large purchase, all issues are voted on by all of the family members.

5) One family member should chair the meeting and one should keep the minutes. The meeting agenda should be set at the beginning of the meeting, and should probably last no more than an hour.

6) When an issue is brought up, it should be discussed by the parties involved as well as other family members. Solutions are then offered, discussed, and negotiated. When an agreement has been reached on a solution to the problem, the meeting moves on. If the agreed upon solution is not working after a fair trial or if one member of the family does not follow through with their commitment, then the issue may be discussed again at the next meeting.

7) Families should plan a pleasant family time at each meeting. This may be as simple as going for a bike ride together or as elaborate as planning a family vacation.

These are the basic rules. Families of two or families that include members of three generations can use them. They are simple and relatively easy to follow, however, a period of time working out the details may be necessary. You will likely be surprised how eager your children are to adopt such meetings, especially when it is their turn to be chairperson, as they are not only heard, but they are also on equal terms with their parents and siblings.

In the event that one family member is resistant, unwilling to attend the meetings or follow the format, go on with the meeting according to the rules, even if that person is a parent. The reluctant person will usually come along, especially when they realize that important decisions are being made without their input.

Modify the format to fit your family; the important thing is to start settling conflicts within the family in a fair and respectful manner. You may be surprised what you learn about yourself and your children in the context of the meetings and how much you will all grow as you learn new problem-solving skills. It is worth a try. You have nothing to lose and much to gain.

New Rule: In our family we settle conflicts as they arise with the use of regular family meetings.

October 7

Old Rule: We don't have rules here.

Some time ago the "enlightened" parenting wisdom held that we should not say "no" to our children. Saying "no" and establishing limits was thought to stunt their intellectual and emotional growth as well as damage self-esteem. Predictably, this anarchy and chaos did not last long and parents returned to attempting to find a balance between anarchy and rigid control.

However, some parents continue to attempt to rear children without rules. Children, likewise, react predictably. They do as they please and when the parent attempts to discipline, they react with anger and defiance. The parent, lacking the ability or will to adequately discipline, gives up in frustration, allowing the children to do as they please. The children may believe they are free, but in actuality they are just loose. They may even feel alone and unloved.

Children do need fair rules, direction, and limits. Not only do they feel safer with such limits and guidance, but they also feel more cared for, for at the root of such "lassiez faire" parenting is the message, "Do whatever you want, just don't bother me." When parents decide to parent and set boundaries and rules, children feel more valued. Although they will continue to test limits, their behavior will generally improve.

Loving parents realize this and are willing to establish appropriate limits for their children. They know and their children will eventually realize that being loose is not the same as being free and that loving children means a willingness to establish and maintain fair and reasonable limits.

New Rule: We accept the responsibility to set fair boundaries and rules for our children. It is an important part of being a parent and helps prepare children for the world beyond their home.

October 8

Old rule: The rules are the rules, but we don't really mean it.

This cousin to "we have no rules" means that parents may set limits with their children, but give in when the child argues, whines, has a temper tantrum, cries, or simply ignores them.

All parents get tired and, at times, give in rather than remain firm and face the often difficult task of setting and holding to reasonable rules and discipline. Nevertheless, when this becomes a consistent pattern, children learn that Mom and Dad may talk a good game, but if the child argues, whines, or even charms their parent, they can easily get their way. They also learn when Mom and Dad are not allied. Therefore, what they may not be able to get from one parent, they may be able to get from the other. They learn if you don't get what you want, get angry, cry, or manipulate your parents by going first to one and then the other. In effect, we teach them to use the very behaviors we find so troublesome. Consequently, small children become little tyrants and older children become rebellious and unpleasant. Having learned such tactics at home, these behaviors will generalize to other circumstances, including school. As a result children may have difficulty accepting the authority of other adults with resulting negative consequences in school, athletic teams, and other social situations.

Being a parent is time and energy consuming. Being a consistent parent, at least initially, takes even more energy. In the long run, consistent parents who set reasonable rules and limits and are willing to enforce those limits are actually saving themselves a great deal difficulty while teaching their children to accept appropriate limits and authority without self-destructive rebellion.

New Rule: We have reasonable rules and limits in our family. When we set a limit we expend the energy necessary to enforce it with our children. We believe that children need consistent, reliable limits.

October 9

Old Rule: The rules are the rules and we do not deviate from them.

As I get older, it becomes more and more apparent to me that healthy functioning at a personal, family, national, and even global level is found in the middle ground. So it is with parenting. We often find that when we operate in the extremes, for instance when we have few positive expectations for our children or we expect them to be perfect, we create problems for our children and ourselves. The same is true with discipline and limit setting.

While children do need clear, consistent rules and limits that parents are willing to enforce, it is also necessary to be flexible. The parent who rigidly enforces the rules no matter what the situation and how well-reasoned the child's protest invites rebellion and secretive behavior. The child must rebel in order to establish their individuality and grow up.

Parents who believe they have complete control over their children are living in a fool's paradise. In actuality, they will eventually have control over what the child allows them to see. Children will usually not live with this rigidity very long before learning to go around their parents and do what they wish in secret. Believing they are in control, the parent misses the opportunity to guide their children in appropriate behavior and sound decision-making.

Listening to children and being flexible when they would like an exception made to the rule is vital. Even if we decide not to change the limit, it gives us an opportunity to talk with the child and tell them the reasons for our decisions. It also allows the child to feel that they have a voice in what happens in the family. Frequently, this is all that is necessary. For children, like adults, feel better about following any rule when they feel they have been heard and their point of view considered. They will also be more apt to come to the parent for permission to deviate from the limits rather than simply doing it and then facing the consequences if and when they are caught. Being flexible gives us the opportunity to establish healthy patterns of interaction and behavior within the family and avoid destructive ones.

New Rule: In our family, we discuss changes in the limits and rules. Sometimes there is a good reason to change them.

October 10

Old Rule: We don't have a schedule. Life just happens here.

As our children have gotten older, my husband and I are again enjoying the freedom we had as newlyweds. We can pretty much do as we please, when we please. However, I also know the value of routines and schedules while rearing children.

Children need predictability in their lives. It helps them feel secure. They also need a parent to schedule time for meals, rest, and homework, as well as extracurricular activities. Limiting computer and TV time is also important. Children may resist efforts to.schedule their time, but they need the predictable security of a schedule in order to function well personally as well as academically. It is part of our job, however unpleasant and exhausting it may become, to create and reasonably maintain a family schedule.

In those homes where children have no schedule other than the one that they set for themselves, children are less healthy, not as well rested, and do not do as well in school. They are less involved in extracurricular activities. They spend more time watching TV (much of it inappropriate programming), playing computer games, and just hanging out. They are also less likely to feel valued and loved by their parents, who for whatever reason, do not expend the effort necessary to help them maintain a healthy schedule.

Maintaining a sane and healthy schedule is sometimes difficult for parents, and frequently not appreciated by or popular with children, but it is part of the responsibilities of parenting.

New Rule: In our home we maintain a schedule that meets the needs of our children for structure, security, and healthy functioning.

October 11 & 12

Old Rule: In our family, we live by a schedule. No matter what happens, we do not deviate from it.

In some families the schedule is law. They eat at a specified time, as well as do homework and go to bed at a specific time. Children must be at home on schedule, chores must be completed on time, and even recreation is rigidly scheduled. The schedule is maintained no matter what else happens within the family or the needs of the individual family members. The schedule is more important than the people.

As children grow older, they chafe against this rigidity. They rebel and there is conflict and resentment resulting in ever-harsher means of controlling the behavior of the children and maintaining the schedule. Parents find they are exhausted from their attempts to enforce rigid order and the children feel less important than the schedule when it is not flexible enough to meet their needs or allow them to make some decisions themselves.

Once again, healthy functioning is found in the middle ground. As parents, we often find ourselves attempting to balance giving our children the space to make their own decisions and to schedule their own time versus closely supervising their activities.

Naturally, schedules change over time. When children are babies and preschoolers, we sense that they are happier when they have regular meal times, naps, and bedtimes. They are less fussy and life with them is more pleasant if they do not become excessively hungry or tired.

As children enter school, they need their parents' guidance in setting a time for homework, as well as regular meal and bedtimes. They will also need to have their recreation time, especially their TV and computer time, monitored to make certain that a healthy balance is maintained between active and passive activities. Chores also need to be figured into the schedule. As much as children might complain or passively rebel against a schedule, they need it for healthy functioning, as they are not yet able to make constructive time decisions for themselves. Children do, of course, need unscheduled time for play by themselves and with others.

As they grow older they can be given greater latitude about when they will do homework, chores, and other activities within appropriate guidelines. They will not always be under our roof and teaching them about sensible schedules and time management should begin as early as possible. This means letting them begin to negotiate and be responsible for getting their chores and schoolwork done on a schedule they helped to create. This process will certainly accelerate as children move through adolescence and prepare to leave our homes and live independently. All of this requires parental time and energy, but it is an important part of our life skills instruction to our children. As a college instructor, I can usually tell which students come from homes in which they were taught to manage their time effectively versus those who were reared with either rigid schedules from which they are glad to escape and do as they please or those who were reared with little or no consistent schedule. Actually, the behavior and challenges of the two later groups are pretty much the same. They struggle to learn in a hurry what the first group learned throughout their childhood and adolescence, to effectively mange their time.

New Rule: While it is important to have a regular schedule when rearing a family, it is also important to be flexible enough to meet the changing needs of the children and to gradually teach them to take control of their own schedule.

October 13

Old Rule: Why can't you be more like …?

As parents we think we use this technique to teach our children about desirable behavior and achievement. In reality, what we do is foster resentment in our children, not only for us as parents because of our unfair comparisons, but also for the potential role model. How many of us have grown up resenting a brother, sister, cousin, schoolmate, or the child of a family friend because we were told that they were a model of what we should aspire to be? Or we might have been the ostracized, resented, or mistreated innocent victim of parental approval and comparisons. This pattern of resentment may continue into adulthood, robbing us of potentially satisfying relationships.

Actually, this is an ineffective way to teach our children about desirable or expected behavior. A far more effective way to teach them about our expectations is to avoid comparisons and to specifically state what behaviors we would like and expect and what logical or natural consequences will take place if these behaviors do not occur. At the same time we need to accept and value our children, realizing each child has a unique set of abilities and focusing not on comparisons, but on helping our children develop their own talents.

New Rule: I teach my children what is expected of them not by comparing them to others, but by being specific about my expectations and setting up reasonable consequences for misbehavior, while supporting the development of their abilities and talents.

October 14

Old Rule: If you do that again, I'm going to …!

We have all done it, threatened our children if they misbehaved one more time. We have all issued unreasonable, absurd threats of punishment that we were in no way prepared to carry out. We knew this almost as we said it and our children knew it, too. They knew these were angry, but empty, threats. Therefore, they felt perfectly safe in ignoring us and continuing the behavior, knowing that once we were less angry the punishment would be relaxed or completely abandoned.

While we have all done this, it is a dangerous habit. Not only does it undermine our authority with our children, it also tells them that behavior really has no consequences other than idle threats that will be forgotten when the authority figure is no longer angry. We certainly do not want these messages to come across, for it makes effective discipline almost impossible and teaches children to ignore other authority figures, including teachers.

We want to teach our children that behavior has consequences; actually that behavior has reasonable consequences. Therefore, we must issue realistic consequences for unacceptable behavior that we are willing to carry out, consequences that teach children about satisfactory behavior.

This might require that we take a breath, perhaps several breaths, or maybe even a whole day for older children before we decide on a reasonable consequence for their misbehavior.

As children get older you might include them in deciding on the consequences for their objectionable behavior. They might come up with something even more severe than what you had in mind. Such discipline teaches children not only that behavior has consequences, but also that you will keep your word and that they can expect fairness and consistency from you. These are important lessons.

New Rule: In our family behavior has consequences that we, as parents, are willing to uphold.

October 15

Old Rule: You are such a whiny face today!

Whining! It drives parents crazy! It drives me crazy! I hate whining when it comes from a child, but even more when it comes from an adult. However most adults whine, at least a little, especially when we feel sick, overtired, hungry, or stressed. Children whine for the same reasons. Most parents understand this kind of whining and take action to remedy the problem. It is the other kind of whining,

whining for attention that causes parents so much frustration and grates on our nerves.

Children need and will seek the attention of their parents. When they cannot get positive attention, they will do something, like whining, to get negative attention. Even negative attention is preferable to no attention from parents. Furthermore, it works for them. We become angry and punish them in some way or we give in to their demands. We do not generally ignore them. By either getting angry or giving in, we reinforce the very behavior that we find so irritating and want to end.

How would it be if we were honest with our children? How might it change their behavior if we told them we find whining very annoying and we are not going to give in to their demands? Would their behavior change if we told them that if they need our attention that they should please use their regular voice and then begin to ignore any bid for attention or request that is whined? As with any change of behavior be prepared for them to try out the old whiny behavior to see if we are serious. If behavior is to change, we must be willing to remind them again and refuse to listen to requests that are whined. While I don't guarantee that this suggestion will be the solution to all whining episodes, it certainly cannot hurt and may actually work to decrease them. Give it a try. What have you got to lose?

New Rule: I choose not to reinforce bids for negative attention by getting angry or giving into unreasonable demands and whining. I try to give my children positive attention and set reasonable limits and hopefully decrease episodes of whiny behavior.

October 16

Old Rule: You are such a whiny face!

If I could wave a magic wand and eliminate three things from family communication they would be: sarcasm, name-calling, and mocking. All of these, whether parents or children use them, are verbally abusive and damage relationships as well as self-esteem.

When we use sarcasm, mocking, or call our children names, we say, in essence, to them, "I don't care about your feelings or our relationship. Because I am your parent, I have the right to say anything to express my anger." If we were honest with ourselves we would admit that when we viciously attack our children and call them names we are often acting out our anger and powerlessness over another situation. Children, being powerless, become the target of our frustration - our helpless victims.

I am aware that these are tough words about a common set of behaviors. However, these are very destructive behaviors that do a great deal of harm and are not appropriate parenting methods.

As adults we are responsible for what comes out of our mouths when we speak to others, including our children. We are also responsible for handling our adult stressors and anger with our children and others in a non-destructive manner. Given that children learn by our actions, if we verbally assault our children they will eventually talk to us, other authority figures, and other children in the same manner. We will then be upset, hurt, and angry, wonder where they got those words, and complain that they are disrespectful and out of control.

If we want respect from our children, just as in any relationship, we must first respect them. If we want to say, "I won't tolerate your speaking to me that way," we had better be able to add, "Because I don't talk to you that way."

New Rule: In our family we do not use name-calling, sarcasm, and mocking to ventilate our anger toward one another. Our relationships with each other are too important to use these destructive weapons.

October 17

Old Rule: My children must do exactly as I say. I am in control and they must obey me without question.

An acquaintance, whose young adult children struggle with low self-esteem, lack of self-confidence, and making good decisions, confided that he guessed, "The Marine way just didn't work." He had reared his children like his Marine trained father had reared him: get in their face, yell, and demand absolute, unquestioning obedience.

What seems perfectly obvious had somehow eluded him. Children are not Marine Corps recruits that must be molded into combat ready soldiers. It is doubtful that such rigid, controlling authoritarian parenting was ever a successful way to rear children. However, today we know that such methods do not work. While they might result in short term compliance out of fear and intimidation, authoritarian parenting will eventually result in rebellion. Today, there are many ways for our children to rebel; most of them (drugs, alcohol, breaking the law, and premature sexuality) are destructive to children and frightening to parents.

Our culture has changed and we must change with it. This is not to say that we should not discipline our children. On the contrary, it is our responsibility to discipline them. Therefore, we must learn about and use parenting methods that teach them to think before they act, respect the right of others, and value and care for themselves. This takes more effort than the authoritarian, "Do it because I said so." In the long run, the more democratic "Do it for these reasons" approach helps rear more responsible, less self-destructive young adults who have high self-esteem and self-respect. This is ultimately what my friend wanted for his children. He simply could not get there from where he was, using the rigid, authoritarian methods he had learned from his father.

New Rule: The culture that we are preparing our children to enter has changed drastically over the past 50 years and continues to change rapidly. We must learn to adapt our parenting to equip them to function productively and wisely when they leave our home.

October 18

Old Rule: I was reared with too many rules. I want my children to be free spirits. I don't want to crush their spirits with too many restrictions and rules.

I know a young mother with two preschool sons. She disciplines them gently, explaining in great detail why they should choose to behave. She wants them to know that she loves them dearly and appreciates their individuality. She does not wish to crush their spirits or hurt their feelings with her disapproval. She also wants them to love her and never feel angry with her. They are terrible! They talk loudly and constantly when others are talking. When they do not get what they want, they ignore all attempts to discipline them. They are rude to adults and bully other children. They are disagreeable little boys that no one, including other children, wants to be around.

Their mother is frustrated and unhappy with them. She is having a great deal of difficulty handling what she believes are unacceptable angry feelings toward them. She is frightened of them and they know it. On a recent occasion, I witnessed them smiling slyly as she removed them from a situation where they did not want to be. They knew if they were unpleasant enough they would be out of there. Their little spirits are not crushed. They are very powerful! They are in control of their mother!

Children need discipline. Children need to learn how to get along with other people. They need to learn that others have rights, including their parents. They need to realize that bullying others into submission will guarantee that no one will want to be around them and that the world was not set up solely to make them happy. Parents need to accept that noble little savages are still savages and though they may be very angry with us at times, it is our responsibility to discipline them. This is love in action.

New Rule: It is part of my responsibility to discipline my children even if it means they do not feel free to do as their spirits move them. I do this even if they become angry with me.

October 19

Old Rule: It is a terrible thing for children to say, "I hate you!" to their parents.

When I teach marriage and family courses, I encourage students to talk about their own families. Invariably, mothers say that one of the most heartrending moments in their lives occurred the first time their toddler said, "I hate you."

As difficult as they are to hear, these words from a little child may signify that we are doing something right. At the same time they present us with a teachable moment, an opportunity to teach our children a valuable lesson about handling anger.

When we must say "no" to a small child instead of permitting them to do exactly as they please, the natural reaction from the child is anger at being frustrated. Anger is an intense feeling and the only word that a small child has that accurately conveys the intensity of that anger is "hate." They "hate" it that we have said "no" and they want us to know it. The worst thing we can do at this point is to take it all personally, respond angrily ourselves, shame the child for being angry, or respond to our own need to be loved by our beloved child by giving in.

"I hate you" actually means "I'm really, really angry with you." An adult response of "I know you are angry with me now. The answer is still 'no', but it is okay to be angry with me." is more appropriate than, "Don't you ever say that to me or anyone else again," or worse, "When I die, you'll be sorry."

Disciplining children is difficult and requires that parents respond as adults and not with our own childlike hurt feelings. When we can remember who is the child and who is the parent, our job is much easier and children will respond more positively.

New Rule: I know the difference between anger and hate. I expect that when I must say "no" to my children they will be angry, but I know that ultimately the loving thing to do is to set firm, reasonable limits for them.

October 20

Old Rule: Oh, okay! Just stop crying!

There is a psychology of learning principle called "selective reinforcement." It says that a behavior that is occasionally rewarded, even though it may be punished or ignored at other times, is virtually guaranteed to reoccur. In other words, selective reinforcement casts behavior in cement!

When we ignore, fail to discipline, or give into undesirable behavior just because we are tired and want it stopped, we are rewarding the behavior, selectively reinforcing it, and virtually guaranteeing that it will happen again.

Being a parent is difficult. Being a parent when you are tired, stressed, have a lot on your mind, and just want a little peace is really difficult. It is just so easy to give in, to let children have their way, or to buy whatever they want. However, getting a little peace in the short run, guarantees that our job will be more difficult in the long term. As tough as it is at times, sticking to "no" means "no," not "maybe if you cry, whine, pitch a tantrum, or keep asking," will make the job of parenting much easier.

New Rule: I do not selectively reinforce undesirable behavior by rewarding it occasionally. Such inconsistencies only make family life more difficult. Clear, consistent expectations and boundaries are less confusing for children and easier for parents to enforce.

October 21

Old Rule: Wait until your father gets home.

Poor Dad! He is set up again to be the bad guy. Mom is exasperated, fed up. Feeling she cannot deal with the children any longer, she threatens them with Dad. Dad, who may not even know what is going on, is about to be ambushed. Mom expects him to do something about the problem, to fix it for her. However, making Dad the bad guy is not effective discipline. When Mom uses this tactic, she is not only setting Dad up, she is also abdicating her adult role. She has become one of the children in a power struggle and expects Dad to referee. There has got to be a better way to solve the problem!

Fortunately there is! What would happen if Mother maintained her adult role and firmly and even loudly (avoiding a glass breaking range) voiced her feelings of frustration and anger and issued a consequence that would teach the children that the current situation is unacceptable to her? It might work and the problem may be resolved until such time that it becomes the topic of a family meeting involving all family members, including Dad. The result might be that Mother and the children are able to work together and Dad is not forced to play the role of bad guy and even "Daddy" to Mother. In this way Mom gets what she really needs from Dad: consistent support and a break from being the chief caretaker and disciplinarian. Try it! It can't hurt and just might work!

New Rule: In our home the parent who is currently upset with the children's behavior deals with them at that time. Serious, ongoing problems are brought to family meetings for input and problem solving by all members of the family.

October 22

Old Rule: I have always felt so guilty about everything. I don't want my children to grow up that way.

What you felt is not guilt, but shame. Shame is believing we are somehow defective as human beings. Shame is given to us in childhood when we are expected to live up to unreasonable expectations, when we are made to feel responsible for the feelings of others, when we are told that others have sacrificed in order to raise us and we should be constantly grateful, or we feel that no matter what we do, it is not quite good enough to win the approval of our overly critical parents. These are the ingredients of shame, the feeling of being defective.

Of course, these are painful feelings and we do not want to burden our children with them, but we do not want them to leave our homes free from feelings of guilt. Guilt is that pang of self-disapproval we feel when we violate the rights of others. We feel guilt when we violate our own value system. Guilt, its attendant pain and resolve to do better, is what keeps civilization civil. We want to free our children from shame, not the sting of conscience and guilt.

We are responsible for giving our children a set of values, values that we live by and give to them as precious gifts. We also have the responsibility to discipline our children when they violate the rights of others, including their parents and siblings. As our children grow in their understanding of the rights of others, we want them to suffer the sting of conscience (guilt) and accept responsibility for their actions while resolving to do better. As we help them understand they cannot always do as they choose, when they choose, and that their rights stop where another's begins, we help them to learn to live productively in a civilized society. We want them to be free of shame, but to have a healthy conscience that guides their behavior in relationships with others.

New Rule: We teach our children to live by a set of values that includes respecting the rights and dignity of others and to feel guilty when they violate these values.

October 23

Old Rule: If you will just behave yourself, I'll buy you something.

Whenever I go into a large discount department store with a huge toy section, I am glad that I do not have to take young children in there anymore. I see parents with their children begging them for a toy and remember those days when my own children, confronted with the vast array of available toys, begged for them. All too frequently, to buy peace and get my shopping done, I gave in. This was easy when they were small and an item for less that $5.00 would satisfy them. However, when buying good behavior became a habit for both them and me, the price inevitably went up.

It is best not to set this up in the first place. Whenever possible do not take children to the store with you, especially when they are small. I found that when my children were little, hiring a baby sitter actually saved money. Not only was I more relaxed and less stressed, I also spent less because I could think while I shopped, rather than buying things just to finish and get out of there.

Second, learn to reward good behavior with other things like trips to the park or library, reading to them, playing games, or doing together whatever the child enjoys. I realize this demands more time from an already crowded schedule and that buying them something is much faster and less taxing for you - initially. Perhaps if we are so busy doing other things that we must throw toys at our children rather than spend time with them, then we are too busy and our priorities are not balanced. What most children need is less stuff and more us!

New Rule: While I do expect my children will behave without rewards, I choose to reward good behavior with family time rather than new toys.

October 24 and 25

Old Rule: Bedtime is such a hassle at our house. I dread putting the children to bed!

How did it get to be this way? Children have been going to sleep for thousands of years, yet in the past few years bedtime has become a virtual battleground between parents and children. Like most people who write about parenting, I have some thoughts on the subject that might help.

First, children need their sleep. They may not think they do, but like food, shelter, and water they need sleep and it is up to us to provide them with the opportunity to get it. This means a scheduled bedtime. While there may be some variations in the routine when circumstances dictate and accommodations to the fact that some children do not need as much sleep as others, children need more sleep than adults. Insisting that they go to bed is not abuse, it is meeting this need.

Bedtime rituals are meant to help children wind down from their day and prepare for sleep. When these rituals become increasingly long or "just one more story or stay with me until I go to sleep" becomes the norm, we are being manipulated and need to set reasonable limits on bedtime routines.

We may let them sleep with us as babies out of convenience or a belief that keeping them close to us is appropriate, nurturing parenting. However, remember they will not give up this privilege willingly until about ages 5 to 7, perhaps even later with particularly dependent children. If we try to end the habit before that time, we can count on loud resistance from them. I am not suggesting that the "family bed" is not appropriate, but if we begin this practice we must realize that breaking the sleeping routine of a 3 or 4 year-old is going to be difficult.

Putting a fed, comfortable, sleepy baby into a safe, warm, familiar bed alone is not abuse. Children need to be able to soothe themselves and allow themselves to rest. This is part of the ongoing process of becoming independent from us. When we must make certain that they are asleep before we put them to bed or we remain with them until they fall asleep, we are interfering with this process.

Parents need adult time together. The time we have after children go to bed is important time for parents. We need not feel guilty when we claim this time for ourselves by putting the children to bed.

It is normal for children to have periods of time when they have difficulty sleeping. For instance, the child who has recently been put into a bed they can easily climb out of will likely go through a period of time when they will make frequent appearances after they have been put to bed to "be with you," have "one more drink of water," or to "tell you one more thing." This can be maddening after a long frustrating day when you are looking forward to some time for yourself, but this is normal limit testing behavior. You might respond by firmly continuing to set limits and put them back to bed without spending undue time.

Children, as part of their normal development, may also fear the dark and have occasional nightmares. Making one check for "monsters" under the bed or in the closet may be part of the bedtime routine. Having a night-light, favorite toy, or special blanket to help soothe the child may also help. Briefly comforting and reassuring the child who has had a nightmare is also appropriate. However, these behaviors can become manipulative and the source of undue attention. Therefore, we should set limits and gently, but firmly, return the child to their bed. (Repeated nightmares or sleep difficulties may signal that children are having difficulty handling changes in their lives or with other problems at home or school and we may need to help them with specific problems or adjusting to change.)

We are the adults; they are the children. We have the right and responsibility to parent them with firm, reasonable limit setting. They need their rest and so do we.

New Rule: We are in charge of setting firm reasonable, limits surrounding bedtime in order to ensure that our children receive needed rest and develop good sleep habits.

October 26 and 27

Old Rule: My children must eat what I want, when I want, and the amount I want.

Parents of small children often face food wars as well as bedtime battles. This clash of wills not only makes home life unpleasant, but their unsuccessful resolution can lead to more and bigger difficulties.

It was so easy when they were infants. At first they ate only breast milk or formula. Later we slowly introduced solid foods. We were in charge and they willingly ate what we offered. Then they learned to talk, to have preferences, to say "no," and the food battle began. They became "picky eaters" and we worried about them getting the nutrition they needed. Such worries led to power struggles and mealtime became a stressful battle for power and control. Food battles can escalate to remarkable heights. I had a neighbor some years ago whose daughter would sit for hours at the dinner table with food in her mouth refusing to swallow and thus give her mother power over what she ate. Mother, unwilling to admit defeat and surrender power, was trapped sitting there with her.

Many of these battles can be avoided when parents understand the bigger picture. Toddlers and small children test their independence and power in many ways. Eating is just one of them. Such limit testing is normal intellectual and emotional development.

It is also normal for small children to be quite hungry at one meal and refuse to eat at another or to go through periods of time when they eat a great deal and followed by periods when they eat very little. Unlike most adults, they want to eat only when they are hungry and not when it is "time." Given today's rates of childhood and adult obesity, this is a habit we might want to encourage rather than discourage. When my first child was about 2 and we were engaged in our own food battles, a friend and mother of five healthy children assured me that erratic eating behavior would end when he went to school. Since I was losing the war, I decided to relax a bit. She was right. As my son grew older, his appetite became more consistent.

It is also normal for small children to have rather odd food preferences, wishing to eat one food almost exclusively for a period of time and then later refuse to eat the same food. They will also eat things at someone else's house that they will not touch at yours, thus making a liar out of you. Don't fight it. You cannot win this one!

Children develop their food habits by observing us. If we eat junk foods and drink sugary, caffeine-laden soft drinks and give such food to them, then they will develop a taste for them. It is very difficult to change the food tastes we develop in early childhood, just ask any adult who has tried to change their eating habits. Therefore, if we want them to eat a variety of healthy foods, it is essential that we eat them ourselves and that we offer them to our children and limit the offering of less nutritious foods.

Even if we offer them nutritious foods and eat them ourselves, we cannot force our children to eat. They are ultimately in charge of this and to engage in a power struggle like my former neighbor is not only pointless but also damaging. I don't care what their grandmother says; children will not starve to death if they are allowed to leave the table without eating very much. They do not need as much as would satisfy us. Their stomachs are small and we do not want them to develop the habit of stuffing themselves and loosing the ability to identify when they have had enough food. When children start eating table foods, a good rule of thumb is one tablespoon of each food served for each year of the child's age.

It is probably a good idea to offer several small meals during the day and certainly a bedtime snack. This schedule is more likely to be in tune with their digestive system and energy requirements.

This does not mean, however, that we need to run our kitchen like a short order grill. We have a right to set reasonable limits on eating schedules. Actually, several small meals a day might also be more in line with our requirements rather than three larger meals.

Eating should be a pleasurable time for families to interact as well as nourish themselves. Ending or maybe even avoiding the food wars altogether can greatly enhance the quality of the precious time we spend with our children.

New Rule: I put an end to the food war by using common sense practices to help my children develop beneficial food habits.

October 28

Old Rule: My child will dress in the clothes that I choose and they will also wear their hair as I want.

The clothes and hair wars have made many families miserable. Parents believe they have the right to dictate to their children what they will wear and how their hair should be cut. Children, especially as they reach adolescence, just as adamantly disagree and the battle is on.

When teaching parenting classes, I have observed that the most successful parents, who not coincidently seem to enjoy parenting, are those who have learned to "pick their battles." They accept that children are not their property to be controlled. While they will insist that some things be done their way, they regard clothing and hair as negotiable items that their children quite naturally use to express their individuality. Within the limits of budget and decency, they allow their children to make their own decisions on these matters, accepting that they will not always like their choices. They know that their children will want to express their individuality or identify themselves with a particular group by how they dress and cut their hair. They accept such expressions as normal development and set fairly loose boundaries, knowing that to set up situations in which their children will feel the need to rebel against too much control invites potentially more extreme and possibly destructive self-expression.

Learn from these successful parents; choose your battles wisely and save your energies and influence for the important issues. Don't sweat the small stuff!

New Rule: I know and appreciate my children's need to express themselves by their clothing and hairstyle. Although I may need to set some limits, I let them decide how they will look. I do not permit clothing and hairstyles to become a family battleground.

October 29

Old Rule: Don't cry when you get a spanking or I'll give you something to really cry about.

When I counsel with those who come from abusive families, I am surprised at how often this rule comes up. Beaten as children, not just spanked but beaten, they were told by their parent that if they cried, it would be worse. In order to survive, they learned to keep their feelings hidden and to push their tears down inside.

I have often wondered why it would matter to an adult who is willing to beat a child if the child cried or not. After all, the purpose is to control the child and to do so by hurting them. Why should it matter if they cry? I have come to feel that in demanding that the child not cry the parent is able to maintain some denial that what they are doing is not hurtful to the child. Frequently, parents are acting not out of anger about what the child actually did, but out of their own frustrations that have nothing to do with the child. The child is merely a convenient and safe outlet for frustration and anger; not to hear crying enables the parent to deny that what they are doing is actually painful.

Whether or not a parent feels that spanking is appropriate discipline is a personal decision. However, to demand that a child not cry when they are being spanked is not discipline, it is emotional abuse. If we can't handle the crying, then we don't need to be spanking.

New Rule: When I feel that it is necessary to spank my children, I do not emotionally abuse them by insisting they hide their feelings and not cry.

October 30 & 31

Old Rule: I don't want my children to grow up feeling about me the way I felt about my parents. I want them to like me. I want to be their friend. I want them to be free spirits. I am afraid if I discipline them too much I might harm them.

Those of us who want to rethink the rules of parenting, especially those who want to limit the use of physical punishment, are often accused of rearing "spoiled," "obnoxious," and "selfish" children. The further criticism is that these children will be totally unprepared to function in a world that holds them accountable for their behavior. Hearing such criticism and fearing these dire predictions might come true, we become afraid to parent. Thus we vacillate between too little discipline and too much discipline, all the while fearing that we are not doing any of this very well.

Let me help set your mind at ease. Once again perfect parents, like perfect children, do not exist. Don't try to be perfect; you will never succeed. What our children need from us is not perfect parenting, but a sense that we love them and ultimately approve of and value them just as they are. With this basic knowledge, they will be okay even when we make mistakes.

Secondly, the people who have the most difficulty functioning in the world are those whose parents have abused, neglected, or abandoned them. Those individuals who were somewhat overly indulged usually learn somewhere along the line that not every one in the world cares whether they are happy or not. Such lessons are generally learned without dire consequences.

It is, however, vitally important that we discipline our children. We are not our children's friends. We are their parents. Parenting is a far more important and responsible role than friendship. As a parent we lovingly teach, guide, and protect our children. This constitutes discipline and it is one of our most important responsibilities. We need to teach them what is dangerous and to protect themselves. We need to teach them how to live and work successfully with others. We need to teach them how to take care of themselves, to make sound decisions, and to discipline themselves. We also need to teach them that almost nothing worthwhile comes without self-discipline and sustained effort and that achieving one's goals and using one's talents and gifts is one of life's greatest pleasures.

All of this is accomplished over time with loving commitment to our children. We will not do this perfectly. Occasionally, we may wish that we had handled a situation or reared an older child differently. We may also find that our children are, at times, angry with us, chafe against our efforts to guide and protect them, accuse us of not loving them, or tell us that they "hate" us. This is just part of being a parent.

Each of us has an intuitive sense about what is right for our children. If your intuition tells you that you should not spank your children, then follow your intuition. Discipline can and is accomplished without physical punishment and don't be intimidated by those who tell you to "spare the rod and spoil the child." If you do spank your children, (remember that a spanking is an open hand on a clothed bottom), you will likely do no harm, but remember that spanking has limited usefulness and you need more than spanking in your arsenal of discipline techniques.

In short, do not be afraid to parent. Relax and enjoy it. Realize that disciplining your children is an imperfect art and as you teach them you will also be learning.

New Rule: We know that we cannot be perfect parents. We also know that we are not our children's friends. We are our children's parents and it is our responsibility to discipline, protect, and prepare them for life beyond our home.

November 1

Old Rule: Holidays should always be spent with the family.

Sometime in October, therapists' offices begin to fill with people dreading the upcoming holidays. Believing the line from Robert Harlings' play *Steel Magnolias,* "Families are about being with people you don't like, doing things that nobody wants to do," many adults feel that they have no choice other than to suffer through the holidays with their extended families. Fearing they might hurt someone's feelings or somehow betray the family, they return home for the holidays, carting their children with them. Hoping that somehow this time will be different, they arrive seeking a loving, nurturing family with whom to enjoy the season, only to find the same family they left the previous holiday season. They grit their teeth and suppress their feelings, except to growl angrily at their children (the only acceptable target for their frustration and anger), and somehow make it through. Returning to the therapist in January, they complain bitterly that nothing, absolutely nothing, has changed.

We have the power to change how we celebrate the holidays. Such change requires that we let go of the old fantasies about returning home to a loving, accepting family and begin new holiday traditions. Maybe it is time to celebrate the holidays with those whose company we enjoy the rest of the year and create a family, not of blood ties but of caring, for our children and ourselves.

New Rule: We can choose to spend the holidays with those who love, accept, and support us throughout the year. These are the people with whom we can truly celebrate the blessings of life.

November 2 & 3

Old Rule: When we have a conflict with another person, especially our extended family, we do not talk directly with that person. It might hurt their feelings. However, we do talk with others about what is bothering us.

This dysfunctional communication rule is, unfortunately, quite prevalent. The scenario generally plays out something like this: You have a conflict with a family member, for instance, a brother who has made a critical remark, hurting your feelings. However, rather than talk about the difficulty with him, you talk with your mother, spouse, and friends, whoever is available to listen. You tell yourself that to talk about the difficulty with your brother would either hurt his feelings, cause additional problems, lead to an uncomfortable scene, or would not do any good. Thus the problem is never resolved because we lack the integrity, courage, and skills to talk directly with the person with whom we have the conflict.

This dysfunctional pattern is called the "drama" or "victim triangle". In the above example, you feel victimized, your brother is your "victimizer," and the people listening to your story are your potential "rescuers." The "rescuer's" job is to say, in effect, "You poor thing. How could he say such an awful thing?!" If you tell enough "rescuers," sooner or later the remarks will get back to your brother, who then gets to play "victim" to your "victimizer" with a whole new set of "rescuers." Thus the drama continues. Conflicts remain unresolved and may, instead, poison relationships for years.

Unfortunately, our children learn this pattern of conflict resolution from us and carry it into their relationships, repeating the cycle. Learning to resolve conflict in a functional, healthy manner is one of the most crucial lessons we teach our children. Since it is virtually impossible to be in relationship with another human being and not experience disagreements, it is important to teach our children how to successfully resolve them.

Conflict resolution requires courageous action, taking responsibility for our feelings, and letting go of attempts to control the reactions and behavior of others. Furthermore, it is important to resolve disagreements instead of avoiding them and prolonging them by drawing others into the battle.

The steps toward effective conflict resolution are simple, yet powerful. First, we should wait, if possible, until some of the emotion has subsided and we are calmer. Then we can ask for a few minutes of private time with the person whom we feel has injured us or with whom we disagree. Using "I" statements, we briefly state the problem as we see it, including our feelings about the situation. We then ask for what we would like to see changed in the relationship.

For instance, if you are annoyed because someone is chronically late, you state your feelings and ask them to be prompt. If the situation warrants and their lateness forces you to be late, you could state what action you will take if their behavior does not change. Lastly, you invite them to respond to your requests with their own ideas. If they become defensive, respond with your thoughts, feelings, or perceptions, remembering to use "I" statements. It is hard to argue with individual perceptions voiced in this way.

Using this method, conflicts are much more likely to be resolved and we improve our chances of getting our needs met. Relationships will also grow because conflicts have been faced and resolved by the parties involved, allowing trust to build in the relationship. However, there is a down side. Not everyone is ready to deal with conflict in a mature and responsible manner. They may find your behavior somewhat threatening and avoid you. There will also be less drama, less gossip, and less complaining in your conversations with others when you refuse to play the "victim" and encourage others to do the same.

This is a powerful skill to teach our children. When they learn to effectively resolve conflicts with their siblings, friends, even their parents and other adults, they make a giant leap in their growth and their ability to create open, trusting, and mutually fulfilling relationships. Such skills are taught not by our words, but instead by our actions. Children must see and experience them in order to learn and to practice the skills necessary for successfully conflict resolution.

New Rule: In our family we deal with conflict by talking directly to the individual with whom we have conflict; thus we are better able to resolve conflicts, get our needs met, and foster growth and trust in relationships.

November 4

Old Rule: Never let go.

One of my most grievous character flaws is my failure to let go of conflicts. No matter what the outcome, I replay them in my mind over and over, nurturing hurt feelings and righteous indignation. While I seldom recall pleasant interactions, I recall conflicts verbatim. I have a "letting go" problem.

My "letting go" problem does not hurt those with whom I have had a conflict. However, it does hurt me. Not letting go means that my mental energy is occupied with replaying the words and the feelings of long ago conflicts, sapping me of the energy necessary to take action and enjoy today. Not letting go puts emotional distance between others and myself. It hurts my working and personal relationships. Learning to let go has been one of the greatest challenges of my adult live. However, to the extent that I have been able to accomplish this, the rewards have been great. My relationships with others and my emotional well-being are markedly improved.

The habit of hanging on to conflicts is not something that I wanted to pass on to my children. Therefore, I worked at modeling for them a more functional style of dealing with problems and conflicts. I hope they learned a different approach and are not plagued by my old emotional habits.

If this habit sounds familiar to you, you probably learned it from your own family. You did not have a choice about this lesson, but you do have the choice today to let go of past conflicts and not pass this energy and relationship draining style on to your children.

Changing these habits is not easy, but we can do it. When I am replaying an old conflict and wasting my mental energy, I ask myself what I am really angry about in the present that I am not willing to deal with. Often, I find I'm avoiding current conflicts by replaying old ones. At this point, I have several choices: I can stay stuck in the old pattern, focus on resolving the current conflict, or let go and turn the situation over to my Higher Power. I can never change the past no matter how much I dwell on it. This is a habit I can no longer afford; the cost in lack of peace of mind is too high. This is what I want my children to learn.

New Rule: I teach my children that letting go of the past, especially conflicts with others, is not only the constructive way of handling such conflicts, but it also results in increased personal freedom and mental energy with which to live more creatively today.

November 5 &6

Old rule: When conflicts arise, fight to win with every weapon at your disposal.

Conflict is inevitable in every family or close relationship. However, resolving conflicts in a constructive manner is a learned skill that, unfortunately, too few of us possess. Too many of us have learned to "go for the jugular." We use all of the weapons at our disposal and attempt to vanquish our foe, including those whom we profess to love, in order to win. This kind of winning results in hurt feelings, lack of trust, and emotional distance. Such behavior virtually guarantees that the issue will not be resolved, but will resurface at another time when the vanquished foe has rearmed. In this manner, conflicts continue in families and especially between couples for long periods of time and may result in severed relationships or a divorce.

In reality, being in an intimate relationship with anyone, especially our spouse and children, means that we know where the vulnerable places are. We know what will hurt. When we choose to use this information to win a conflict we are choosing to deliberately wound that person. This is dirty, unfair fighting. It destroys the basic trust that all intimate relationships need in order to survive. It does no good to apologize after the hurtful words are out of our mouths by asserting, "I was angry and didn't know what I was saying. I didn't mean it." Of course we meant what we said. Furthermore, we are responsible for what we say, even in anger. Using these tactics to win an argument is quite risky. We may end up winning the battle and losing the war.

Another destructive habit is to accuse another of "always" or "never" doing something. Since no one "always" or "never" does anything, this is like throwing gasoline on the fire. The accused then has the right to point out the times when they did or did not do what they are accused of, further derailing resolution of the conflict. Thus, we find ourselves mired in a swamp of unresolved conflicts.

Instead of using destructive behaviors, why not focus on "win-win" conflict resolution. "Win- win" means that we stay with the present problem and not muddy the waters with past conflict. It also means that we focus on the problem not the personality and supposed character flaws of the other person. It also requires that we clearly state what we want to happen. Finally, we learn to either compromise and find a solution in which each person gets some of what they want or negotiate a new solution to the problem.

Some of us relish the thrill of winning arguments, vanquishing our foe with our clever words. Some of us believe we are always right and, therefore, should have our way. We may even secretly desire to end the relationship, but lack the courage to say it outright and, therefore, chose to destroy it slowly with our words. In any case, is this the conflict resolution style you want to pass to your children? If so, then stick to the old rules. If you want to resolve conflicts, while preserving relationships, and teach your children how to resolve differences in a fair, constructive, and effective manner, then try using win-win conflict resolution. We do have a choice.

New Rule: In our family we attempt to resolve conflicts using the win-win conflict resolution strategy. Our relationships with one another and the well being of each family member is too important to deliberately wound each other in unending conflict.

November 7

Old Rule: Don't be different.

Each of us is unique; we have a combination of genetic material and experiences different from anyone who has ever lived or will ever live. This fact gives human experience its complexity and vitality. Indeed, those of us who study human behavior find people, in all of their diversity, infinitely fascinating.

However, our culture values only certain combinations of physical features, talents, abilities, and experiences. To be different, to be unique, often leads to criticism and even ostracism. The pressure for children to fit a certain well behaved, physically attractive, academic, and athletic mold is enormous. Children who fail to fit this societal mold often experience difficulty finding a comfortable, accepting place in our culture. For instance, the boy who is not athletic, but prefers music or art, or the girl who is not petite and shapely but has, instead, a sturdy, athletic body may find acceptance difficult to come by. Being considered different may result in rejection, emotional pain, decreased self-esteem, and devaluation of one's talents and abilities.

It is painful for parents to watch children experience rejection as a result of such differences. In our well-intended efforts to help them fit in, we may be adding our own voices to the larger chorus that says to the child, "You might fit in (be more acceptable) if only you were a little more or less...." It is important that we accept, affirm, and value our children as they are with their unique talents, abilities, and interests. This acceptance is even more important if a child's attributes do not correspond to the cultural mold of the ideal. To do otherwise is to rob them of our needed support in discovering and using their talents and abilities to realize their full potential.

New Rule: Our children are unique and together we value, nurture, and celebrate their individuality.

November 8

Old Rule: It is acceptable to have a physical illness, but it is shameful to have a mental illness or emotional difficulties.

We have come a long way from the time when people believed that mental illness and emotional difficulties were the result of sin, demon possession, or some character flaw on the part of the sufferer. However, mental illness still carries with it stigma and embarrassment. We talk openly about our family members with diabetes, cancer, or heart disease, but we continue to be reluctant to discuss those with depression, schizophrenia, or addiction. We are particularly embarrassed and silent when our children suffer from emotional difficulties. Believing that such difficulties are a reflection on our parenting or evidence of defect, we are often so ashamed that we enter into a form of denial and refuse to even acknowledge the possibility that our children may need professional assistance. Thus we deny them treatment in a manner that we would never consider for a physical problem.

Much of the latest research on mental illness points to abnormalities in the chemistry of the brain, just as diabetes is characterized by abnormalities in the way that the body uses sugar. Even emotional problems caused by difficult circumstances are not shameful, but instead, part of being human. However, our denial can be so stubborn that we fail to seek treatment for emotional difficulties ourselves, as well as provide treatment for our children. Thus avoidable suffering continues and may ultimately result in tragedy. It is time to emerge from the ignorance and darkness of past attitudes and beliefs and treat mental illness, like physical illness, as a problem to be dealt with openly, not consigned to silence and shame.

New Rule: It is no more shameful to have a mental illness than to have a physical problem. In order to ease human suffering, it is necessary to openly acknowledge and seek treatment for mental disorders and emotional difficulties.

November 9

Old Rule: The world is a rotten place and there is nothing that anyone can do about it.

I am often amazed and saddened by the cynicism of the students in my classes. These young adults are disdainful, critical, and disappointed. While they tend to be personally optimistic, they are pessimistic about other people and the world as a whole. This pessimism is often an excuse for lack of action and withdrawal from the larger world.

It is true that there are monumental problems in this world and it sometimes seems that the phrase "human progress" is a contradiction in terms. Perhaps it is my own overly optimistic point of view, but I do believe that it is possible for individuals to make a difference in the world. Giving up is no more a realistic response to the difficulties we face than to view the situation with cheery, starry-eyed optimism.

We can alleviate the distressing cynicism of our children by our example and by helping them to take individual action. We can show them that what they do does make a difference. We can show them with such simple things as not littering, recycling, and being good stewards of the planet. We can demonstrate good citizenship by informing ourselves about the issues and voting. We can show them that when people join together they can make a difference. Individuals can accomplish what they believe to be important whether it be coaching children's athletics, volunteering at a school, or giving time to any of the many worthwhile organizations that help to make our world a bit better place to live.

It is vitally important that we teach our children that they do have the power by their actions to either make the world a better place in which to live. Our only power may be in the kindness and consideration we show others today, but each of us does have the power to make a difference in someone's life each day.

New Rule: I do not allow myself to slide into cynicism. I teach my children that they can, by their actions, make the world a better place in which to live.

November 10 & 11

Old Rule: I am not interested in politics. All politicians are dishonest! I don't bother to vote. My vote doesn't really make a difference.

Granted, our national, state, and local governments are far from perfect and there are many situations about which to be disillusioned and frustrated. Governments at every level are run by people, and therefore, imperfect and sometimes corrupt. It often seems that our voice and wishes get lost in the shuffle. In addition, most issues are extremely complex and we hear so many opposing points of view that the temptation is to throw up our hands in confusion. However, ignoring governmental matters and failing to vote sets a negative example for our children.

Before you decide not to vote in the next election, allow me to present some thoughts for your consideration.

First, we live in the wealthiest and most free nation that has ever existed on this planet. In truth, all of us have greater civil liberties than our grandparents. (My grandmother could neither vote nor serve on a jury when she was a young mother.)

Second, while many countries have large numbers of people who wish to leave, our country experiences enormous pressure to admit more and more people. Few other countries offer such economic opportunities and political freedoms that people risk their lives or imprisonment to come there. Citizens of western European democracies that have comparable standards of living are often eager to come and study and work in the United States. While far from perfect, our system of government provides the greatest amount of freedom and opportunity to the most number of people regardless of their heritage and the circumstances of their birth.

Third, while we say that our opinions and actions do not matter, many of the truly revolutionary changes in the past 75 years have come about as a result of ordinary citizens banding together to take action. These changes have included civil rights laws (When I moved to Atlanta in 1956, there were "whites only" and "colored" restrooms, fountains, restaurants, hotels, schools, and colleges.); gender equality laws (In the 1960's it was perfectly acceptable to pay a woman less than a man for the same job, if a woman could get hired at all, because those in power believed that a man needed money to take care of his family, while a woman was only working for spending money or because she was selfishly escaping her family responsibilities,); child labor laws (In the early part of the 20th century millions of children under the age of 16 worked 12 hour days in factories, mines, and mills in dangerous conditions for minute wages which not only shortened their education, but also destroyed their health and frequently led to an early death.); and the passage of environmental protection laws (In many areas of the country, the air and water are actually cleaner than they were 50 years ago.) This list is far from complete, but it does illustrate the power of committed individuals working together.

Even though we have immense political power and personal liberty, we have become a nation of non-voters. Only about 48% of registered voters go to the polls during a Presidential election. This percentage is dropping and an increasing number do not even bother to register to vote. In 1998, according to *U.S. News and World Report,* only about 1 in 6 or 17.4% of eligible voters voted in the congressional and gubernatorial primaries. In contrast, people all over the world are fighting for the right to cast ballots in free and fair elections. Indeed, when other countries wish to institute such election practices they often ask the United States to send observers to ensure the fairness of their elections. Furthermore, their citizens come out to cast their ballots in amazing numbers. For instance, people in South Africa traveled long distances and stood in line for hours waiting to cast their ballot for the first time. Our freedom to vote without coercion and the relative lack of corruption of our elections are the envy of much of the world.

When we say that we are not interested in politics, when we do not vote and say that it doesn't matter, when being interested in government and voting is equated with either being an idealistic fool or having "dirty hands," then we are in serious trouble and we are passing that trouble on to our children.

Government at all levels is our business. Voting is our duty as citizens. Being a responsible, voting citizen is part of being a good parent and modeling responsible behavior to our children.

New Rule: As parents we are interested in and vitally concerned with our government. Our <u>minimal</u> responsibility is to inform ourselves about issues crucial to our well-being and to vote whenever the opportunity arises.

November 12

Old Rule: The only achievements in life that really count are those that make money. The more money you make the more successful you are.

Who defines success for you? By whose yardstick are you measuring your choices? In many families the spoken and unspoken rules say, "Make money and be important," or "Make money and you will prove yourself worthy of respect, approval, and love."

Following this rule, we make career choices based primarily on the amount of financial reward. We do not seriously consider careers that do not pay well, even though they might be more appealing and emotionally rewarding. By our attitudes and actions, we pass these beliefs on to our children, thus limiting their choices as they search for careers.

Taking responsibility for our choices means using our own yardstick to define success. It also means having the courage to risk doing that which is genuinely important to us, not what is valuable to someone else. Financial success is but one indicator of success; the real tragedy is achieving financial success without satisfaction and meaning. Failure is being a slave to someone else's definition of success.

New Rule: I measure success by my own yardstick. How much money I earn is not the only indicator of how successful I am. Living by this new rule, I can teach my children to place money in its proper place as only one measure of success.

November 13

Old Rule: I love you, just look at all I have given you.

When parents are in the midst of their own worries, addictions, emotional pain, or excessively busy schedules, children's needs do not get met. There is simply not enough time and energy left over from the stress of just getting through the day to attend to children's needs on a consistent basis. However, parents can assuage their own feelings of guilt and inadequacy by buying all that they can for the child. With this behavior parents say in effect, "I do not know how or cannot give of myself emotionally, but I will give you material possessions and you should be satisfied and grateful."

This is a powerful legacy handed down through the generations. Money and providing things comes to equal love. Money and gifts are used to control children and to silence the desire that parents give of themselves emotionally. This pattern may continue as adult children continue to receive things rather than enjoying a caring relationship with their parents.

While it is true that children need and desire material things, what they truly need from us is something far more difficult to give, ultimate and consistent concern for developing and maintaining a relationship with the child that says, "You are worth more than my money, you are worth my time."

New Rule: Children need time and attention more than the material things that parents give them.

November 14

Old Rule: I love my children so much! I have trouble saying "no" to them. I can't stand to see them upset. They always come first in my life.

Is it possible to love children too much? Is it possible to be an overly dedicated and loving parent?

It depends upon what you are calling "love." If you are unwilling to say "no" even when you know it is in the child's long-term interest, is that love or wishing to avoid a tantrum? If we do our children's chores rather than insist that they do them, is that love or condoning defiance? If we do not expect our children to assume increasing amounts of responsibility for their behavior, is that love or neglect? When we insist that others cater to our children and never permit them to work out problems with other children or adults, is this love or teaching them that the world revolves around them and their wishes? When we buy our children everything they ask for, is this love or teaching them that money is limitless and they are entitled to have everything they want?

When we spend all of our time and energy on our children and have no adult interests or time for ourselves, is this love or martyrdom? When we ignore our relationship with our spouse and allow our homes to be completely child-centered, is that love or teaching them to be self-centered and to disregard the needs of others?

Being a loving parent is often about setting limits and boundaries, including limits on spending, limits on having one's way, and even limits on parental time and energy. Giving without limits is not loving, but is instead dangerous. It teaches children that they can live without boundaries on their demands of others. How shocked and unprepared they will be when they leave our "loving" home and find that the world does not operate in this way.

New Rule: Loving my children means saying "no," setting limits, and maintaining a personal life and relationships that does not revolve around them. In actuality, such limits are a superb gift to give my children, while I try to maintain the middle ground between too much and too little attention and devotion.

November 15

Old Rule: I want what I want, when I want it!

We all know adults who behave this way. They want what they want now and see virtually no reason why others should not cater to their demands. When they do not immediately get what they want, they are prone to throw monumental temper tantrums. They are two- year-olds in adult bodies and they are very unpleasant to have around.

How did this behavior develop? Perhaps in childhood. Babies and small children are normally demanding. They want to be entertained and have their needs met immediately. Since crying is the only way they have to communicate, they cry to let us know their wants and needs. Lacking a sense of time and the resulting inability to delay gratification, life for babies and small children is intense and immediate. This is a part of normal development.

As children grow older, they gradually develop a sense of time and the ability to communicate their wants and needs and to delay gratification. These abilities grow slowly and imperfectly as any parent of a two or three-year-old knows. However, children do mature if parents help them. Parents do this by setting limits on demands, saying "no" and sticking to it, and not responding to demands, but rather to requests. Gradually, children learn to delay gratification and to wait without complaining for what they want for a reasonable length of time. They learn that while their needs will be met their wants may not always be fulfilled. Becoming a reasonable, patient, considerate adult begins in early childhood. When parents do not set limits on demanding behavior, rush to fulfill a child's every want, tolerate rude demanding language, and capitulate to demands, children grow into self-centered adolescents and young adults.

Helping children to mature and prepare for the larger world is the essential work of parenting. It may be difficult and tiring, but the alternative may be that we create a 35- year-old who demands from us and from everyone around them what they want when they want it.

New Rule: Children do not need to have all of their wishes met immediately. They need to learn to delay gratification and to be patient and reasonable in their requests of others.

November 16

Old Rule: You think you had a bad day! Wait till you hear what happened to me!

This maddening, dysfunctional pattern of family communication is rooted in a strange competition for the worst day, the worst physical problem, and the worst difficulties. This attention-seeking pattern is learned, for in such families being sick, sad, or having a crisis is the only way to get attention. Those who are feeling and doing well are simply ignored. Thus, children in the family learn this disaster one-up-man-ship in order to get attention.

In such families, conversation centers on complaining. Nothing is ever going right, especially for "us." It may be going well for others who are more privileged, luckier, or more fortunate, but not for us. No one is ever doing their job correctly, the government is not working as it should, and the neighbors are deliberately annoying us. There is always something to complain about. These folks are also chronic victims. Everyone is taking advantage of them and they are powerless to stop it (so they say). If anyone would be so bold as to suggest a solution to any one of their problems or illnesses, the suggestion would most likely be met with a "Yes, but…." This way of remaining a victim is passed down from generation to generation.

Such people are stuck in their misery, refusing to resolve any issue in their lives and choosing instead to complain and justify lack of action. Not only is life difficult for them, it is extremely frustrating for those who must listen to them.

If this is the pattern in your family, it is not too late to change and pass on a more functional way of communicating to your children. It will take a determined effort to stop yourself and move away from the chronic complainer role. The first step is to stop one's self when one is into the old pattern. Next begin to develop an "attitude of gratitude" and a willingness to change what one does not like and letting go of what one cannot change. Actually, gratitude and action are the exact opposites of chronic complaining. While these changes may be initially difficult, they are well worth the effort.

New Rule: In our family, we do not have to have terrible problems in order to get attention. We take action where we can and let go of those things we cannot change.

November 17

Old Rule: I'm in control of my family.

Sure you are! Many people were reared in homes where parents, perhaps one parent, believed they were in control of the family. This parent often believed they were entitled to be in control of the children and sometimes the other parent. If this old method of authoritarian parenting ever worked, and this is debatable, it certainly does not work now. We live in vastly different times than our grandparents and even our parents. We are rearing children in a world that is actually quite different than the one in which we were reared. In reality, the ability to totally control the behavior of another human being, even a child, is an illusion.

When children are babies, we have some control. They stay where we put them and we feed them and bathe them when we want, but that control fades quickly. Parenting is about the gradual loss of power over our children. What we do have as parents is the power of influence and persuasion. Because they want to please us, we have the power to mold and shape their behavior. We have the power to teach them and to impose limits, boundaries, and consequences. We have some power to protect them from that which we consider harmful. While all of these powers will diminish over time, we will always be powerful in our children's lives.

In other words, we have the power that comes from a loving parent - child relationship, but we do not have control.

New Rule: I realize that I do not have control over my children and do not seek it, but what I do seek is the power to teach them and to influence their actions so that they will grow into self-reliant, productive adults.

November 18 and 19

Old Rule: Girls are fragile and need to be protected. Boys are strong and should be given maximum independence and freedom.

The role of women in our culture has changed dramatically in the past 50 years, but we still have many vestiges of this old rule. In my marriage and family classes, young women often complain that they were reared differently from their brothers. They had less freedom to come and go as they pleased. Their friends and whereabouts were more closely monitored. They were more protected than their brothers and they were considered more fragile. Often, they were not encouraged to be physically active and competitive.

Young men, on the other hand, often relate that many of their activities were not supervised. They did not have a curfew and were pretty much on their own from middle adolescence. They were expected to take care of themselves financially much earlier and to be strong and self-reliant. They were also expected to be inclined toward athletic pursuits and to be competitive with other males.

This continuing double standard has the effect of over-restricting girls. It limits their experiences and they are less likely to feel that they can take care of themselves. They may feel less competent and independent. In short, such restrictions have a tendency to decrease the self-esteem and confidence of young women.

Boys are not as closely supervised and are often permitted to be on their own without supervision before they are prepared to make sound decisions without appropriate parental support and input. They may often encounter situations that are risky and potentially harmful. They tend to go to work earlier than girls and are more likely to encounter employers who take advantage of them and place them in potentially dangerous situations. Boys, in general, do not receive as much emotional support even early in childhood. This lack of parental involvement may increase their alienation, while decreasing self-esteem. It contributes to the tendency of young men to find deviant sub-cultures, especially if they do not feel they fit in with the usual adolescent male culture.

Parenting is a balancing act. How much freedom do we grant? How much protection do we give? How soon do we allow them to go to work and make their own decisions and handle situations that arise with other adults? Once again, healthy functioning occurs somewhere in the middle between overprotection and under protection, between pushing our children out in the adult world to deal with problems on their own too soon and keeping them at home where parents deal with these issues. A balancing act to be sure, but an essential part of rearing children to leave our homes as confident, self-reliant young people.

New rule: We offer protection to our daughter while encouraging her to pursue a wide variety of interests and experiences, even though they may not be traditionally feminine. We also protect our son from making decisions independently for which he may not be ready. At the same time we try to protect him from adults who might take advantage of his inexperience. We also encourage him to pursue a wide range of interests, even those that might not be traditionally masculine. Our goal as parents is to rear self-confident

425

and self-reliant young adults who are adequately prepared to deal with the many choices and situations they will encounter as they move from our home into the wider world.

November 20

Old Rule: Now color in the lines, children.

From time to time, most of us encourage our children to "color in the lines," not just with their art projects, but in the rest of their lives as well. We tell them not to take risks, not to experiment with new ideas, not to be too bold or too different. We teach them to be like others and to fit in. In doing this, we stifle their creativity. We teach them not to use their ideas, but to blindly follow the mind-set of the crowd, to follow the old acceptable ways.

The parents of Alexandra Nechita, a promising young Russian artist, reportedly took her coloring books away at age 4. Replacing them with blank paper, they made it impossible for her to stay within other people's lines, but only within those she created for herself.

Would our children be more creative if we took away their "coloring books" in many areas of their lives and encouraged them to think and create for themselves? Given such freedom, what might they achieve? Would they be less influenced by peer pressure and less likely to say, "Everybody else is doing it so why can't I?"

Indeed, how might our own lives be different if we were able to free our own creativity from staying within the lines and begin to think, do, and create for ourselves? Would we continue to follow the ideas of the majority? Would we follow our own inner creativity and allow ourselves to be just who we are and in the process allow our children to do the same?

New Rule: My children and I do not always color within the lines. I give myself and my children permission to take the risk to think and create independently from the constraining opinions of others.

November 21

Old Rule: This is our athletic child, this is our smart child, and this is our other child.

We've all heard parents introduce their children by their role or label in the family. Naturally, parents are proud of the achievements of their children and want friends and acquaintances to know about them. But what of the "other child," the one who is not quite so athletic or academically gifted? Often this child is the recipient of false compliments and praise that the parent makes in order for the child not to feel bad or left out. But the child knows. That child knows that parents are really proud of the star children. They are the ones who make the family (parents) look good. They are where the action is and the other child knows they cannot compete, thus their self-esteem suffers.

Although there is a temptation to see the "athletic child" or the "gifted child" as privileged, they also pay a price for their role. They are not really free to be themselves and there can be an enormous amount of pressure to keep doing what they are doing. They also suffer from the suspicion that parental love and approval is contingent on their performance. They may have anxiety about what will happen if they fail to perform. What if they mess up, simply do not want to keep on being an athlete, or want to take a different turn in life, for instance become a teacher rather than a doctor?

Parents have enormous power to influence the self-image of their children. We have the power to enhance self-image or damage it. Valuing each child is crucial to its self-esteem and self-image. It is important for them to know that they are loved just as they are, not just for the accomplishments that make us look good and enhance our self-image. It is not "all about us;" it is about them.

New Rule: I want you to meet my children. I am proud of all of them.

November 22

Old Rule: I want my children to have and to do the things that I didn't.

It is natural for parents to want their children to have what they wanted during their own childhood, but where unable to obtain.

For generations, parents have worked to make a better life for their children. This is part of being a loving parent, as well as, the way of upward mobility for many families.

The problems arise when we, as parents, become too preoccupied with what we wanted and do not stop to consider what our children want. If we always wanted to be an athlete or a beauty queen, play in the band, take dance or piano lessons, or be the editor of the school newspaper, we might pressure our children to do what we could not. In this way we might re-capture a bit of that dream for ourselves and live out that old dream through our children. Still, these are our dreams and may not be our children's.

Growing up in a family where money was scarce, a parent will frequently focus on giving their children all of the material things they did not have. They work many hours. Believing that more money will make their children's lives better than their own, they forget that children also need their parents' presence and time. A vacation or an extravagant Christmas may be terrific, but not with a parent who is exhausted and resentful because children are not appreciative.

Once again healthy functioning is in the middle ground. Parents need to find the balance between pushing children into activities they wanted to pursue and encouraging children to choose for themselves. There is also a balance between working to give your family material possessions and making time to be with them and enjoying the pleasures of life together. Along the way parents might find time to focus on themselves. Parents need to dream new dreams and work to make those dreams come true for themselves.

New rule: Although I want my children to have more opportunities than I, I want them to choose their own dreams. While giving my family material things is important, time spent together is more important than the extra things I buy them. I also realize that even though I am an adult and a parent with many responsibilities, I need to have my own dreams and invest some of my energy into making them come true.

November 23

Old rule: I'm afraid my child is going to have problems with … just like I did.

No matter how old we get, we all have childhood wounds. Many of them reflect perceived childhood and adolescent inadequacies. We may believe we have left these feelings behind, but they may resurface when we begin to observe in our children the same behavioral or physical characteristics that caused us so much difficulty.

When we begin to worry aloud that our children have the same difficulties, we, in effect, point out a liability the child may not realize they had or about which they had no sense of inadequacy. By projecting our feelings onto them, we may cause the child to focus on the prospective problem and to feel our disappointment for having this flaw. There may also be a feeling of resignation that the supposed defect must be hereditary and therefore, nothing can be done.

For instance, because our culture values physical appearance in women, many mothers worry about their daughters' physical defects, tending to pass their own insecurities on to them. Small breasts, large hips or thighs, and non-perfect noses are all cause for concern. No wonder so many teenage girls seek plastic surgery to correct these supposed defects and less than perfect bodies.

Like female physical beauty, our culture reveres male athletic achievement. The father who felt inadequate with respect to athletics may pass feelings of inadequacy on to his sons who may be discouraged from even trying any form of athletic endeavor.

Both men and women may have feelings of inadequacy concerning some area of academic achievement, for instance math or science. They may pass onto their children the doubts they had about their own ability to master these subjects.

When we project our unresolved shame and pain onto our children, believing that we are being empathetic and realistic, we damage their self-image. It is more beneficial to separate our feelings about our own supposed inadequacies from our feelings about our children, thus freeing ourselves to take realistic positive action when our children encounter difficulties in their lives.

New Rule: Although I have contributed one-half of my child's genetic material, they are not me and I am not them.

November 24

Old Rule: It is silly to have lofty goals and aspirations. After all, remember who you are and where you come from. Don't rise above your raisin'.

Seems strange, doesn't it? Most parents claim to value education. They want their children to have a quality education in order to compete successfully in the world. However, in some families there are spoken, as well as subtle unspoken, messages that to achieve or to even aspire to achieve beyond a certain level is not only foolhardy, but also disloyal to the family. In effect, children are given the message, "Don't be too much better than your parents." This message usually results from the parents' shame about their own lack of achievement, as well as the family's perceived status in society.

Growing up with conflicting feelings of shame and pride concerning their family as well as their own accomplishments, parents pass this conflict along to their children. They are saying in effect, "If you achieve too much I will feel that I am a failure and you will hurt me. Protect me. Don't achieve too much." These messages are usually unspoken; indeed, children may be overtly encouraged to achieve, while getting covert subtle, often sarcastic, remarks about not becoming too smart or too educated. Wishing to maintain a relationship with the family, children learn early to scale back ambitions and hide or stunt abilities. All of these contradictory messages can leave them feeling confused and conflicted as they move into adulthood. This subtle tragedy is repeated throughout the generations, resulting in frustration and unused talents and abilities.

We can help our children by first examining our family messages about achievement and adopting new rules for ourselves about our possibilities and dreams. By changing our attitudes and perhaps deciding that the price of such family inclusion and approval is too high, we are then able to pass on to our children a new legacy of freedom and support for using all of their abilities and talents.

New Rule: The price for following this rule and keeping family approval is too dear. I choose to use the gifts and capabilities I have been given and encourage my children to use theirs. They will never lose me if they soar higher. I will always be there, cheering them on.

November 25

Old Rule: Hitch your wagon to a star.

My father was a great one for mottos. This was one of his favorites. It means to aim high and to set lofty goals for yourself. This sounds like good advice and a way to inspire children to use their abilities to the fullest.

However, problems arise when the expectations are too lofty, too ambitious. When expectations are unrealistic, children are set up to fail. No matter what they achieve, it is never enough. They can never meet parental and later their own extreme expectations. Such persons go through life feeling that no matter what they accomplish it is not quite good enough and they should have done more.

Let me give you an example. In my counseling practice, I encountered two men from politically oriented families who were told from earliest childhood that they could be President of the United States. This is actually what they were supposed to do! Talk about hitching your wagon to a star! A very lofty goal indeed, but not achievable by most people, no matter how focused and talented. These men felt that no matter what they did in their lives it would never be enough. They felt they had failed by not fulfilling the promise of their childhood. Because of overly lofty family goals, both of them gave up early in life. They were not only unhappy, but they felt they had failed no matter what they achieved. They probably did not achieve what they might have if they had not been burdened by unreasonable expectations.

Once again emotional health is found in the middle between expectations that are too low and those that are too high. When children set goals (they should be theirs not ours), help them to set achievable goals. Let us permit them to dream big dreams and support those dreams, but, as the parents, let us keep our feet firmly on the ground and help them to know that success can be found in many forms.

New Rule: It is my job to assist my children in setting achievable goals and to help them feel successful when they achieve even the smallest of these.

November 26

Old Rule: Prove yourself.

This is one of those powerful, unspoken rules perpetuated by families who have high expectations for their children. Such parents believe the way to get their children to work hard and achieve is to be very stingy with praise, dispensing it sparingly, if at all. They also tend to be quite critical and often respond to their children's achievements with, "That was pretty good, but…"

As a result, these children come to believe, "Do well and Mom and Dad will approve of me. Do well and they will be proud I am their child. Do well and they will love me." These children are driven to succeed, but no achievement is ever enough. Their self-esteem is contingent upon their latest accomplishment. Feelings of self-worth evaporate rapidly after each accomplishment and must be bolstered by the next one. They may ultimately give up, deciding they can never be good enough or achieve enough to win their parents' approval and love. Both of these patterns, which are usually carried into adulthood, are extremely destructive.

The world outside our homes gives the message to our children that if they wish to be accepted they must prove themselves. This starts in preschool and continues throughout adulthood. Our children get an abundance of these messages in our extremely competitive and goal-oriented culture, but home needs to be a haven from the voices urging constant striving. Home needs to be a place where we love our children, approve of them and are glad they are ours no matter how much they achieve. In such a home, high self-esteem and confidence are born and nurtured.

New Rule: While I want my children to use their talents and assets, they do not need to prove themselves by constant achievement in order to win my love. They will always have my love just for being themselves.

November 27

Old Rule: Children and adults grieve in the same ways.

Loss and grief are part of life, even in childhood. Children may lose important people in their lives to death and friends when families move. Many children must grieve the loss of their home, as they have known it, when parents divorce. Children grieve, but their grief may look and sound differently from that of adults.

The ways in which children understand loss changes as they age. Very young children may have a difficult time understanding that death is permanent or that parents will not reunite after a divorce. They may ask questions at irregular, sometimes puzzling, intervals as they try to make sense of what has happened. They may have periods when they seem to disregard the loss and will go on as usual and other times when they will misbehave or have fears and concerns that seemingly have nothing to do with the loss.

As children grow older, they begin to understand more about the nature of loss. They may not, however, display intense emotion at the time. They may be quiet, withdrawn, or seem pretty much the same. This behavior leads some to believe that children are quite resilient and do not feel the pain of loss. Therefore, parents may be surprised when a child misbehaves, regresses to an earlier stage of development, or becomes angry or upset about a situation they might have previously handled well. However, all of these behaviors are normal manifestations of children's grief.

How do we help children cope with the inevitable losses of life? First of all, we give the child permission to talk about the loss when they are ready, not when we think they should be ready. We leave the door open, but we do not force them to go through it on our timetable. We can also leave the door open for questions, no matter how uncomfortable. We might also talk about our own feelings. Talking about loss does not re-traumatize the child. Not talking about loss says to the child that we are too upset to discuss it and they must protect us or that there is something wrong with such discussions. Lastly, we can show them through our expressions of grief and ultimate healing that one can recover from loss, while remembering that we do not move rigidly through "stages" of grief and neither will they. Each of us grieves differently and it is all okay.

New Rule: Children experience loss and grief differently than adults. Therefore, we are patient with their varying expressions of grief and open to opportunities to help them heal from loss.

November 28

Old Rule: My baby should be completely off the bottle by a year and not dependent on the pacifier by nine months.

Whenever parents of babies meet, the talk quickly turns to their babies' latest achievements. This leads to inevitable comparisons concerning the behavioral milestones of each baby. While developmental and behavioral milestones such as using a cup, rolling over, and sitting up are important to judge if there is a problem with the child's development, rigidly applying such milestones to an individual child may be harmful and unnecessarily upsetting to you and your child. For instance, trying to force a 10-month-old who loves their bottle to give it up completely sets up an unnecessary battle of wills between you and the baby. There will be tears, screaming, frustration, and you will likely lose the war if not the battle. All of this is unnecessary.

Relax! Enjoy your baby! Stop trying to fit your child into some rigid developmental time schedule. Avoid comparisons and stop listening to other anxious parents, your mother, mother-in-law, or baby-sitter about what the baby should be doing. Back off and try new things like the cup or giving up the pacifier later. Follow your own intuition about what your baby needs and when they need it. Growing up is difficult and babies need to be allowed to take it at their own pace. They will grow up. After all, few kids take their bottle and pacifier to kindergarten and almost no one takes their favorite blanket to the prom!

As pediatrician Dr. Sanford Matthews said in an Oct., 1982 *Redbook* article, "If you are not enjoying motherhood then you are putting too much pressure on yourself. If you are putting too much pressure on yourself you are likely putting too much pressure on your child. Remember that the time that we have our children with us is short, so take pleasure from being a parent."

New Rule: We try to relax and allow our children to grow up at their own pace. Childhood is short. Why rush it? Enjoy it!

November 29

Old Rule: Toilet training is serious business and needs to be done properly.

Toilet training anxiety is a fairly recent phenomenon on the parenting front. Thanks to Sigmund Freud and other psychoanalysts, parents fear that terrible consequences will result from improper toilet training. There are a multitude of books and articles that seek to help parents get through this serious business without doing irreparable psychological damage to their children.

Experienced parents know that toilet training really just takes patience and empathy. Look at the situation from the baby's point of view. You are a 2-year-old. Having recently learned to walk, you are able to go just about anywhere. Every day is a new adventure. So many things to explore. So many places to go. From sun up to sun down life is all go, go, go. You have also recently discovered that when you make certain sounds people respond, so that getting the food and drink one wants has become much easier. Life is great!

Now all of a sudden Mom is talking about sitting down on this thing she calls a "potty" and putting your pee and pooh into it. First of all, you are much too busy to sit down and worse; they want you to hold it until you get to the potty. Ever since you were born your parents and others have changed your diaper. Hold it? Hold what? Though you have never actually seen it, whatever they took away in that old diaper came out whenever it was ready and most of the time you didn't even know it until someone laid you down and changed the old diaper and put on a clean one. A pretty good system from your point of view. Granted those who do the changing have not been as happy lately as when you were a new baby and they laughed and talked to you and tickled your tummy, but they still give you something to play with because you really haven't the time to stop and lay down to be changed. Now they want all of this to change. No way!

It takes patience and time to train a child, but few children go off to kindergarten without the whole idea down pat. Relax! Generations of parents and children before you managed to get through this successfully and you will, too.

New Rule: Toilet training is best accomplished with empathy, a sense of humor, and patience. Relax!

November 30

Old Rule: Money = Power

It is virtually impossible to live without money. Its presence or absence influences the quality of our lives as well as our survival. Money is power, even in families. Whoever has the power to make decisions about money influences family decisions as a whole.

Many disagreements among couples, including divorced couples, are about money. These disagreements are actually power struggles. Many marriages end and divorces are made even more traumatic because the person who controls the money uses this power inappropriately to control or punish the other. Many of our disagreements and struggles with our children are about money. There is a tension between the parents who have money and the children who have none, but wish to have certain things.

It is impossible to eradicate the power of money. Previously, most monetary power rested with men. They were the "breadwinners." Often the husband and father not only had the power to make decisions, but he could also conceal from the family the details of their financial situation. With the advent of two income households, the partner who makes the most money often has the lion's share of the power. No wonder many men are uncomfortable when women make more money. They lose power and no human being wants to lose such power. Couples who successfully work out the issues surrounding power and money usually come to a sense of shared power and cooperation with respect to money management.

While shared power between spouses is widely accepted, giving children some power in managing the family finances is less common. Children need to begin to learn the complex topic of money management when they are quite young; preschool is not too early. Allowing children to share some of the responsibility for making financial decisions within the family, like spending money for recreation or where to go on family vacations, teaches them about the realities of the family financial resources. Children might also be given an allowance to spend as they choose while learning to save for things they want. It is in sharing money management power with them that they can begin to acquire the skills necessary to use this power wisely.

New Rule: While money will always equal power, we share this power within our family.

December 1

Old Rule: Don't discuss money with the children

I am infamous in my family for an incident that took place when I was preparing to graduate from high school and enter college. Having been kept ignorant of my family's financial situation, I told my high school guidance counselor that money was not an issue with respect to my college choice. When my parents heard this, they were justifiably appalled. Money was most definitely an issue.

My parents, like many others, believed that family financial matters were strictly the business of the parents. While this comes from an attitude of not wishing to worry children about money problems coupled with the belief that children are not able to understand financial matters, keeping children ignorant about finances does them a disservice.

Having been kept ignorant of family finances, not only did I make a foolish statement to my guidance counselor, I also had to learn about money management as a semi-independent adult in college at 18 and as a more independent adult when I was 20 and married. Many of those spending and budgeting lessons came at a rather high cost with numerous financial mistakes.

I believe we can begin to teach our children about money as soon as they are old enough to understand that we have to have money in order to purchase the things that we need as well as those things that we want. Simple lessons in money management might begin within the context of the family meetings. (See the description of the family meeting format on October 5 and 6)

Many child-rearing experts recommend that even young children be given an allowance to be used as they want, while learning to save a portion of their money for things they want later. Beginning in their early teens, children might also start to earn money outside of their home or by doing extra household chores, provided it does not interfere with schoolwork and activities.

How we use our money reflects our values. We impart these values to our children, including our feelings about the importance of saving and giving to religious organizations or others who are less fortunate. Family discussions about money are valuable lessons not only in learning to handle money, but also in developing values.

New Rule: It is important for children to learn money management and money values. Such lessons are an important part of their preparation for becoming independent, successful adults.

December 2

Old Rule: God expects you to …

Discovering and living by the will of God, or however one refers to a Supreme Being, is a central issue of the human spiritual journey. The commandments to "Love the Lord your God with all your heart, all of your soul, and all of your might" and "To love your neighbor as yourself" can provide a lifetime of spiritual discovery. Attempting to live out these commandments in our daily lives and in our dealings with others is the essential the task of ongoing spiritual growth.

However, some parents use God as a disciplinary ally, telling children that God wants or desires a behavior when it is really the parents' desire. While we need to teach our children about God and the way in which they might live according to the will of God, we should always allow the child to define that relationship and give them the freedom to decide what God wants for them to do, think, or be. Such decisions are not our right or our responsibility; it is theirs as they mature in their faith.

We should, however, have the courage to tell them what we think is right or ethical. They may not always follow the path we would have them take, but we need to give them the freedom and dignity to discover for themselves their purpose and develop their own relationship with God.

New Rule: My children have the freedom to develop their own relationship with God in which they can discover for themselves what God wants for them. It is my task as a parent to foster that relationship by living by my sense of the purpose God has for me. I try to provide my children with the opportunity to learn about God and the relationship God has with all human beings.

December 3

Old Rule: It is appropriate for children to know about their parent's painful histories. It makes them grateful for what they have.

Talking about family history is not only fun, it is also important. It gives children a sense of connectedness to an ongoing family as well as valuable information about themselves.

However, many children grow up hearing the horror stories of their parent's painful childhood. By telling these stories, the parent often conveys the unspoken messages: "Don't expect too much of me, I'm wounded, "Be grateful you don't have it as rough as I did," or "I'm fragile, take care of me."

Hearing these stories, children grow up feeling that they must somehow make up for their parent's unhappy and painful past. They may feel that their needs are not as important as those of the wounded parent or that they have no right to have their needs met. In effect, children become an emotional parent attempting to take care of their own parent. As a result, children grow up not only putting their needs consistently second to those of others, but in many cases not even acknowledging that their emotional needs exist. Thus their relationships tend to be one-sided and self-destructive. This painful pattern may be passed on from generation to generation.

Children are not responsible for healing the emotional wounds of their parents. This is the parent's responsibility. Children can know about their parents' painful history, but only if parents are willing to accept responsibility for their own healing and recovery.

New Rule: I am responsible for healing from my childhood emotional trauma. I take care of my children's emotional needs; they do not take care of mine.

December 4

Old Rule: Old people don't count.

Some time ago, my husband and I were visiting in the home of one of our children's friends. The great-grandmother of our son's friend made her home with them and when we entered she was in the kitchen. Not only did we as a group of younger adults not talk with her, we did not even acknowledge her presence. Quickly, she retired to her room. We had treated her as though she did not exist, as though she was not important enough to deserve the respect of an acknowledging greeting. I cringe when I think about the hurt we so callously inflicted.

Attitudes and behaviors that say that older people are not interesting or worthy of notice are certainly not ones we wish to model for our children, but when we behave in this manner we speak volumes to them about the value of such people.

A friend routinely takes her daughter to a local nursing home to do simple tasks or take small gifts to the residents. They have gotten to know many of these elderly adults quite well and look forward to their once or twice a month visits. She does this despite the fact that her daughter sees her own grandparents frequently. She is saying to her child that community service is important, but also that older people, even those who are infirm, are valuable human beings worthy of care and respect.

During this holiday season I encourage you to seek out older people who may need a bit of company and attention. I further challenge you to keep up this practice throughout the rest of the year when giving to others may not be so paramount in our thinking. Such lessons regarding caring and respect are invaluable to our children.

New Rule: All people, whether young or old, healthy or infirm, are worthy of attention and respect.

December 5

Old Rule: Home is not a haven.

We all know the saying "Home is the place that when you go there they have to take you in." We may provide physical space for our family, but are we creating a haven, a home where everyone can feel safe?

Some of us were fortunate enough to come from homes where we were safe. We were safe from violence, both physical and verbal. Our bodies were our own, not to be violated sexually by others. We were accepted and valued for whom we were and not criticized or devalued for being different. Home was a place where mistakes were learning opportunities and not evidence of incompetence and failure. Home was a place where they supported and took care of you when you needed it and encouraged you to go back out and try again when you experienced difficulties and disappointments.

Others of us came from homes where violence could occur at any time. Our bodies and our spirits were not safe. Our bodies might be violated sexually for the gratification of others. We might have been ridiculed and told we were ugly or stupid. Mistakes were evidence of stupidity or the folly of lofty aspirations. Home was a place where they might take you in but where your woundedness was ridiculed or you were allowed to slip into fearful, passive dependency rather that encouraged to try again.

Which sort of home do we wish to create for our children? When we were children we had no choice in the matter, but as adult parents we have many choices about the type of home we create.

New Rule: Our home is a haven of love and support for our family.

December 6

Old Rule: It is up to mother to make the holidays wonderful for everyone in the family.

Some years ago, I had a client who dreaded Christmas. She felt she had to decorate her home elaborately with several different Christmas trees, participate in the many children's Christmas activities, bake elaborate pastries, entertain her husband's business associates, have the extended family in for a celebration, and purchase, wrap, and deliver Christmas presents for over 60 different people. She also had to prepare to travel to her parents' home to participate in the Christmas Eve celebration and gift giving. She believed all of this activity was her responsibility and absolutely vital to making the holidays wonderful, indeed perfect, for everyone. Everyone, that is, except herself.

By the time the holidays arrived she was exhausted, and though she did not admit it, resentful and angry. Her children were unhappy because she was constantly rushing about and irritable. She and her husband were at odds, mostly because he seemed to think that all of this was truly her responsibility and she wasn't doing enough. There was nothing that remotely resembled holiday cheer in their house. Peace on earth, good will to men? Bah humbug!

While this harried woman is an extreme example, she is definitely not unique. Many mothers dread Christmas because of the expectations to make the holidays joyful for everyone around them.

Early this month, while there is still time, decide what you would like to do for the holidays. Not what you feel duty bound to do, but what you would like to do. Decide what is important for you. Begin to scale back some of the activities, learn to say "no" to those who wish to entangle you in their elaborate plans. Spend time with your children while planning for the holidays. Teach them that the season is not about party after party and obtaining a multitude of gifts. The holidays are far more significant than decorations, presents, and food. Take time for yourself and do those things that are meaningful for you and bring you joy. Perfect holidays do not exist, but enjoyable and meaningful holidays are created in warm and caring relationships with others.

New Rule: I accept that only I can bring sanity into my holiday preparations. I do not attempt to create a perfect holiday for those around me. During the holiday season, I express my love for others without exhausting myself with overwhelming tasks.

December 7

Old Rule: I know they love me, they just don't show it.

Many of us heard this message as children, "You know your mother/father loves you, they just don't show it." Believing this rule, we enter into adult relationships in which we are abused or ignored, but tell ourselves, "They love me, they just don't show it." What a terrible lie! Yet, we go on for years getting an occasional crumb of affection and approval and waiting for someone to express the love we tell ourselves must exist. Worse yet we pass this legacy on to our children, telling them the same lie.

Being in what is supposed to be a loving relationship with someone who is incapable of expressing love is one of life's most painful circumstances. We cannot force someone to love us. We probably cannot teach an adult to express love who is incapable of doing so. The only power we have is to decide if we want to continue to wait. Refusing to wait and letting go of this fantasy means accepting the painful reality that love unexpressed is love that does not exist. With this realization, we can decide when it is time to stop waiting for love in such relationships and begin to invest our love in relationships with those who are willing and capable of returning it.

New Rule: I choose to relinquish this family excuse for being abused and neglected. I am unwilling to pass this painful legacy on to my children. I choose to enter into relationships with those who are willing and capable of returning my love.

December 8

Old Rule: I'll teach my children right from wrong! If they disobey, they get a good smack!

Well, that is one way to teach children. It gets their attention. It will stop, at least temporarily, almost any behavior. However, parents must have more tools at their disposal in order to discipline their children, for there will come a day when spanking will not work or even be appropriate.

The first tool is an understanding and appreciation for how children develop a sense of right and wrong. How do they learn to do the right thing? How do they develop a conscience? After all, we want them to leave our homes as young adults not with just a set of rules, but with a conscience and the ability to think through a moral problem.

Young children, under the age of five or six, have an external conscience. They have learned that doing certain things will result in negative consequences. At this stage, most behavior is guided by what they want with little thought to the needs or wants of others. They want what they want, when they want it. It is not that they are "bad" or "mean"; this behavior is simply the result of an immature brain. The only reason they can see for not doing what they want is that they will be punished. They will test us to see if the results are the same every time. This is normal behavior, but it is also the reason why it is important to be consistent in our discipline.

We all know people who are stuck in this first· stage of moral development. The prisons are full of people who do what they want, hoping they will not be caught and punished. Fortunately, most of us move to the next stage of development. As the brain matures the ability to understand time and the use of language develops. Children begin to learn that some behaviors might bring future reward. Five-to-ten year-olds are moving from an external to internal control of their behavior. Still, avoiding punishment is dominant at this age, coupled with the desire to have what they want now. Talking with them and giving consequences for undesirable behavior (discipline) becomes more effective than physical punishment. Indeed, the overly critical or inconsistent parent is laying a defective foundation for the years that lie ahead.

These early years are the time to lay down a foundation for internal moral control, a conscience, by beginning to instill the idea that behavior has consequences.

New Rule: Morality and conscience begin to develop early in childhood, but it is important to respect children's normal development and not expect too much too soon.

December 9

Old Rule: You are not being fair! You have to be fair!

This is not a parental rule. Rather, it reflects the moral focus of children between the ages of 10 to 13, as they begin to internalize the rules of fair play. During this stage of moral and intellectual development, they enjoy making up games with complex rules, and become irate when someone violates them. They become particularly outraged at favoritism, especially when they are not on the receiving end of the favors.

These children are concrete, black and white thinkers. Something is good or bad, right or wrong, fair or unfair. They tend to either idolize or condemn others, and have difficulty accepting that a person can be both good and bad. This is the age when they begin to identify with peers and adults outside of their home. Their ethical behavior is motivated by the expectations of others and a personal respect for authority. They have internalized the rules of conduct, but they still have not developed the ability to understand the concept of private ethical beliefs that governs one's behavior and thinking.

At this age parents can help their child to continue their ethical and moral development by talking with them about what characteristics they admire or find objectionable in others. They can also continue to talk with them about being honest, especially with respect to schoolwork. At this stage of development children will have much difficulty tolerating even a little white lie from their parents. They may focus on the simplest untruth with a great deal of moral indignation. If we keep our cool, parents can help by explaining the difference between the little white lies that spare the feelings of another and being dishonest in order to avoid consequences or gain a desired outcome for oneself.

Many adults remain at this stage of moral development. They behave according to the rules of society not only to avoid punishment, but also because others may think badly of them for breaking the rules. These are the people who will act unethically or immorally if they believe they will not be found out. They have not matured to the next stage of ethical development, where decisions are made in accordance with an inner moral compass. If we are stuck here, our children will be stuck here also, for we cannot teach them what we do not practice ourselves.

New Rule: During late childhood and early adolescence, children are focused on the rules and become upset when they are not followed. I allow them to express their feelings while helping them to focus on their own behavior.

December 10 & 11

Old Rule: My teenagers focus solely on the opinions of their friends. They don't care what I think. They disagree with everything I say!

The parents of teenagers often worry about their seeming loss of influence over their children. Some parents give up and allow their children almost complete freedom with little attempt at limit setting and guidance. Such adolescents are not free, just loose, and the consequences can be disastrous.

Other parents respond by setting overly strict limits with threats of dire consequences for violating the rules. They make decisions for their adolescents, allowing them little or no input into the choices that affect them. They are overprotective and hope to keep their adolescents children as long as possible. Such parents unwittingly invite rebellion because their treatment of these young adults is not age appropriate. They are also inviting their children to deceive them by simply limiting what they know, thus avoiding punishment while gaining some freedom.

Once again, the middle ground is probably the wisest course. Adolescents have before them an amazing number of choices about what to think, how to act, what to buy, and what to believe. They have emerged from the black or white thinking of late childhood and early adolescence into a confusing world in which most things are neither black nor white, but gray. They are coming to know that even the best people have flaws. This realization may be upsetting and disillusioning to them. No wonder they can, at times, be so cynical. The time from 13 to 17 is a period of intense confusion and change. It is a time of trying on new ideas just as they try different clothes and hairstyles.

Their brains are maturing and they have developed the skills to argue and debate. While this can be tiresome for parents, it is a sign that they are using these new skills. At the same time, they face many choices every day. The new ideas and different lifestyles they are exposed to in school and by the culture, in general, makes this a turbulent and stressful time for adolescents and parents alike. Parents often feel they have lost all control and, indeed, they no longer know this person who lives in their home.

Knowing all of this, parents can make this time easier by keeping their cool and reminding themselves that all of this is part of normal development. This is the point where much of the work we have tried to do as parents pays off, for we can call on the loving, accepting relationship we have built with them to continue to be a steadying influence in their lives. However, if they doubt our love and acceptance and have been unable to please us for as long as they can remember, they will stop trying to win our approval and love and do what they want and, not coincidentally, wins the approval of their peers. This situation can have long-lasting, harmful consequences. On the other hand, if adolescents find that they have the love, respect, approval, and trust of their parents, they may, as I have heard many young adults say, refrain from doing something wrong or self-destructive because their parents would be "terribly disappointed." When kids make decisions based on this belief, parents have done their job well.

New Rule: Adolescence is a morally confusing time for our children, but if we have a positive open relationship with our adolescents, we can keep the door open for them to talk with us about their choices and seek our input when they are faced with troubling decisions.

December 12 and 13

Old Rule: We are 24/7 parents.

I am embarrassed urging parents to find a balance between being a parent and an individual with personal interests and activities. I have never felt I was successful at finding the balance between fulfilling my own needs and desires and being a 24 hours a day, 7 days a week parent.

Like most parents, I wanted to be the best parent I could be. I also worked outside of the home and wanted to be successful in my career. In addition, I did the usual household chores. Sound familiar? Perhaps painfully familiar?

My husband and I also tried, with limited success, to find time to be a couple as well as Mom and Dad. Yet, our relationship was often way down on the priority list. What was even further down on this list was being an individual with friends and interests that did not involve being a mom or wife. I was often resentful and angry as well as exhausted. I felt I was on a treadmill and it was impossible to get off. I often felt guilty for being angry and wanting time to pursue more adult interests.

When I was at work I felt I should be more dedicated to home and children, while believing that I was not more successful in my career because I was not sufficiently focused. I felt pulled in so many different directions, no wonder it was difficult for me to enjoy either family or work.

I would like to tell you that I successfully resolved this dilemma. Looking back on those years with the perspective of my last child leaving home, I think there is great value in doing those things you can do and let the rest, like a well-kept home, slide. I also think that my children did not suffer so much from my working outside of the home and having interests besides mothering, but rather more from my anger and resentment about my life being so out of balance.

When I look back, what I recall most fondly is not the clean and tidy house or the praise from my supervisor for a job well done, or even the expensive vacations or other luxuries, but having fun with the kids on a day-to-day basis. I treasure the afternoons in the park and the time spent reading stories and playing games. What I regret is not taking the time for the little moments when we could have had more fun if I had not been preoccupied.

I also regret wasting emotional energy on feeling guilty when I wanted to do things that did not involve being a parent. Being a 24/7 parent is a prescription for feeling burnt out and angry. It is also a prescription for having a marriage that is totally subsumed by parenting and rearing children who believe the world revolves around them. Such children tend to believe they should not only have what they want, but they should also be able to command the attention of their parents whenever they please.

It is natural to want time for oneself and for being a couple. It is normal to have interests that have nothing to do with children. It is normal to want time, romance, and uninterrupted lovemaking with the person you married.

Once again, there is a need for balance between being a loving, involved parent and being an adult human being and spouse. Make time for yourself. A few hours pursuing your own interests will do wonders. Have a date with your spouse at least twice a month (once a week is better). Be a couple, not just Mom and Dad. You will probably spend time talking about the kids, but at least you will be alone and having an uninterrupted conversation. Have fun together! It doesn't need to be expensive. All it takes is being together away from the interruptions of children. As a matter of fact, you had better do this if you expect to have a marriage when the children begin to have interests and lives of their own and leave you behind.

Give this parenting business the dedication it deserves, but also dedicate yourself to yourself and to your marriage. Work toward a balance, it is worth the effort.

New Rule: We try to maintain a healthy balance between being parents and employees as well spouses and individuals. At times it is difficult, but the effort does pay off.

December 14

Old Rule: You should find your ultimate fulfillment in being a parent.

This rule, a corollary to the previous one, is seldom applied to fathers but rather to mothers. Mothers often hear the message that everything in their lives should pale in comparison to the fulfillment they find in mothering.

Even today when over 50% of mothers with young children are in the workforce, mothers continue to be pulled between the desire to be with their children, the desire to have a fulfilling career, and the need to work outside of their home. Mothers often feel guilty because they feel they short change both parenting and work.

Cultural messages about parenting still put the lion's share of the responsibility on mothers. While being a mother is fulfilling and satisfying, it does not complete a woman's life. Indeed, many of those cultural messages about motherhood as the ultimate fulfillment of one's life date back to the time when large families were the norm, women often died in childbirth, and many women died shortly after their last child left home.

I can clearly recall, shortly after the birth of our first son, when my husband got his first promotion. He came home excited and pleased with his success and accomplishment, ate dinner, kissed us both, and went off to his graduate school class. I was left at home, bathing the baby, playing with him, and putting him to bed. I can still recall sitting by that bathtub feeling so left behind, frustrated, and angry.

At the same time, I felt guilty for wanting to work on my own career and go to graduate school myself when I had this wonderful baby boy that I loved with all my heart. I decided that night that I needed to go back to school even if it was part time. Beginning to consider what I needed in my life as an individual worked. I can truthfully say that the mother who came to pick up my son after class was a much better mother than the one who left him. I was certainly a better mother than the one who stayed home with him all of the time battling feelings of guilt for wanting to have more in her life than being a mother. Once again, an emotionally healthy life is found in seeking a balance between two extremes.

New Rule: Being a parent is just a part of life. There is no need to feel guilty or to stop yourself from having more in your life than motherhood.

December 15

Old Rule: Play is for children. Adults have better and more important things to do.

This is a reminder concerning bringing sanity into our holiday celebrations. We want our children to have joyful and memorable holidays. We frequently spend more money than we actually have, running up credit card debt. We exhaust ourselves attempting to make everything perfect. We even try to make up to them for our shortcomings during the rest of the year.

Sometimes, we forget that loving our children does not necessarily mean giving them things. Loving our children means that we spend time with them, fun time, playtime, when we drop our serious parent role and just be with them. As adults, we need to retain a sense of fun and play. What better way to continue to fulfill our own need for fun than to learn to play and be silly with our kids?

Think back to your favorite childhood holidays. You will probably recall time spent with those who loved you. You may recall a few exceptional presents that were bought just because your parents knew they were exactly what you really wanted. However, special holiday memories are more likely to involve having fun as a family. Joyful holidays are created in relationships, relationships between children and adults who take pleasure in each other's company.

It is vitally important that we retain our ability to have fun. What better way than to play with our kids? Today and the rest of the holiday season, take some time to enjoy yourself with your children. These are the moments that you and they will recall come July.

New Rule: Children and adults both need to play and have fun. This is an important part of being a healthy family.

December 16

Old Rule: When members of the family make mistakes, don't hold them accountable. Make excuses for them.

Unwilling to admit their children's imperfections, parents often make excuses for their unacceptable behavior. One hears such excuses as, "He didn't mean to do that," "She was only teasing," "He is having difficulties adjusting to the new baby, school, the recent move," or "The teacher just doesn't like her."

This sets up a pattern in the lives of these children that allows them to escape responsibility for their actions. It also allows them to blame others for their behavior: "If you had not done this, then I wouldn't have been forced to do that." In other words, "You made me do it and you are responsible for my behavior."

We all know parents who blame others or otherwise make excuses for their children's behavior and we all know adults who continue to operate this way. Such adults do not take responsibility for their behavior whether it is failure to perform at work, spouse abuse, or drug abuse. Instead, they blame their behavior on others or their life circumstances. When one continues this pattern from childhood into adulthood, it becomes more entrenched as the consequences become more serious.

It is part of our parental responsibilities to hold our children accountable for their inappropriate behavior and to help them learn more acceptable and responsible ways of behaving. We can do this by first modeling a willingness to take responsibility for our own mistakes. We can also hold our children accountable and give them consequences for inappropriate behavior, thus helping them to grow up to be responsible, successful adults.

New Rule: We admit imperfection and mistakes and take responsibility for them and make an effort to correct them. We do not blame others or circumstances for our inappropriate behavior.

December 17, 18, and 19

Old Rule: It is possible to be perfect, if you try hard enough.

We are human beings and, by definition, not perfectible. Perfection is reserved for the angels, but many of us were reared by parents who demanded perfection. As a result, we have become "perfectionists." Most perfectionists have mixed feelings about their predicament. On one hand, they know that such expectations are not only unrealistic and painful, but they also tend to hold on to their perfectionism as a mark of high standards and superiority. They also tend to have unrealistic expectations of others, especially their children and spouses, whom they view as extensions of themselves and their achievements. Obviously, perfectionism is especially hazardous to the emotional health of a family.

According to Stephen J. Hendlin, PhD, clinical psychologist and author of the book <u>When Good Enough is Never Enough,</u> "Perfectionism comes about in human beings when we are able to conceive of perfection but fail to understand the impossibility of actualizing this image in reality." I would add that much perfectionism stems from critical, demanding parents who expect perfection of themselves and their children. While we can strive for excellence, we can as human beings only approach the perfect body, the perfect relationship, the perfect lifestyle, the perfect performance review, or even the perfect spiritual experience. For the perfectionist, good enough is never enough. No matter how positive the experience or how lofty the achievement, the perfectionist will come away feeling empty and inadequate.

Our achievement-oriented culture reinforces these beliefs concerning the ability to achieve perfection. For instance, athletic performance or ones' appearance are rated as a "10" (perfect) or less than noteworthy.

Perfectionists are overwhelmingly concerned about their performance. They are "human doings" as opposed to human beings. They are often driven, constantly working toward some new goal.

According to Dr. Hendlin, "Perfectionists set unrealistically, even impossibly, high goals for themselves. There is little or no room for accepting achievement without perfection." This can take on near ridiculous proportions. When I was in college and at my perfectionistic worst, I felt I had to make not only "A's," but the highest "A" in the class. If I failed to achieve the highest "A," I felt as though I had failed. Emotionally, there was literally no room between the second highest "A" and an "F." They both felt the same.

Perfectionists cannot tolerate coming close to a goal and they cannot celebrate achieving the successive steps leading up to goal. They either achieve all of it or feel as though nothing was achieved. They tend to give themselves little time to learn or to be a beginner. Perfectionists tend to be impatient with themselves while learning a new skill. They want to be expert from the start. They also tend to carry these unrealistic expectations over into their relationship with their children, allowing them very little time to learn a new skill. Believing that they should be able to master a skill very quickly, perfectionists tend to avoid seeking help from others. To ask for help would not only force them to acknowledge their own limitations, but also the superior skills of another. Actually, we perfectionists tend to be an arrogant lot.

Because the perfectionist does not tolerate the frustration of being a learner, they also tend to shy away from things they have not mastered, especially when there is a potential for public revelation of a less than masterful performance. They tend to have little sense of humor about themselves and suffer from a seriously impaired ability to laugh at themselves. Perfectionists take their public image very seriously.

This thinking often leads to procrastination and reluctance to try new things. Despite a show of indifference, what is really at work is a paralyzing fear of failure and public humiliation. Perfectionists seek to avoid the excruciatingly painful feelings of shame and inadequacy. They have experienced these feelings before and believe it is better not to try anything new rather than to risk feeling them again.

When perfectionists do achieve their lofty goals, they often report a feeling of emptiness or numbness. They find it very difficult to celebrate accomplishments and will instead tell themselves, "It wasn't that hard." or "It really wasn't such a great accomplishment, anyone can do this." Weary from this striving, perfectionists often want things to be accomplished magically, but discount any achievement that seems too easy. Thus the perfectionist is in a lose/lose situation. If something comes too easy, it is not of value and does not, even for a moment, fill the void that the perfectionist hopes to fill with achievement.

Aside from a terror of failure and public humiliation, the perfectionist also fears being found out as an imposter. Because the perfectionist's expectations are so high, there is a fear that others will discover that they are not as competent, worthy, or capable as they appear. Perfectionists tend to be self-critical and lacking in self-esteem. They are often unable to tolerate criticism from others. When others are critical, the perfectionist feels the burning shame of humiliation at having been found out and perceived as less than perfect. Since they are so self-critical when they make a mistake or are less than perfect, criticism from others seems like too much. Thus, they may initially react to criticism with dejection, but later with anger, blame, and defensiveness.

Part of the perfectionist's inability to enjoy what they do achieve is a belief that says, "So what have I done lately?" They have at their very core a belief that love and worth must be constantly earned. They tend to move very quickly to the next goal, failing to enjoy their achievements and feeling driven to achieve in a new way. Our performance driven society reinforces this with a "you are only as good (valuable) as your last performance" mentality. It is never enough to have an outstanding performance; the culture says that in order to be noticed (the perfectionist wants desperately to be noticed and to be thought of as extraordinary) one must continue to achieve at an even higher level. The perfectionist takes in these cultural messages and internalizes them, believing that they are only as good as their last achievement, victory, or performance.

The engine that drives the perfectionist is a firmly held belief that they are not currently loveable and worthwhile, but that if they keep trying and keep achieving, somehow they can earn love and approval from others. While this began with the desire to win approval from critical, demanding, withholding parents, this desire for approval generalizes into a desire to be seen by virtually everyone as capable and extraordinary (the perfectionist has a great fear of being considered ordinary) and, therefore, worthy of love and approval.

Surely, we do not wish to pass this painful circumstance on to our children, especially if we are living in this situation ourselves. We can start to dismantle this old rule in our families by first breaking the hold that perfectionism has on us. Even if it means that we go to a therapist to help us ease up on ourselves, it is worth the effort and the expense. For not only will we be happier and healthier, we can then help our children break these patterns. We cannot give to our children what we do not have.

We can also give our children learning time and permission to have fun and to be less than perfect at an activity. We can also act as a buffer between our children and the culture, especially other adults, who would demand perfection and criticize the lack of it. We can criticize less and praise more, making certain to give genuine praise. Children are smart. They know the difference between genuine praise and praising just because we feel we ought to. Look for things to praise in your child. When you honestly look without perfectionist eyes, you will see your children and their efforts much differently. Open your mouth and let them know you are proud of them. Let them know your love is given freely and not earned by perfect performance

New Rule: Perfectionism is a painful, but preventable condition. It can be cured and prevented with knowledge, love, and patience.

December 20

Old Rule: Stop crying! You are not hurt! If you don't stop crying, I'll give you something to cry about!

Crying is annoying, especially when parents believe that the child has absolutely nothing to cry about and is crying in an effort to get attention. Having not as yet been indoctrinated by the cultural messages, "Don't cry, it makes others uncomfortable, shows that you are weak, and makes you vulnerable," crying is the way children communicate hurt and anger.

When we shame children for their tears and tell them not to cry, the pain does not go away. Instead, the child swallows the feelings, which may come out later as sadness or defiance. Having heard this message in childhood, adults take over the job of telling themselves not to cry when they are hurt. The pain does not go away. It continues to reside in the body. Having been denied, hurt may resurface later as resentment, depression, emotional numbness, anger, or physical illness. This is particularly true of those who were told not to cry when they were spanked or hurt in other ways by their parents. Often the first step in healing old emotional scars is giving yourself permission to cry about them.

By our willingness to be vulnerable, we can show our children that it is okay to cry when you are hurt, even if you are a man. We know that boys are often shamed early in childhood for their tears and told to, "Be a man, don't cry." They need to know that hurt that is expressed is hurt that heals. Allowing our children and ourselves the freedom to express the full range of human emotions is a powerful and valuable legacy to pass on to them. Expression of feelings creates, indeed defines, emotionally healthy families.

New Rule: I know that emotions are neither positive nor negative; they are merely temporary responses to perceptions of events. I also know that emotional expression is healthy. I can teach my children, by my example and permission, that it is okay to cry.

December 21

Old Rule: Having a conflict means that we are forever estranged. Never let go! Never forgive!

A friend taught me a lesson about the power of forgiveness. A brother betrayed her. His betrayal was conscious and deliberate. It took place over a period of time and resulted in lasting consequences to her. It was serious business.

She was hurt and angry. She held him accountable. She allowed him to suffer the consequences both personal and legal. She refused to continue to be his victim. Then she did a truly courageous thing. She forgave him and took him back into her life! Such forgiveness was in no way a signal to him that what he had done was all right or that he could do it again without suffering the consequences. She did not make herself his victim. She forgave him, not for his sake, but for herself. She knew that to harbor anger, no matter how justified, would ultimately hurt her. She knew that such anger ultimately hardens into bitterness and resentment. She knew that bitterness saps the energy of the one who harbors it and diminishes the quality of their life.

I know that my reaction to such a betrayal would have been unrelenting anger and estrangement from the offender. I know I would have permitted this to drain my energy and occupy my thinking for years to come, but her behavior taught me about the power of forgiveness and the freedom that is possible when one is willing to let go of blame and resentment. What a wonderful gift!

What a magnificent lesson to teach one's children. To hold accountable, but not to permit wrongs to forever poison relationships. To use anger to defend one's self, but to refuse to let anger harden into resentment and bitterness. To give the gift of forgiveness freely and without expectation of return. To love oneself enough to refuse to allow one's life to be poisoned with the pollution of harboring past hurts and wrongs.

New Rule: When we are wronged, we hold others accountable and then we forgive and let go. We cannot afford to harbor old hurts. We have too much living to do!

December 22

Old Rule: Attendance at religious services is for children and old people.

Many adults can recall going to religious services by themselves or with a grandparent. In effect, they received the unspoken message that it was important for children to learn about religion and, more importantly, how to behave properly. Thus religion became an adjunct to parental discipline. The other part of the message was that it was important for old people to go to services. They were, after all, preparing to go to an afterlife, just in case there might be such a thing. Besides old people had nothing better to do and might as well go to religious services.

However, religious services and spirituality were not really important for younger adults. They had better things to do, more significant things to occupy their minds. Therefore, children learned that religion and spirituality are not significant concerns in busy, adult lives. They believed it was not essential to be concerned about such things and that religion holds little value for adults.

When we continue to behave in this manner, we rob our children of learning about and developing their spiritual and religious lives. We deprive them of an example of growing, vital adult spirituality. We also rob ourselves of the comfort and grounding of a belief in something greater than ourselves. When we begin to focus on our own spirituality, we not only cease to send our children a mixed message about the significance of religion, but we also add to the quality of our lives and to the lives of our family.

New Rule: It is vitally important that each member of the family has a relationship with a power greater than themselves and is encouraged to develop spiritually. Parental leadership in this area is meaningful and precious.

December 23 & 24

Old Rule: Growing old is a terrible thing.

In Eastern cultures, growing old is a wonderful thing. The old are venerated for their experience and wisdom. When friends greet one another they might say, "Oh, how old you are looking!" This is a complement!

Think what might happen if you greeted a friend in this manner! In Western countries, especially the United States, we would view this as insult. In our youth-worshiping culture, we tend to view age as a tragedy, something to be struggled against and avoided. Indeed, getting older is viewed as some sort of personal failing; if one had been smarter, faster, or wiser, it would not be happening at all.

Yet aging does happen to all of us. While the last quarter of life can be healthy and productive, the ravages of age do take their toll and sometimes the results are not attractive or easily dealt with. There is a story by Leo Tolstoy that considers how the less desirable side of aging might be viewed in a family.

There was a family of a mother, father, a young boy, and an old grandfather. The grandfather was very old and his hands trembled. He broke the mother's china cups. She was very angry and gave him tin plates and cups to eat from. The grandfather was messy when he ate, soiling the tablecloth. He was banished to the cellar to take his meals and his food was served from a wooden bowl behind the furnace.

The young boy felt sorry for the old man and often visited him in the cellar. One day his parents saw him making a bowl out of wood. They asked what he was doing and he replied, "Dear parents, I am making a bowl for you for when you are old and I must feed you."

471

We teach our children about aging and the aged by our own actions toward them. When we are patient and considerate, we teach patience and consideration. When we practice love and concern, we teach those virtues. Likewise when we are impatient, neglectful or push the elderly into a corner and treat them as though they not only have nothing to offer, but are instead a nuisance, we teach those attitudes.

What do we want our children to learn? Do we want them to understand aging as a part of life, not as frightening or disgusting, but accepted and maybe even welcomed? Do we want them to accept us as we age and continue to welcome us into their homes or ignore us as they go about their busy lives? The instruction is up to us. What do we wish them to know?

New Rule: I want my children to understand that getting old is a part of life, not something to be feared or denied. I also want my children to practice compassion and acceptance when the results of aging are inconvenient and unattractive.

December 25

Old Rule: The holidays should be different. We should all get along and show our love for one another.

Even if you have made time for your daily reading, you are probably feeling worn out and slightly let down. Perhaps it has been a good day, but not the wonderful, magical time you tried so hard to create. You may feel taken for granted. The children are grumpy and discontent, even though they received all that you can possibly afford and maybe then some. Adults are overfed and lying on the couch. Some family members are mesmerized by yet another football game. The usual family conflicts may have arisen or are lurking just under the surface. This is not what you had in mind! What went wrong?!

Nothing really went wrong. Your family is being human. Human beings experience few magical moments and most are not planned. They just happen. Your family is only being who they are. Children have been conditioned for weeks by television and their surroundings to expect a truly magical day, when they will get all that they want and this will make them blissfully happy. Although they do not as yet have the words to express it, they have just been given a lesson in the reality of the limitations of things to make one truly happy, even things one desires mightily.

Adults have also been conditioned to believe that this will be a day of joy and that they and others will be different, only to discover that nothing about themselves and others has changed. Although they might do a better job of articulating this than children, adults too experience a sense of disappointment. If you have been the one to plan what was supposed to be a wonderful, joyous day, you have likely had a lesson in the limitations of your ability to change your family even for a day. All of the shiny decorations, good food, and beautifully wrapped presents do not change who we are and certainly do not change our relationships.

So relax, let go of your expectations about the holidays and please yourself. What do you want to do to make this day meaningful for you? You might do well to remember the reasons why we celebrate the holidays and nurture your relationship with the God of your understanding. Deepening this relationship may be the finest gift that you can give yourself and ultimately those you love.

New Rule: While the holidays may be very pleasant, they are a reflection of the relationships we have all year long. Next year when I plan for the holidays, I will remember that over-work, over-spending, and over-expectations can ruin what can be a pleasant time of relaxation and renewal.

December 26

Old Rule: Don't upset your mother/father!

Many of us come from homes where the "do not upset" rule was in force. We knew what would happen if we disturbed the "don't upset" parent. That parent would fall apart, get sick, cry, become hysterical, or uncontrollably angry. All of which would get us into trouble, especially with the parent who had to calm down the upset parent. Complicated, isn't it? It is really confusing for a small child, but many children find that their survival depends on navigating this system.

Living in this situation, we were taught to put the needs of others before our own, to keep secrets, to protect others from our "upsetting" emotions, and to feel guilty if we bother others with our needs and feelings.

When we stop to look back at the situation, what was really going on here had little to do with the child, but with the relationship between the parents. One parent was deemed by the other to be either too fragile or too explosive to know the routine concerns of the family. Thus, one parent filtered information going to the other. This cut the children off from the "don't upset parent" and gave the filtering parent a great deal of power in the relationship. This parent allowed the "don't upset" parent to be protected from actually being a parent, because they did not have to deal with the problems of family life. They could be either sick and fragile or the blustering monarch feared by everyone. Of course, the real power lay with the one who decided what the fragile one or the monarch should hear.

These beliefs and communication rules lead to massive dysfunction within the family. During the holidays you may have been confronted again with this insane situation. This pattern will change only when one person sees the game clearly, is willing to break the rules, and begins to talk honestly with the "upsettable" parent. We also have the power to change this within the families we are creating by refusing to maintain this pattern. In our own families, we can create a system where anyone can talk with anybody about anything. This is truly a free and functional family system.

New Rule: In our family, we are able to discuss problems and concerns openly, without fear or shame.

December 27

Old Rule: Leaving home is a betrayal of the family.

In some families, children are not expected to leave home. They may marry, but they always stay in close proximity to their parents, maintaining their primary commitment not to the family they are creating, but to the family in which they were reared. While this dysfunctional pattern is not the norm, we do occasionally witness the pain and turmoil this causes. Most of us expect our children to leave our homes and create their own lives apart from us. This is the natural course of things. However, leaving home is more than just moving one's place of residence. Leaving home is living our own life, even if that life is quite different from one's parents. Thus as we grow into adulthood, we leave home not only physically, but also emotionally, intellectually, and spirituality.

Tension arises in families when leaving home means that one lives a vastly different life with different beliefs and values from ones' parents. For the parents this may feel like a betrayal of them and the way they have attempted to rear their children. It can be quite stressful, especially when children are living in ways that violate important family values and principles. These differences may involve religious values, career choices, choice of a mate, rearing of children, financial choices, or even political beliefs.

We know that becoming independent and leaving home is the goal of adulthood, but letting go is difficult. Letting go and maintaining a loving, respectful relationship when we do not approve is even more difficult. Nevertheless, to do otherwise is to create a painful distance between our children and ourselves as they move into young adulthood.

New Rule: I accept that my children will leave home and while I may not always approve of their actions, they will always have my love.

476

December 28

Old Rule: Don't question your religion.

Many parents feel that formal religious instruction and attendance at religious services is an important part of family life. Indeed, religious faith does seem to have a stabilizing influence on children and make a positive contribution to their well-being both now and in the future.

While we feel quite comfortable answering the questions of small children about religious beliefs and practices, we tend to feel less comfortable when our older children begin to question their faith and religious instruction. When they begin to challenge us and our religious beliefs as well as the religious traditions in which they were reared, we may feel threatened and shame them for even thinking about these questions. We may tell them that such questioning is morally wrong and that they risk the severest religious consequences, perhaps even eternal damnation, for questioning what they have been told is true.

Most religions view this time of questioning with tolerance. Indeed, most religions see such questioning by the young as a prerequisite for developing mature faith. Sometimes less well-informed and insecure parents or religious leaders feel threatened by these questions. Rather than dealing with their own doubts that the young person's questions have brought to the surface, they shame the questioner. While it may temporarily silence the questioner, this tactic does not make the questions go away. It stops growth within faith and leads to a stunted, immature faith that has difficulty withstanding the tests that will eventually come. Such shaming tactics may also lead to rebellion and angry rejection of faith and religion. Having been silenced and shamed for questioning the young person wants no part of a dogmatic religion that does not allow them to question and inquire more deeply into matters of faith.

Wise parents and religious leaders know that questioning is a healthy sign of growth in faith. They view such times as opportunities to teach their children about their religious traditions and beliefs as well as a time to grow in their own beliefs. Additionally, they see this as a marvelous opportunity to enhance their relationship with the questioner. They welcome and rejoice in this time! It is an answer to the prayer, "Help me to train my child up in the right way."

New Rule: As teachers of our religious heritage, we welcome our children's questions as evidence of growth and maturity in religious faith.

December 29

Old Rule: Honor thy Father and thy Mother

This is a difficult commandment for many of us. What does it mean to honor one's parents? Does it mean that I will always agree with them, at least in their presence? Does it mean that I will never get angry with them and let them know it? Does it mean that I will live my life as they want? Does it mean that I will not hold them accountable for what they do, allowing them to hide behind "I did the best I could," no matter how miserable the job?

Considering that many of us have so much emotional baggage and ambivalence concerning our relationship with our parents, perhaps it is best to sort out this "honoring" business from the other end. How would we like for our children to honor us?

While I would like for my sons to live their lives as I see best, not to disagree with me or become angry with me, and to certainly never hold me accountable for the mistakes that I made while rearing them, I know that this is not truly honoring me. Instead, to really honor me they will live their lives as they see fit, use their talents and abilities wisely, think for themselves, express their feelings and opinions openly, and live according to their own set of values. If they can accomplish these things, if they are kind in their relationships with others, seek to do the "right thing," and if they can pass these things on to their own children, then I will be honored beyond my deserving.

New Rule: Honor thy Father and thy Mother.

December 30

Old Rule: If you confront me, you will lose me.

No matter how old we get, we still desire our parents' love and approval. Nevertheless, many adults have never experienced this in their relationship with their parents. When they attempt to talk with their parents about their feelings, their usual purpose is to improve the relationship. Their secret dream is that the parent will see them differently and the relationship will be transformed into what they always wanted it to be - loving, nurturing, and supportive.

All too often these children, now adults, meet with rejection in the form of silence or condemnation. ("How could you talk to me this way?") While the shaming words may be difficult to hear, silence is probably worse, for in the silence the child is left with nowhere to turn. They are powerless except to continue the relationship as it has been, one in which they are not accepted for who they are, or they can distance themselves from their parents, giving up on having the close relationship they desire. Both options are extremely painful.

This pattern in the relationship between the parent and child does not begin when the child becomes an adult. It starts in earliest childhood with a parent who believes that children have no right to disagree or to form opinions of their own, even about themselves. The patterns continue through a stormy and painful adolescence and young adulthood, in which the shaming and critical parent does not accept the child as they develop into an individual while the child fights to assert their individuality and freedom to be who they are becoming. The conflict continues until the child lets go of the pursuit of the parent's love and acceptance or abandons their individuality and attempts to become what the parent says they want.

This family dysfunction and pain is passed on from generation to generation. If you find yourself in this situation, I urge you to seek help in letting go of your pursuit of your parents' affection and approval. Free yourself in order to give your children the love and approval that they so much want from you. Let them know that they are free to speak their truth to you and let you know who they are without the fear of losing you.

New Rule: I will allow my children to be who they are and to talk freely to me about how they feel, even their negative feelings about me. I will not turn away in silence or shame them when they are honest with me.

December 31

Old Rule: If you love me, you will…

How did this sentence end in the family you grew up in? It may have been: "Believe as I do, do as I say, never question or challenge me, keep quiet about what is happening in this family, or never leave me." The variations are endless.

However, the unspoken threat at the end of the message is always the same: "If you love me, you will… and if you don't, I will abandon you." Whether we are conscious of it or not, the unspoken ending, implying loss of the parental love, is what we respond to when we continue in our attempt to prove our love. Fearing the loss of the love and support of our parent, we comply with this demand, abandoning what is best for us and acceding to the demands and needs of another.

In essence, we abandon ourselves, our dreams, our potential, and even our relationships in order to hang on to what we believe we desperately need and cannot live without - the illusion of parental love.

Refusing to betray ourselves and not respond to this emotional blackmail carries with it the real possibility of abandonment. However, not to refuse is to allow ourselves to remain an emotional hostage to those who do not truly love us, but who may be using our love to protect themselves from emotional pain. When we refuse to continue to be controlled in this manner, we are able to focus our energies on rearing our own children with emotional honesty and discipline rather than control through emotional blackmail.

New Rule: I will not pass on this dysfunctional method of controlling others to my children. I refuse to accept or demand love that is conditional on silence or blind compliance. The price is too high. I cannot afford this kind of expensive, conditional love.

Epilogue

Rearing a family is one of life's most important responsibilities. It can also be one of the most rewarding and joyful. I hope that this book has given you some new ideas and skills to make this responsibility a little lighter and a lot more fun.

Enjoy your children. The troublesome situations will pass as well as the good times. So learn to savor the good moments and relax during the more difficult. They all pass so quickly!

About the Author

Gay Moore M.Ed., RNC has enjoyed a varied career as a nurse, counselor, and educator. She is certified in adult mental health nursing and is a licensed drug and alcohol abuse counselor. Currently an assistant professor in the behavioral and social sciences division of a community college, she teaches interpersonal communications, sociology, and substance abuse counseling courses.

A frequent speaker at civic organizations and churches on such topics as parenting, enriching the couple relationship, and resolving family conflicts, she has authored several articles on mental health and spiritual issues. New Rules To Live By is her first book.

Gay is also a wife and the mother of two grown sons.

9 781418 413156